CHAUCER'S PROBLEM OF PROSE

Media, History, and *The Canterbury Tales*

CHAUCER'S PROBLEM OF POPE

Media, History, and Representation

Chaucer's Problem of Prose

Media, History, and The Canterbury Tales

STEPHEN M. YEAGER

UNIVERSITY OF TORONTO PRESS
Toronto Buffalo London

© University of Toronto Press 2025
Toronto Buffalo London
utppublishing.com
Printed in the USA

ISBN 978-1-4875-0406-9 (cloth)   ISBN 978-1-4875-1937-7 (EPUB)
                                 ISBN 978-1-4875-1936-0 (PDF)

Library and Archives Canada Cataloguing in Publication

Title: Chaucer's problem of prose : media, history, and the Canterbury tales / Stephen Yeager.
Names: Yeager, Stephen M., 1979– author
Description: Includes bibliographical references and index.
Identifiers: Canadiana (print) 20240483006 | Canadiana (ebook) 20240482484 | ISBN 9781487504069 (cloth) | ISBN 9781487519360 (PDF) | ISBN 9781487519377 (EPUB)
Subjects: LCSH: Chaucer, Geoffrey, –1400. Canterbury tales – Criticism, Textual. | LCGFT: Literary criticism.
Classification: LCC PR1874 .Y33 2025 | DDC 821/.1–dc23

Cover design: Liz Harasymczuk
Cover image: The Wilton Diptych (c1395–1399): left inside panel. King Richard II of England is depicted kneeling before the Virgin and Child. He is presented to them by (right to left) his patron saint, John the Baptist, and by the English saints King Edward the Confessor and King Edmund the Martyr. Alamy Stock Photo.

We wish to acknowledge the land on which the University of Toronto Press operates. This land is the traditional territory of the Wendat, the Anishnaabeg, the Haudenosaunee, the Métis, and the Mississaugas of the Credit First Nation.

University of Toronto Press acknowledges the financial support of the Government of Canada, the Canada Council for the Arts, and the Ontario Arts Council, an agency of the Government of Ontario, for its publishing activities.

Contents

Acknowledgments   vii

Abbreviations   ix

Critical Introduction   3

1 The Problem of Prose in Fragments II and VII:
An Overview   29

2 Saxon Script and Chaucerian Verse in London BL Add.
MS 14848   44

3 The Text, the Gloss, and Fragment III   60

4 Tragedy and the Law of Edward in *The Monk's Tale*   79

5 Chronicles and Customary Law: Chaucer's Tale of
Custaunce   100

6 The Problem of Prose and the Prose *Canterbury Tales*:
Melibee and the Parson   121

Conclusion   140

Notes   149

Bibliography   169

Index   197

Acknowledgments

Concordia University, where most of this book was written, is located on unceded Indigenous lands. The Kanien'kehá:ka Nation is recognized as the custodians of the lands and waters on which I work and teach. Tiohtià:ke/Montréal is historically known as a gathering place for many First Nations. Today, it is home to a diverse population of Indigenous and other peoples. We respect the continued connections with the past, present, and future in our ongoing relationships with Indigenous and other peoples within the Montreal community.

Funding for this project was provided by the Fonds de recherche du Québec – Société et culture and by the Social Sciences and Humanities Research Council of Canada, which among other things paid for the essential contributions of Katheryne Morrissette, Katrina Tsimiklis, Olivier Pelletier, and Ghislaine Comeau to the project as research assistants. Thank you to Tarren Andrews, Susan Nakley, and Manish Sharma for reading drafts and early versions of particular chapters, and also to the two anonymous readers for their many helpful suggestions. There are too many colleagues to count whose feedback on the project in conversations and at conferences over the years has been so essential in helping me get it to this form, but some of the many I deeply appreciate (in no particular order) include Liz Reich, Jonathan Newman, Magda Hayton, Kathleen Kennedy, Dan Kline, Michael Van Dussen, Shannon McSheffrey, Mary Kate Hurley, Alex Gillespie, Suzanne Akbari, Will Robins, Robert Epstein, Sarah Star, Jessica Lockhart, Breann Leake, Holly Crocker, Matthew X Vernon, Brantley Bryant, Fiona Somerset, Virginia Blanton, Patricia Dailey, Thora Brylowe, Alice Sharp, Eric Weiskott, Arthur Bahr, Laura Ashe, Kathy Cawsey, James Simpson, Daniel Donoghue, Richard Newhauser, Ingrid Nelson, Kathleen Tonry, Brandon Hawk, Tiffany Beechy, Dana Oswald, Erin Sweany, Jordan Zweck, Irina Dumitrescu, and Matthew Hussey. Thanks finally

viii   Acknowledgments

to Suzanne Rancourt and everyone at University of Toronto Press for their work in producing this beautiful volume.

Archival research for this book was conducted at the British Library, at the Bodleian Library in Oxford, at the Huntington Library in San Marino California, and in the archives at Worcester Cathedral and Westminster Abbey. Thank you to the archivists and librarians in those institutions for their suggestions and support. Conventional citation is also insufficient for acknowledging the value of the digital archives and research tools I relied upon to finish this book. If I had not been able to access the Electronic Sawyer, the Early English Laws site, the Chaucer Concordance at Columbia University, the Parker Library on the Web, the British Library's digital collections, the Dictionary of Old English and DOE web corpus, the Middle English Dictionary, Logeion, and Brepols' International Medieval Bibliography, this project would have been much poorer.

I would also like to thank my family and friends – my parents, my siblings David and Christine and their families, my Montreal neighbours, my community of faculty and staff colleagues at Concordia, and all the former students and classmates around the world. You have enriched this project, and me. My son Sam and daughter Clara are both younger than some of first Word documents drafting the chapters that follow, and they have shaped not only the words of this book but the man who wrote it. Thank you finally to my wife and colleague Cynthia Quarrie, for everything.

Abbreviations

AND	*Anglo-Norman Dictionary (AND² Online Edition)*. 2021. Aberystwyth University. https://anglo-norman.net.
ASE	*Anglo-Saxon England*
DIMEV	*Digital Index of Middle English Verse*. Compiled, edited, and supplemented by Lynne R. Mooney, Daniel W. Mosser, Elizabeth Solopova, Deborah Thorpe, David Hill Radcliffe, Len Hatfield. http://www.dimev.net.
DMF	*Dictionnaire du Moyen Français*, version 2020. ATILF – CNRS & Université de Lorraine. http://www.atilf.fr/dmf.
ChauR	*Chaucer Review*
EETS	Early English Text Society
EHR	*English Historical Review*
JEGP	*Journal of English and Germanic Philology*
Mann	Geoffrey Chaucer. *The Canterbury Tales*, edited by Jill Mann. New York: Penguin Classics, 2005.
MED	*Middle English Dictionary*, edited by Robert E. Lewis et al. Ann Arbor: University of Michigan Press, 1952–2001. Online edition in Middle English Compendium, edited by Frances McSparran et al. Ann Arbor: University of Michigan Library, 2000–18. http://quod.lib.umich.edu/m/middle-english-dictionary.
OED	*Oxford English Dictionary*. https://www.oed.com.
PMLA	*Publication of the Modern Language Association*
RES	*Review of English Studies*
Riverside	*The Riverside Chaucer*, edited by Larry Benson. 3rd ed. Boston: Houghton Mifflin, 1987.
S&A	*Sources and Analogues of The Canterbury Tales*, edited by Robert M. Correale and Mary Hamel. 2 vols. Cambridge: D.S. Brewer, 2002 and 2005.
SAC	*Studies in the Age of Chaucer*

CHAUCER'S PROBLEM OF PROSE

Critical Introduction

Since my first reading of *The Canterbury Tales*, I have always thought it to be a strange and noteworthy feature of the frame narrative that at two key structural moments – the ending, and Chaucer's own appearance as a tale-teller – the text turns to prose, in a flagrant violation of its establishing fiction that everyone in fourteenth-century England naturally speaks in rhyming iambic pentameter couplets. The violation is explicitly acknowledged by the tale tellers, whose announcements that they will tell prose tales include three of the five appearances of the word "prose" in the entire *Canterbury Tales*.[1] A fourth occurrence of the word appears at the "second beginning" of fragment II, where the Man of Law announces an intention to tell a tale in prose that parallels in many particulars the Parson's own announcement in fragment X, suggesting that at one time prose tales were supposed to bookend the collection. The fifth and final occurrence of the word "prose" is in *The Monk's Prologue* (*MkP*, VII.1980), where the Monk says that tragedies may be written in hexameter, prose, or any other form.

Though these moments of beginning, ending, and authorial self-analysis are clearly marked as important to the structure of the text as we have it, they do not reveal much to readers about a coherent authorial plan for the structure of *The Canterbury Tales*. If anything, the appearances of the word "prose" are the parts of the frame narrative where its various aporia and unresolved contradictions are especially emergent. Fragment II is the most difficult to make sense of in the entire collection, the prose *Melibee* (*Mel*) probably used to be *The Man of Law's Tale* (*MLT*) but its new assignment to Chaucer gives it a particular metafictional importance, *The Monk's Tale* (*MkT*) is possibly unfinished and has a very unusual metrical structure, and *The Parson's Tale* (*ParsT*) feels so distinct from the rest of *The Canterbury Tales* that there is a plausible case to be made that it was not even intended for the collection.[2] Prose,

4   Chaucer's Problem of Prose

then, is less a problem in *The Canterbury Tales* than it is a problem for it, as it appears in the collection at moments that clearly signal a structural logic in its ordering though at the same time these moments offer very few clues for figuring out what that logic is supposed to be.

In her 2012 dissertation, correctly self-described as "the first full-length study of Geoffrey Chaucer's prose," Dawn Colley suggests that Chaucer's prose works all deliberately play off of the incomplete authority of the translator to invite readers to critique Chaucer's own authority.[3] Like many medieval translators, Chaucer used prose to render texts from other languages as precisely as possible in their content, because verse imposes limitations on word choices that will necessarily lead to imprecisions. That said, prose translations of verse from other languages hardly serve to eliminate the traces of those verse forms, as redundancies and elisions and figures of speech that have resulted from the economies of prosody remain in the text of those statements as clear signs of the prosody that has not been translated. In other words "prose" is no abandonment of the mediating form of poetic *solaas* to present the unvarnished content of *sentence*, whatever some of Chaucer's characters may suggest. Rather, we should imagine the prose *Canterbury Tales* to be moments where *mediation itself* – particularly the mediating effects of written language and literary form – becomes the content under consideration.

In the present study, I will build on Colley's argument by demonstrating how Chaucer's use of prose calls attention not only to the formal features of the language of a text (especially when it is a translation), but also to the layout of manuscript page on which *The Canterbury Tales* appears, as the structural unit of the line dissolves and takes with it a clear sense of the text's formatting.[4] Certainly *Mel* and *ParsT* are always the easiest tales for readers to find by flipping through a copy of *The Canterbury Tales*, in paper as in parchment. In this book, then, I posit that the inclusion of prose in *The Canterbury Tales* helps it to represent a set of problems that the fragmentary, incomplete collection does not resolve, and that indeed inspires its most vexed fissures and contradictions. At the core of these problems is that central contradiction: texts that claim to represent and so protect human diversity and autonomy often contribute to the precise processes of consolidating power whereby that diversity and autonomy is undermined and eliminated. The problem of prose encoded in the structure of *The Canterbury Tales* articulates and manages an anxiety in the text that it too may ultimately fall into precisely this trap, which possibility can only be managed by empowering readers to assume a critical distance from not only the content of *The Canterbury Tales* but also its mediating form.

Critical Introduction   5

In his recent book *The Logic of Love in The Canterbury Tales*, Manish Sharma has argued that throughout *The Canterbury Tales* Chaucer draws on medieval formal logic to figure his own authorial control over texts and their meanings as paradoxical, in a way that empowers readers to make their own interpretive decisions. Sharma begins with a famously suggestive passage from *The General Prologue* (*GP*), where Chaucer claims to be a transparent, non-distorting reporter of the tales and cites both Christ and Plato to justify this self-representation (I.725–42).[5] Sharma summarizes the paradox laid out in these lines as follows: "The author of *The Canterbury Tales* invokes the towering authority of [Christ and Plato] to legitimate the abdication of his own authority. He may relinquish his own authority by claiming to be a mere reporter, subordinate to his own fictive constructions, but he does so *authoritatively*" (his emphasis).[6] *Chaucer's Problem of Prose* will apply Sharma's reading to identify the prose *Canterbury Tales* as moments where Chaucer authoritatively abdicates not only his own authority, but the authority of the written literary (and, we shall see, legal) form and formats that are the basis for that authority. The most obvious indication in *The Canterbury Tales* that its reportage is mediated by Chaucer's own poetic authority is the fact that it is, mostly, poetry. When Chaucer switches to prose in *Mel* and *ParsT*, he reconfigures the totality of what he calls at precisely these moments his "litel tretys" (VII.957, X.1081), which cannot be referred to in the singular as a "poem."[7]

Chaucer's abdication of specifically poetic authority informs my approach to another key theme in *The Canterbury Tales*, which is its persistent critique of the cultural and political institutions in late medieval England that used formal strictures in writing to control the medium of the written word and in particular its power to memorialize and assert ownership. In brief, my reading of Chaucer's "anti-clerical" critiques of ecclesiastical professionalism is focused not on their theological implications for salvation (as clerical sacraments mediate between lay believers and the divine), but rather on their material implications for political life (as clerical documents mediate between individual right-holders and the official recognition of those rights). In her recent article on media theory and *The House of Fame*, Ingrid Nelson argues persuasively that Chaucer and other medieval thinkers did in fact have a "media concept" for thinking about the impact of media technology on the transmission of messages, conceptualized in relation not only to human speech and rhetoric but also to the air's mediation of light and sound.[8] Nelson writes: "since sensory perception is central to aesthetic experience, the medieval theory of mediated perception enables Chaucer to understand the literary work as that which emerges from the sensory

6   Chaucer's Problem of Prose

effects of environmental and conventional aesthetic media."[9] *The House of Fame* of her reading instantiates the larger theme in all of Chaucer's poetry, concerning his profound "anxiety over the distortions of mediated perception" as they pertain especially to "his own poetic practice of making."[10] Such anxieties are pertinent to not only Chaucer the poet, but also to Chaucer the courtier and controller of petty custom.

In these terms *The Canterbury Tales* is particularly attuned to the particular aesthetic experiences related to the sensory perception of poetic form, both auditory and in its appearance on the page. The text's structural anxieties about the distortions of poetry and prose express larger political anxieties about the technical apparatus of writing, archiving, publication, and circulation that define "media" in our modern sense. There is a substantial body of criticism that draws attention to the connection between social unrest in late fourteenth-century England and the increased reliance on legal documentation and literate institutions of government.[11] Chaucer's authoritative abdication of poetic authority in the prose *Canterbury Tales* deploys this paradox to pose questions about the uses and abuses of authority in writing more generally, since of course these are the conditions within which his own poetic project took place.

As I will detail in chapter 3, the symbolic framework within which Chaucer expresses his anxiety about authority in writing is that of the old dichotomy between text and gloss.[12] I will argue that the recourse to prose in *The Canterbury Tales* serves to express the unresolvable contradiction between the glosses that need texts and the texts that need glosses, as textual literalism and contextual glossing are consistently represented as opposing strategies for identifying and correcting deviations from the laws of church and crown, though in fact they are mutually reinforcing aspects of the same continuous process of centralizing, consolidating power. Though the most direct representation of the text/gloss dualism is the unresolved debate between the "glosing" Friar and the strictly literalist Summoner, my reading will demonstrate that the same dualism is also expressed in the contrast between *Mel* and the *Tale of Sir Thopas* that precedes it; in the contrast between *ParsT* and the *Retraction* that follows it; in the contrast between the two prose tales themselves; and, most suggestively, in the contrast between the two pilgrims who talk about prose but do not use it, the Man of Law and the Monk. The tale that immediately precedes *MkP* in fragment VII is the prose *Mel*, which may at one time have been assigned to the Man of Law, and which in this way suggests a dialogue between the characters that is either semi-effaced or accidentally emergent in the current ordering.[13]

In these various re-stagings of the text/gloss contradiction, Chaucer's anxiety about authority and writing is often framed as an anxiety about authority in specifically English language writing, with its particular implications for the imperial ambitions of the English king. Chaucer's concern for "Englishness" is a well-known feature of his work,[14] and his exclusive use of the English language in his poetry is most commonly read as expressive of his aspirations to be a "European" poet, as his primary interlocutors and models are continental authors who similarly wrote in their own primary spoken languages.[15] As Susan Nakley compellingly argues, this internationalism in *The Canterbury Tales* encodes claims to English national sovereignty on the world stage that anticipate the British imperial ideology, which itself defines the entire history of Chaucer's reception in England into the present.[16] Though Chaucer's title as "father of English poetry" is imposed by later readers, it is reasonable to assume that it was imposed because they found Chaucer's work amenable to the task of representing and critiquing their emergent worldview.[17]

My own reading of Chaucer's "Englishness" proceeds from Wendy Scase's recent study of English scribal identity, *Visible English: Graphic Culture, Scribal Practice, and Identity c. 700–c. 1500*. Scase's comprehensive survey demonstrates that virtually all formal training in reading and writing in England throughout the medieval period focused primarily on reading and writing in Latin. By implication, reading and writing in English appears to have been "rare and specialist skills" in Chaucer's lifetime, as they had been since English writing was first produced in the seventh century.[18] Chaucer's project was therefore defined by a contradiction: the spoken English he claimed to report was the language of everyday life and the audience he wished to find for his poetry was international and contemporary, though at the same time even that small percentage of medieval English speakers who read Latin may have found it difficult to understand the written English of his works or to reproduce it in their own manuscripts. As we can confirm with hindsight, Chaucer's English language poetry did not so much serve to make the inner workings of literate bureaucracy transparent to everyday people as it did to aid the ongoing transformation of the written English literature into a tool for literate bureaucrats, who for example used their poetry to secure patronage and improve their careers, with the ultimate effect that literacy in England became an increasingly necessary survival skill.

By far, the most rarified, technical, and inaccessible English texts in circulation in Chaucer's lifetime were the oldest ones, originally written in the pre-Conquest dialect generally called "Saxon" in the fourteenth

8 Chaucer's Problem of Prose

century but now called "Old English."[19] Though the Old English poetic corpus was not in wide or active circulation during Chaucer's lifetime, English monasteries founded before approximately 1100 CE took great pains to copy and use legal texts that included Old English in many forms: legal formulae ("sake and soke"), boundary clauses, and in some cases complete English translations. Throughout this study and especially in chapter 2, I will lay out in more detail the evidence demonstrating that Chaucer and his audience would have had an historical awareness of the Old English law codes, chronicles, writs, and charters kept by England's oldest corporate entities as proof for their privileges and exemptions, shaping the subtext of the anxieties about authority in literacy that are expressed through the problem of prose in *The Canterbury Tales*. For all that these institutions were at the vanguard of the bureaucratization of the English language, their local and traditional power was by its very existence antagonistic to the imperial aspirations of the emerging institutions of government. As a result Chaucer's own attempts at revisioning English writing had to contend with the resulting contradictions between the highly specialized and local administrative language that English writing had been and the elevated literary language on continental models that Chaucer would see it become. Hence the premise of this study, that English monastic exemption is a key theme in *The Canterbury Tales* for understanding Chaucer's self-conception as an English author, and is predicated on the historical claim that Old English legal documentary writing was not only copied and used in Chaucer's lifetime, but that Chaucer himself was very likely aware of it and in conversation with it.

In chapters 4 and 5, I will argue that Chaucer's likely awareness of this early, institutional context for English writing is important context for reading the Man of Law and the Monk's staging of the text/gloss dichotomy, and for contextualizing their uses of the word and concept "prose." The Monk's first instinct, quickly abandoned, is to tell a life of Edward the Confessor (VII.1970). Meanwhile, there is a direct reference to Edward's direct antecedent William the Conqueror in the *GP*'s description of the Man of Law (I.324), and the tale that the Man of Law actually tells is a legend of England's conversion to Christianity that gives an English origin to the Roman emperor Mauritius who approved Augustine of Canterbury's conversion mission. I argue that these glances back to moments of origin and/or rupture in early English political history are part of a structural ambivalence in *The Canterbury Tales* about the assimilation of long-standing, autonomous, material communities of local power centres into the emergent, national, imagined communities of the English crown and the papacy. The anxieties about reception that famously animate Chaucer's poetry are concerned less with his own personal authority as a poet and prince pleaser than they are with the structural authority of the written medium whereby he practiced these crafts, as the ever-evolving apparatus of English writing and its circulation produced embodied artifacts that would go on to circulate in forms and formats he could not imagine.[20]

In her study of French prose texts, Gabrielle Spiegel suggests that the medieval understanding of the formal category "prose" is more commonly related to the historical veracity of a text's contents than it is to the presence or absence of specific metrical forms.[21] *Chaucer's Problem of Prose* will proceed from this framing to read the opposing valuations of "prose" in the statements by the Man of Law and the Monk – where the former carefully explains why he must use it, and the latter offhandedly names it as one of many appropriate forms – as expressing their contrary affective framings of the history of English law between the Saxon and Norman Conquests. For most of the medieval period, the techniques of media creation and storage in England were tightly controlled by ecclesiastical institutions. But by Chaucer's time, it was increasingly common for manuscripts to be produced and circulated in secular institutional and commercial contexts, without direct ecclesiastical oversight.[22] Both a cause and an effect of this change was the economic decline of the English church, well advanced by the fourteenth century.[23] Chaucer himself was a witness of and participant in this shift.[24] As controller of wool customs for the London port, Chaucer imposed a relatively novel infringement upon the liberties of the city, by ensuring that export duties due to the crown were properly collected.[25] And as an inhabitant of Westminster who remains buried there to this day – not far from both the remains of Edward the Confessor, who established the church as the traditional site of English coronations, and also the houses of the "Westminster" Parliament whose widely adopted system of government is named still for its proximity to this monastic cloister – there is every reason to believe that Chaucer would have not only considered English monastic history to be central to his understanding of English political history, but that he would have also been surprised by the historical forgetting that might lead twenty-first-century scholars of his period to consider this centrality counterintuitive.

It is no surprise, then, that Chaucer's literary work exhibits a keen awareness of how institutions of power can manipulate the production and storage of media objects to their own advantage, and so how the organizational forms of the archive can be such an intensely political site of struggle. *The Canterbury Tales* was directly imbricated in these processes by two opposing facts: first, that archival struggles on the

10   Chaucer's Problem of Prose

continent were accompanied by an increased use of "vulgar" spoken languages for poetic expression; second, that the largest known corpus of early English writing in Chaucer's own lifetime survived almost entirely in monastic archives (kept and used by monks like the Monk), in texts that only circulated when they were needed to protect their traditional rights from the encroachment of especially secular and royal institutions (represented in court by lawyers like the Man of Law).[26]

This framing of *MLT* and *MkT* may seem like a departure from the dominant approaches to these texts in recent scholarship, which have generally focused on what we may call their proto-colonial (or, as I will say from now on, "imperial") representations of gender and race.[27] In particular the figures of Cenobia in *MkT* and the Sultaness in *MLT* are some of the most striking instances of racialized and gendered "othering" in *The Canterbury Tales*, in a manner which clearly anticipates the strategies of representation that will characterize English "orientalism" in later eras.[28] In the rest of this introduction, I will step back to plot out the starting theoretical and methodological premises of my approach, to explain why I believe my reading reinforces these studies of Chaucer and adds new historical context in support of their claims. Because these premises are somewhat far flung in their disciplinary origins, I have decided that the most concise way of situating my approach in relation to its various influences will be to briefly paraphrase the main ideas from five key works of scholarship from the relevant disciplines and subdisciplines: Chaucer studies, critical race theory, media studies, critical historiography, and Indigenous studies. The last of these defines my key concept of "the politics of recognition," which I will use to explain how precisely Chaucer's expressions of ambivalence about the centralization of secular administration and the corresponding erosion of monastic exemption should be expressed in his poetry by means of symbolic terms that twenty-first-century critics recognize correctly as the antecedents for early-modern fantasies of imperial subjugation. The other four studies will lay the foundations for explaining how I have arrived at my premise, that this Indigenous studies concept can be productively applied in this way.

Media, History, and Empire: A Critical Background for The Problem of Prose

The first book I will use to map my starting premises is Lee Patterson's *Chaucer and the Subject of History*. As the title of this generation-defining study indicates, Patterson argues that *The Canterbury Tales* is built around a tension between the emergent modern "subject" and the

Critical Introduction   11

theme of "history," by which he means not only Chaucer's sense of past events but also the poet's sense of the "historical world" of his own contemporary milieu.[29] Splitting the difference between Jill Mann's synthetic study of estates satire in *GP* and H. Marshall Leicester's analysis of "the disenchanted self" in Chaucer's modes of narration, Patterson argues that the interplay between the pilgrims' different voices at the level of dialogue is in productive tension with the different levels of the social hierarchy they allegorize on the level of structure, so that the frame narrative sets up "a socially undetermined subjectivity in opposition to the social definition entailed by the estates theory" implicit in the *Canterbury Tales'* genre.[30] Patterson therefore problematizes but ultimately reinforces the long-standing narrative whereby Chaucer, "father of English poetry," is held to anticipate and even originate the philosophical, artistic, and cultural conditions of secular bourgeois "liberalism" in England, which would come to their full fruition in the centuries after his death.[31] Patterson proceeds in his efforts by "locating each of [Chaucer's] texts in relation to a discourse – a specific set of texts and practices – that can make explicit the social meaning of his poetry."[32]

Patterson applied this approach against the backdrop of then-emergent post-colonial, critical-race-theory, and Indigenous-studies approaches to Chaucer's poetry, which have since done much to interrogate the ways in which *The Canterbury Tales* participates in (and, in some accounts, resists) the fourteenth-century discourses of race and gender that anticipate later colonizer and settler-colonizer distinctions between the subjects who deserve liberty and the racialized Others who do not.[33] As stated above, such readings have circulated in conversation with similarly "new historicist" studies of Chaucer's "Englishness," which have considered how this political and linguistic construct emerged in relation to the parallel identities of other proto-colonizer nations. These studies are often informed by Patterson's arguments, but they typically withdraw from his claims about subjectivity and individuality to focus rather on what Patterson calls the more "social" dimensions of Chaucer's poetry.

In his afterword, Patterson appears to anticipate the reasons for this withdrawal, and defends his own position in a passage worth quoting at length:

> However much they may have served to mystify the concrete relations of social power, neither liberalism nor individualism can be simply banished into the outer darkness of the politically incorrect. One of the lessons we can learn from late medieval writing is that there are moments in

12   Chaucer's Problem of Prose

history when individualism is a powerful liberating force: in a society in which identity is restricted to social function, and in which functions are assigned in radically unequal ways, to think individually is to think progressively. Nor can we be certain that today is not one of those moments. The culture industry that so profoundly and pervasively shapes contemporary life imposes upon us all homogenized identities that can resisted only by an insistence on heterogeneity and specificity – on, in effect, individuality. Moreover, to foreclose the possibility of acting for other than group reasons is to make inescapable an identity politics that undermines the coalition-building that the progressive forces of our society desperately need.[34]

Thus for Patterson, Chaucer's poetry is not only of *historical* interest – since it records the emergence of liberal individualism at an historical moment in the history of the European intellectual tradition – but also of *political* interest today, because it provides a model for how liberals in the present may balance the tension between individual needs and social pressures to bring about progressive change.

This view of Chaucer's contribution to Patterson's own historical context is a remarkable one, given especially the prominence in his earlier chapters of the various revisions to Marx's account of "primitive accumulation" in England in the 200 years after Chaucer's death, summarily referred to now as "the Brenner Debate."[35] It takes a liberal reading of Marxist historiography, in more than one sense, to argue on its basis that the invention of capital and the rise of the bourgeoisie provide a useful pattern for imagining how political systems may be altered to better respect the heterogeneities and specificities of human experiences.[36] The present book aims to proceed somewhat less liberally, to read Chaucer's anticipation of modernity not as a manifestation of his admirable personal genius but as a form of (admittedly ambivalent) complicity on his part in the establishment of what Sylvia Wynter calls "the Overrepresentation of Man."[37]

Wynter dates this overrepresentation back to the Gregorian Reform of the eleventh century, which in her telling – following Jacques LeGoff – institutionalized a systematic divide between the pure and the impure to confer political power only on the former.[38] In Wynter's terms the project of Chaucer and the other (proto-) "humanists" of his age merely secularized and so broadened the application of these divisions, so that "impurity" was no longer a moral category related to behaviour but an essential one related to genetic and cultural identity. The result was the erasure of the heterogeneity and specificity of marginalized and colonized peoples, who would find their "interests, reality, and

Critical Introduction 13

wellbeing ... to be imperatively subordinated" to the needs of Man – which is to say, to the construct of "pure" humanity that applies only to the white, the masculine, and the rational.[39]

Wynter's term "overrepresentation" is useful here because it exposes Patterson's primary error in the passage quoted above. Scholars like Wynter do not always aim to "banish" liberalism and individualism. Often, they aim to re-contextualize and even renovate these constructs, drawing attention in this way to the absences of the underrepresented identities and practices that liberalism and individualism have themselves banished in contradiction with their own stated values. Again, the titular insight of Patterson's book is that there is a tight correlation between Chaucer's amenability to the ideology of modern liberalism and subjectivity and his representations of history and historicity in his poetry. My study will proceed from the assumption that Chaucer is somewhat self-aware and perturbed by the contradictions of his ideology that scholars like Wynter have exposed, and that this self-awareness is manifest in the text in the various contradictions and questions that surround its problem of prose.

My framework for describing this apparent self-awareness draws from my second book, Lisa Lowe's *The Intimacies of Four Continents*. Lowe directly challenges the starting premises of scholarship like Patterson's to argue that the philosophical, artistic, and cultural conditions of liberalism are not only the products of exploitation, slavery, and colonial genocide, but indeed contributed directly to the normalization of human suffering that has allowed these atrocities to continue into the present. Building on the historiographic tradition of scholars like Wynter, Saidiya Hartman, Paul Gilroy, Cedric Robinson, and C.L.R. James, Lowe aims to describe "the economy of affirmation and forgetting that structures and formalizes the archives of liberalism, and liberal ways of understanding."[40] More specifically, she holds that "we can link the emergence of liberties defined in the abstract terms of citizenship, rights, wage labor, free trade, and sovereignty with the attribution of racial difference to those subjects, regions, and populations that liberal doctrine describes as 'unfit for liberty' or 'incapable of civilization,' placed at the margins of liberal humanity."[41] Through identifying these links she aims to demonstrate that "the colonial state archive both mediates and subsumes the uncertainties of liberal and imperial governance; in it, one reads the predicaments, both known and unknown, that gives rise to the calculations, strategies, forms, and practices of imperial rule."[42] The "intimacies" of her title are the hidden connections that the archive of modern liberal humanism works to hide or even erase, by applying "a formalism that translates the world

14 Chaucer's Problem of Prose

through an economy of affirmation and forgetting within a regime of desiring freedom."[43] In these terms, then, *Chaucer's Problem of Prose* will proceed to identify the predicaments in early English historical legal texts and documents that gave rise to the calculations, strategies, forms, and practices of subjective sovereignty in *The Canterbury Tales*, in the hopes that I may frame systemically not only the world of this text but also the modern tradition of Chaucerian criticism that Patterson's work has shaped so indelibly.

A key passage in Lowe's book for applying her concept of "intimacies" to my own study of Chaucer's *Canterbury Tales* appears in her analysis of a quirk from James' biography, that this foundational contributor to critical race theory loved the novel *Vanity Fair* and even claimed that "Thackeray, not Marx, bears the heaviest responsibility for me."[44] Lowe argues that in context, this comment is less a criticism of Marx than it is a celebration of Thackeray, and generally of how "*Vanity Fair* represented the emerging 'cultural dominant' of English bourgeois consumer society and British aspirations as a world empire," as "it also disclosed how the conception of Britain as a world power within a changing political economy constituted aesthetic and epistemological problems, as well." It is in this sense that the novel (and, Lowe suggests, literature generally) mediates the "asymmetries of dominant, residual, and emergent forces, inasmuch as it may portray that such conditions were more often grasped as isolated effects, glimpsed in particular objects in the social fabric, rather than seized totally or framed systemically."[45]

In the present study, then, I will follow the pattern of Lowe and James to read *The Canterbury Tales* as a work analogous to the *Vanity Fair* of this account. I argue that Chaucer does not so much "father" a new literary tradition as he addresses the aesthetic and epistemological problems of his time with useful economy and thoroughness, mediating in this way the asymmetries of dominant, residual, and emergent forces in fourteenth-century English writing that were shaped by the various conflicts between exempt monasteries and the emerging systems that eventually swallowed them, and that went on to formatively influence the imperial asymmetries already emergent in Chaucer's lifetime in England's ventures into Wales, Scotland, Ireland, and the Levant. In particular, I will follow Lowe's method to consider Chaucer's "anticlerical" media criticism as a form of engagement with the proto-"state archive" of medieval England, which already worked in Chaucer's time to mediate and subsume the uncertainties of that nation's (still mostly aspirational) imperial governance.

My third book, Lisa Gitelman's *Paper Knowledge: Towards a Media History of Documents*, informs the category of "documentary media" I

Critical Introduction   15

will apply in my reading of this theme, as a continuation of Gitelman's critique of media history periodization in her important introductory chapter. Gitelman de-emphasizes the grand teleologies of technical production (whereby, for example, manuscripts begat print media which begat the internet) to look rather at local histories of genres and formats in specific communities of practice. In a modern office a "document" can be a memo, a PDF, a legal pad of minutes taken in shorthand, a carbon copy of a handwritten receipt, or any number of objects in any number of formats, whose protocols of documentation may have arisen at any number of recent or distant historical moments. In all cases the material composition of the document is secondary to its authorizing form, whose consistency with established precedent marks it as useful for storing some discreet unit(s) of information.

Gitelman observes that "documents are epistemic objects; they are the recognizable sites and subjects of interpretation across the disciplines and beyond, evidential structures in the long human history of clues."[46] More specifically, they "belong to that ubiquitous subcategory of texts that embraces the subjects and instruments of bureaucracy or of systematic knowledge generally."[47] To the extent that "modernity" is a useful term for dividing and categorizing the evidence of historical phenomena, it is useful as a term for a stage in the accretion and organization of discrete material documents, whose production and storage is the method and purpose of day-to-day life in modern institutions and especially of the colonial and settler-colonial state archives that are the objects of Lowe's investigations.

Attention to genres like "the document" is particularly useful to critics for the way it enables them to organize history without falling back on problematic period categories like "print culture," which have applied a circular logic to invalidate medieval media studies on the grounds that its institutions had not yet passed some invisible threshold of commercialism or regularity. Gitelman writes:

> We might likewise be wary of recent claims that "the Age of Print is passing" ... Not only do statements like these tend to reify (to default to?) print as one thing instead of many, but they also impute a generalized cultural logic for print and – by extension – other media, at the same time that they fall back on the old Romantic trick by which Western modernity forever periodizes itself as modern. Better instead to resist any but local and contrastive logics for media; better to look for meanings that arise, shift, and persist according to the uses that media – emergent, dominant, and residual – familiarly have. Better, indeed, to admit that no medium has a single, particular logic, while every genre does and is.[48]

16   Chaucer's Problem of Prose

This observation is helpful for framing my own departures from the traditional periodizations of media histories. Gitelman's cautions against "the Age of Print" are directly applicable to the term and concept of "manuscript culture," which similarly reifies Chaucer's media ecology and so obscures the historical contrast between the residual institutions of manuscript production and storage (e.g., exempt English monasteries and other local power centres) and the emergent institutions and markets that employed and/or served literate bureaucrats (e.g., petty custom and the English common law), as they produced and consumed official documents and English language poetry.

Second, I will follow Gitelman to look at the "logic" of the document genre and its persistence, which indeed is precisely what Chaucer repeatedly attempts to articulate throughout the Canterbury Tales surveyed in this book. Though studies like Patterson's presuppose with some justification that when Chaucer wrote "manuscript culture" was evolving out of existence, I believe that such presumptions belie the extent to which Chaucer is troubled less by the oft-cited religious and political instability of his era than he is by the consistent, implacable *continuity* of English documentary authority throughout recorded English history, which may be manifest in different sorts of systems and controlled by different sorts of powers, but that has nonetheless extended from the first known works of written English to our present moment not despite but precisely because of the perpetual state of systemic instability engendered by the perpetual dissatisfaction of the governed. As I will explain, Chaucer figures "glosing" as a critique of strict adherence to the text at the same time that he figures strict adherence to a document's text as a critique of creative glossing, and the inexhaustibility of the resulting dynamic of mutual revision figures how *critique is itself* the engine that drives the consolidation of administrative power in late medieval England, as it also drives the reification and preservation of the contradictions in his proto-liberal humanist ideology. Hence the conversation between text and gloss in *The Canterbury Tales* does so much to vex its ability to materially document the pilgrimage it claims to record.

The fourth book, Kathleen Davis' *Periodization and Sovereignty: How Ideas of Feudalism and Secularism Govern the Politics of Time*, historicizes my connection between Gitelman's comments about the "old Romantic trick" of periodizing modernity and Lowe's "economy of affirmation and forgetting that structures and formalizes the archives of liberalism," by demonstrating how both relate to specifically modern historiography of the medieval period.[49] The explicitly political strategies used by medieval archives to order and narrativize their documents is a

Critical Introduction   17

key Chaucerian concern, and Davis' account of the continuity between those strategies and their modern counterparts will help me to unpack the implications of this concern for *The Canterbury Tales*.

As the subtitle of her book indicates, Davis' study unpacks and challenges two received notions: first, that European "feudalism" was a more or less coherent economic system that was slowly replaced in the modern period by capitalism; and second, that "secularization" slowly undermined and supplanted the "religious" governing apparatus of European Christianity – presumptions, we should note, that clearly underpin Patterson's arguments in the study cited above. Through Davis we see that the *historical* question of whether a feudal, Christian, and medieval Europe was transformed by revolution into a proto-capitalist, secular, and modern seat of global civilization has long been subsumed by a *political* question about the legacy of European imperialism and whether or not there are forms of reparation that ought to contend with that legacy. Again, Davis' points about early-modern colonial historiography apply also to Chaucer's engagement with English history, as crucial context for my application of Lowe's critical-race and Gitelman's media-studies methodologies to rethink the relationship between history and the subject in *The Canterbury Tales*.

For Davis, the term periodization "does not refer to a mere back-description that divides history into segments, but to a fundamental political technique – a way to moderate, divide, and regulate – always rendering its services *now*" (Davis' emphasis).[50] In a chapter titled "Sovereign Subjects, Feudal Law, and the Writing of History," Davis argues that the modern periodization of English "feudal" law contributed directly to the processes of specifically colonial archive formalization which created the standard periodizations of media history interrogated by Gitelman.[51] As she summarizes: "at the very moment when the colonial slave trade began to soar, feudal law and slavery were grouped together and identified as characteristic of Europe's past and of a non-European present."[52] In other words "'feudal law,' historicized into a debate about origins and simultaneously mapped onto conquered territory, negotiates the difference in the exercise of the sovereign exception between its presence (spatial and temporal) and its imagined foundation."[53] And as I will argue, this use for early English feudal law and its precedents is already manifest in the portions of *The Canterbury Tales* surveyed by this study and in the representations of the Man of Law and the Monk in particular.

My argument proceeds from Davis' account of the early-modern historians Henry Spelman and John Selden and their debate about dividing the periods of medieval English history around the arrival

18   Chaucer's Problem of Prose

of William the Conqueror in 1066.[54] In the sixteenth and seventeenth centuries, the question of whether to divide the English Middle Ages at this point had important implications for the struggle between the king and Parliament that culminated in the English Civil War.[55] Selden's view was that English feudal law originated well before 1066, and in this way his account favoured the notion of a prehistoric constitution, which Magna Carta only articulated and reiterated.[56] Spelman, meanwhile, argued forcefully that English feudal precedent traced back only to William, who in his account made English land and title (i.e., "feuds" or fees) hereditary.[57] By implication, the king decides the law, and so Magna Carta matters only because a later king signed it. My argument, then, is that we see precisely this same disagreement about the Conquest in the contrasting memories of the Man of Law – who anticipates Spelman's royalism by using his knowledge of case law back to William the Conqueror (I.324) to dissolve feudal entailments (I.319) – and the Monk, whose Selden-like investment in continuity over the longue duree is suggested by the great age of England's wealthiest monastic foundations and, further, is directly signalled by his plan to tell a life of William's immediate predecessor Edward the Confessor (VII.1970).

To paraphrase, then, my argument will suggest that the double-bind of feudal law and slavery – mythic origins in the past and conquered territory in the future – that helped to codify and normalize the structures of British colonialism through the apparatus of English documentary media were already central to Chaucer's negotiations between "the subject" and history, and hence that Chaucer's evocations of early English historical media (Bede's chronicle, Edward's *vitae* and charters, William's Domesday book) express the asymmetries of dominant, residual, and emergent forces in the organization and governance of England, as these are figured in *The Canterbury Tales*. I believe that Patterson is correct to read a dialogue about "feudalism" between the Knight and the Miller that expresses "powerful ambivalence" about the waning of an old political system that is surely coloured by Chaucer's memories of the 1381 Uprising.[58] But I also think that he does not fully engage with the powerful ambivalence about the Uprising suggested by fact that Chaucer's sole mention of the summer of 1381 references only the xenophobic massacre of Flemish immigrants (VII.3394–6).[59] More generally, Patterson makes the common mistake of medievalists described by Susan Reynolds of concentrating on "dyadic, interpersonal relations, and especially on relations between lords and their followers" in a way that distorts "the strong collectivist ideas that informed secular [medieval] society and politics, the emphasis on government by consultation and consensus, on collective judgements, and the belief in peoples as natural, given units of societies and politics bound together by descent, law, and customs."[60] Accordingly, Patterson's focus on the explicit pairing of the Knight's secular aristocracy and the Miller's peasant revolutionaries misses the slower-moving but bigger crisis in *The Canterbury Tales*, wherein the more traditional and collectivist forms of local identity were eroding in favour of more centralized and imperial forms of national identity, as document-based governing practices became both more sophisticated and also more frustratingly unjust, in a widely acknowledged but apparently unavoidable inversion of the ostensible motives for increasing their sophistication. It is in this sense that the politics of periodization surveyed by Davis were already underway in Chaucer's poetry, waiting only for the conjoined processes of monastic disendowment and global colonization to generate the systemic forms of writing and living that would cultivate the later forms of modern English identity enjoyed by the later generations of readers who would recognize Chaucer as the father of their poetic tradition.

It is against this backdrop that I will complete this introduction by defining the key concept of the "politics of recognition," as manifest in the title to Glen Coulthard's influential study *Red Skin White Masks: Rejecting the Colonial Politics of Recognition*. Coulthard's title itself echoes the title of Frantz Fanon's transformative work *Black Skins White Masks*, signalling his application of Fanon's critique of colonial governance to the specific circumstances of settler-Canadian reconciliation politics.[61] The specific form of recognition that Coulthard critiques is the "asymmetrical recognition" of Indigenous nations by the Canadian state, who does not ask to be recognized in turn by the Indigenous nations.[62] Even when treaties, official policies, and court decisions uphold the rights of Indigenous nations to hunt, adjudicate crimes, choose tenants, approve construction projects, and allocate resources in their territories, they do so in the context of the Canadian court of law, whose presumption of authority transforms and assimilates Indigenous nations in subtle and not-so-subtle ways. A similar impasse faced the medieval monasteries whose own (in many cases strikingly similar) exemptions were asymmetrically contingent on externally granted licenses, which was similarly subject to constant encroachment and renegotiation with the crown and papacy who granted them.

In the next section I will flesh out this analogy by juxtaposing a summary of Coulthard's primary example, his own Dene nation, with the example of Worcester cathedral's monastic priory. It bears emphasizing at the start that I posit no direct analogy between Denendeh and Worcester that might compare the actual cultures, beliefs, or lifeways of

20   Chaucer's Problem of Prose

the communities inhabiting these territories. Indeed, from my subject position, I would be astonished to learn of a single productive point of real similarity between them of this kind. The analogy that I find in *The Canterbury Tales* between medieval monks and colonized peoples is wholly mediated by the parallels between their situations before the apparatus of imperial governance, where both monasteries and Indigenous nations have claims to territorial rights that pre-date the literate institutions with whom they must contend, which institutions exist precisely in order to erode and eventually subvert not only the long-standing territorial rights of unassimilated communities but also the internal cohesion of the communities themselves. The reliance of this imperial apparatus on literary form as a mode of authentication and authorization is the reason that the themes of history, media, and the problem of prose in *The Canterbury Tales* should help to make the similarity between these situations visible.

The Politics of Recognition in English Monastic History

Coulthard's description of the colonial politics of recognition draws on the same Marxist historiography of sixteenth-century England cited by Patterson above to argue that the so-called primitive accumulation of capital in this era of Reformation and Dissolution was not specific to a transitional moment in "modern" history (as Marx argued in *Capital*) but has rather always been a basic feature of capitalist exploitation.[63] More specifically, Coulthard argues that "the history and experience of *dispossession*, not proletarianization, has been the dominant background structure shaping the character of the historical relationship between Indigenous peoples and the Canadian state."[64] By applying this insight to the historical relationship between the British imperial state and all of the various local exempt entities it has recognized over the course of its existence, *Chaucer's Problem of Prose* will turn away from Patterson's focus on proletarianization in *The Canterbury Tales* to consider rather Chaucer's representation of dispossession, continuing Coulthard's challenge to Marxist periodization to interrogate the historical boundedness of primitive accumulation from the other, earlier end.[65] Certainly one of the most dramatic and consequential acts of dispossession in English history is the Dissolution of the monasteries, whose long-term significance is indicated by the fact that the grand English country houses symbolizing English colonial wealth to this day are typically built on the estates alienated from English monasteries out of the stone that was taken from the destroyed monastic churches and cloisters. In Chaucer's time of course the Dissolution was over a century in the future, and the historical processes that Marx would aim to describe through his hypothesis of primitive accumulation had not yet begun. Nonetheless, the dispossessing politics of recognition that would make the Dissolution possible were already deeply imbricated in the discourse of monastic satire in his time, and their imperial logic of subjugating and assimilating autonomy and exemption wherever it is encountered help to explain why the tales told by the Man of Law and the Monk specifically should anticipate the orientalism of later generations so strikingly.

Though Coulthard does not emphasize this aspect of his analysis himself, the colonial politics of recognition practiced by the Canadian state are made possible by their reliance on the long-standing English common law systems of written documentation to formalize agreements and to ensure that they carry forward into the future. Since John of Salisbury at least, it has been self-evident that the need to reinforce the fragmentary record provided by early English epistolary documents inspired the great post-Conquest explosion in English monastic chronicle literature, and that secular English common law emerged with the more or less explicit purpose of eroding the political claims made in these quasi-official histories.[66] For example Bruce O'Brien has compellingly argued that this purpose was an obvious motive behind Glanville's original formulation of the English common law as a *lex non scripta* that nonetheless required one to document one's claims in official writing.[67] Even when particular rights are recognized as originating in "time out of mind" and explicitly affirmed as such in a document, the document is not itself eternally applicable (the law, after all, is "unwritten") and so the terms are subject to gradual evolution as new precedents replace the old ones. If the law itself is always evolving, no claim to possession can ever be settled, and every decision is always open for re-consideration. As a consequence, a king who swore in his coronation oath to uphold the laws of Edward the Confessor may nonetheless ignore a text like *The Laws of Edward the Confessor*, with its curtailments of royal authority over ecclesiastical institutions.

In this common law system, the politics of recognition unfold as follows. Communities are granted official recognition of their inherited rights, as the results of proceedings that are typically framed as victories. However the communities quickly discover that these rights need to be exercised, renewed, and otherwise protected if they are to be maintained. Once the rights are lost, there is no getting them back, and so constant vigilance is required. The long-term consequence is that the vigilant policing of rights becomes itself a basic constitutive aspect of life within the right-holding community, in a manner that is detrimental

22   Chaucer's Problem of Prose

both to internal cohesion of the community itself and to the prestige of the community among its neighbours. If all a community cared about were holding on to its wealth, then why does that community continue to deserve its special dispensations? If they are not morally excellent, then shouldn't they be treated like everyone else? Thus it is the case that even when the documents and systems that nominally exist to protect traditional rights to title are successful in doing so, they subtly assimilate the spirit of the traditions and the communities they shape and so change the way those communities are perceived, in ways that viewers both internal and external to the communities sometimes describe as "corruption." Communities therefore find themselves fighting on two fronts: first to preserve the traditional claims that sustain them, and second to avoid the actual and perceived harms to their community that are inevitably done by the pragmatic necessities of the first struggle.

To clarify the parallels, I will begin with my own summary of Coulthard's account of his own Dene nation, reflecting his own investments in that nation's history and future. In 1973, the Fort Smith chief François Paulette filed with fifteen other chiefs a caveat with the Northwest Territory of Land Titles, claiming a Dene interest in more than one million square kilometres of the Northwest Territory in an effort to resist the construction of a natural gas pipeline in the Mackenzie valley.[68] Their right to file the caveat was contested, and the question culminated in the 1973 decision by the Supreme Court of the Northwest Territories "Re: Paulette and Registrar of Land Titles." In this decision Justice William G. Morrow examined the available historical record to determine that the Dene had likely not intended to passively surrender their title to lands covered by Treaties 8 and 11, negotiated with the crown in 1900 and 1921 respectively, and so that their current leaders had the right to file the caveat.[69]

Morrow's ruling contributed to two major developments. The first was a comprehensive federal overview of land-claims policy across the settler nation of Canada, intended to "exchange the claims to undefined Aboriginal rights for a clearly defined package of rights and benefits set out in a settlement agreement."[70] As Coulthard emphasizes, these clearly defined and documented rights were specifically articulated as rights of ownership over territories, not as political rights to self-governance.[71] The second development was the famous "Berger inquiry," which consulted heavily with Indigenous communities before finally recommending a 10-year moratorium on the pipeline.

Coulthard argues that "one of the negative effects of this power-laden process of discursive translation has been a reorientation of the meaning of self-determination for many (but not all) Indigenous people in the North; a reorientation of Indigenous struggle from one that was once deeply informed by the land as a system of reciprocal relations and obligations (grounded normativity) ... to a struggle that is now increasingly for land, understood now as a material resource to be exploited in the capital accumulation process."[72] If the Dene had true political autonomy, they could have simply decided to ignore the question of whether or not a pipeline would be built in the Mackenzie Valley and devoted their time and energy to other questions. As it was, the Dene were not only forced to consider the pipeline proposal, but also to learn and internalize the rules of the settler-colonial legal processes through which their resistance to the pipeline could be efficaciously expressed. As a consequence, their right to live without reference to a possible pipeline was replaced by a new right to either build a pipeline or not build one, circumscribed by settler-colonial frameworks for assessing the advantages and disadvantages of each course of action. More to the point, the sheer logistics of organizing resistance and communicating arguments within and beyond Denendeh came to shape Dene communal life, so that even their political victories brought about the very forms of assimilation that their struggles started out attempting to resist. When the pipeline project was finally resurrected in the early 2000s, it had the consent of many Indigenous communities along the Mackenzie corridor, before it was ultimately abandoned in 2017 for financial reasons.[73]

There are many analogous narratives of asymmetrical recognition in the histories of English monasteries, including the institutions of Bury St. Edmunds, St. Albans, and Westminster, which are discussed in later chapters. But rather than repeat myself in those later discussions, I will use the example here of Worcester cathedral priory. St. Oswald of Worcester was one of three saints who were remembered in subsequent generations as the architects of the so-called Benedictine Reform, whose major consequences included the establishment of monastic priories as cathedral chapters in a number of important dioceses, including Worcester.[74] Domesday Book claims that during Oswald's episcopacy, in the year 964, King Edgar gave Worcester the right to administer justice in the so-called Oswaldslow triple hundred. Because the articulation of these rights in Domesday is so unusually favourable to Worcester, contemporary scholars have generally followed Patrick Wormald to believe that the immunity was an invention of the Worcester church dictated to the Domesday inquest by their representative.[75]

For now, we can set aside the question of what sorts of rights Worcester might have actually had to govern Oswaldslow before Domesday, to simply note the parallel between this question and the question of

24   Chaucer's Problem of Prose

the Dene nation's rights in Coulthard's account. Just like Justice Morrow, so also did the Domesday inquest set aside Worcester's undefined pre-Conquest rights to govern Oswaldslow for a clearly defined package of rights and benefits that enabled the self-determination of its community. And just like the Dene nation, so also did Worcester priory find itself constrained by the necessity of continuously defending these rights in later eras, as they could not simply administer justice in Oswaldslow without re-orienting the meaning of their monastic self-determination.

The text describing the Oswaldslow rights is recorded three times in the Worcester cartulary London British Library MS Cotton Tiberius A.xiii. Worcester has the largest archive of charters of any ecclesiastical institution before the Conquest, and the first part of Tiberius A.xiii (referred to by modern scholars as the *Liber Wigorniensis*) is the earliest known cartulary in medieval England.[76] The second part appears to have been commissioned by St. Wulfstan, who also appears to have commissioned John of Worcester to write his *Chronicon ex chronicis*, a history of the world that ends in their own lifetime. Wulfstan's chaplain and chancellor Coleman also wrote an Old English life of St. Wulfstan that was later translated into Latin by William of Malmesbury.[77] Together these historiographic projects suggest a concerted effort in eleventh- and twelfth-century Worcester to produce summative and authoritative records of pertinent documentary, narrative-historical, and hagiographic narratives in both English and Latin, whose exhaustiveness is paralleled by the similarly thorough fact-finding methods of the Berger inquiry. And though Worcester was particularly early in cultivating this practice of historical writing, other monasteries across England quickly followed, to produce a similarly wide variety of the sorts of historical accounts that might allow them to preserve (or, when necessary, invent) clearly defined benefits for their communities in the wake of the Conquest's many disruptions.[78]

Applying Coulthard, then, we may observe that one of the negative effects of this power-laden process of discursive translation was a reorientation of the meaning of self-determination for many (but not all) medieval English monasteries, away from their spiritual mission and towards a struggle that was increasingly for land. Historians have observed that the century following the Norman Conquest saw the English landscape more dramatically transformed than it was in any recorded period before the Industrial Revolution, which changes put pressure on not only monastic land rights but also on the practices of monastic land use.[79] New forms of exploitation created new opportunities for the neighbours of monasteries to create precedents that would

Critical Introduction 25

allow them to profit off of monastic land and also for monasteries to profit themselves. Conflicts arose and went before the courts, and their results were recorded. Coleman's life of St. Wulfstan would not be the last biography of a medieval English abbot that praised not only his holiness but his shrewdness as a litigator – if anything, the second trait was more important to the communities.[80] As the great legal historian Patrick Wormald has generalized, the common thread in our records of disputes involving ecclesiastical institutions from the earliest era of monastic historiography is that "the Church always wins; the stories would not otherwise survive."[81]

A monastic history that represents the transformations in monastic life resulting from this new pressure is Thomas of Marlborough's *History of the Abbey of Evesham*, documenting a conflict between this exempt monastery and Worcester where Worcester was in the position of the aggressor. In 1203, Mauger, the bishop of Worcester, wished to visit Evesham and correct the abbot Roger Norreis, who wasted the abbey's wealth and lived in flagrant violation of the Benedictine rule.[82] Though the monks of Evesham agreed that Roger should be corrected – and had, indeed, already made their case for this correction to the papal legate Hubert Walter – they wished to prevent the bishop of Worcester from providing the correction, because this would establish a precedent that would turn Evesham from an independent, autonomous institution into one of Worcester's dependent houses.[83] Alain Boureau documents how in the years-long conflict that followed, the improbable victory of Evesham over Worcester was predicated on the advantage given to their advocate Thomas of Marlborough by his formal education in civil law, which would soon become a standard, necessary requirement for holding monastic office.[84] Roger then continued to serve as abbot of Evesham until 1213, when he was finally deposed not because of his ongoing corruption and immorality as because he had refused to repay a loan.[85]

Thomas wrote his chronicle documenting the case during his own abbacy, 1230–6 CE, in an apparent effort to both preserve his institutional knowledge as a protection against future encroachments from Worcester and also to build community at Evesham. Be that as it may, he could not help but document the obvious contradiction in his actions, between his ostensible commitment to the religious purpose of Evesham monastery and his active protection of the corrupt abbot Roger, made necessary by his wish to maintain Evesham's recognized autonomy from Worcester, who themselves seemed much more interested in Evesham's wealth than they were in the moral rectitude of its leader. The blatant worldliness on display in this conflict is not unusual

26 Chaucer's Problem of Prose

in monastic histories of the period, and Roger Norreis is hardly the only historical template that may have informed the portrait of the worldly Monk in the *GP* (I.165–207) and its many satirical analogues.[86] The insight we gain from Coulthard's analysis is that this worldliness was a direct consequence of the imperial politics of recognition informing the emergence of the English common law, which required monks to organize their communities around the preservation of rights if they were to have any hope of preserving them and so transformed the nature of the communities in the process.

This, then, is the context for my starting supposition, that Coulthard's insightful analysis of the colonial politics of recognition in the Northwest Territories is applicable to Chaucer's understanding of the histories of medieval English monasteries. And as I have already stated, the analogy helps us to make sense of what might otherwise be a surprising aspect of *The Canterbury Tales*, that the sections of the text where it demonstrates a thematic concern for monasteries and their worldliness should also be the sections of the text where Chaucer uses orientalist and anti-feminist tropes in stories about the spread of Roman imperialism. As I will argue in more detail in subsequent chapters, the anti-clericalism in *The Canterbury Tales* is less concerned with the moral corruption of individual clerics than it is with the subtle structural mechanisms that have brought that corruption about, whereby the documentation of rights and privileges can serve not only as the very means whereby those rights and privileges are eroded, but also whereby the communities holding those rights and privileges are debased and so subsumed into larger forms of national collective identity. The problem of prose in *The Canterbury Tales* emerges from its self-representation as a document that may be used for precisely this purpose, but that individual readers could choose to learn from differently, in a way that may finally break or at least give some perspective on the ongoing cycles of textual production, dissemination, and reproduction that the collection represents.

Summary of the Chapters

In the first chapter, I will establish the basic facts informing the structure of this book with a reading of the *Man of Law's Introduction* (*MLI*). This text is the start of the problematic fragment II, and it also contains a meta-textual passage where the Man of Law first mocks the poet Geoffrey Chaucer and then promises to tell a tale in prose, before proceeding to tell a story set in conversion-era England instead. Indeed, the entirety of this book's argument may be imagined as a commentary on

Critical Introduction   27

and contextualization of this particular crux, where the themes of history, media, and the problem of prose are all established.

The next two chapters provide the historical context and heuristic respectively that I will apply to read *MkT* and *MLT* in chapters 4 and 5. Chapter 2 turns to a Bury St. Edmunds register that contains Lydgate's rhyme royal translations of Old English charters, alongside transcriptions of the Old English written in insular letterforms. The cartulary witnesses both the continued importance of Old English legal documents in Chaucer's own time period, and the ways in which the precedent of the charters exerted pressure on Chaucer's own English language poetry.

Chapter 3, meanwhile, reads the dialogue between the Friar and Summoner in fragment III as a representation of the text/gloss contradiction that, in Chaucer's telling, drives the production of text. The Friar embodies a critical openness to the interpretations of the gloss and the Summoner personifies a critical adherence to the precise letter of the text. Both positions are defined by their opposition to each other, and neither position can promise, finally, to lead towards "correct" interpretation and away from obvious abuses. My own reading of the fragment argues that ultimately, the squabble finds no resolution because it turns out that the distinction occasioning it is ultimately false: the text requires the gloss every bit as much as the gloss requires text, and each is generative of the other. This leads me to propose a new implication of Carolyn Dinshaw's reading of the Loathly Lady (and Wife of Bath) and the Rapist Knight (and Jenkyn) as personifications of the text and gloss respectively.[87] The Wife of Bath's unhealthy marriage fantasies allegorizes the same problem for writing that the Friar and the Summoner allegorize, and so they reveal that the target of satire is not so much the hypocrisy of ecclesiastical governance as it is the structural flaws in literate apparatus of that governance itself.

Chapters 4 turns finally to *MkP* and *MkT*. Where the contrast between the Friar and the Summoner is concerned with official ecclesiastical texts more generally, the contrast between Monk and the Man of Law is especially concerned with approaches to early English historical documents. In this instance, the text/gloss contradiction contributes to an inexorable dynamic of alienation and dispossession, expressive of the politics of recognition. My reading of the Monk begins with the subtle continuities between *MkP*, *Mel*, and the *Man of Law's Prologue* (*MLP*) that may have preceded *Mel* in some earlier ordering. The Monk's plan to tell a Life of Edward the Confessor is realized in the tragedy of Cenobia, which allegorizes the subjugation of the monastic life to centralized, secular, and in those senses imperial rule. In chapter 5, meanwhile,

28 Chaucer's Problem of Prose

I will argue that the marriages of Custaunce in *MLT* similarly occasion subjugations and assimilations, where (as in the tragedy of Cenobia) the assimilated cultures are personified by "virago" women. Cenobia's subjection to secular imperial authority and Custaunce's miraculous elevation at her trial represent the same historical dynamic with different affective framings. The Monk remains melancholically attached to a past that the Man of Law blithely abandons, as he focuses instead on the future of imperial destiny.

The sixth and final chapter will turn finally to a reading of the two prose tales, *Mel* and *ParsT*. Once again, we see a polarity between text and gloss collapse into a single whole, in this instance of *The Canterbury Tales*. Chaucer the pilgrim is a glossator, like the Friar and the Man of Law, and he uses the figure of Prudence to represent an ideal form of glossing that affirms a spirit of generosity and non-violence towards others. The Parson, meanwhile, may not be "textueel" but he is nonetheless a man of the text, whose conventional confessional manual represents an ideal mode of textual authority concerned not with punishment but with consensual accountability, repair, and recognition. Of course neither of these visions resolve the contradictions in the rest of the collection, and indeed my readings of *Thopas* and the *Retraction* will argue that they call readerly attention to the true source of the problem: *The Canterbury Tales* is exactly the sort of text whose problems it aims to document, and whose imperfect material mediation of its intended contents instantiates the larger problem for social justice posed by England's reliance on written media to record and apply history.

Chapter One

The Problem of Prose in Fragments II and VII: An Overview

The description of the Man of Law from the *GP* reads as follows:

> So greet a purchasour was nowher noon:
> Al was fee symple to hym in effect;
> His purchasyng mighte nat been infect.
> Nowher so bisy a man as he ther nas,
> and yet he semed bisier than he was.
> In termes had he caas and doomes alle
> That from the tyme of kyng William were falle.
> Therto he koude endite and make a thyng,
> Ther koude no wight pynche at his writyng;
> And every statut koude he pleyn by rote. (I.309–27)[1]

The key statements for the present study are that the Man of Law is a "purchasour" of land, that "al was fee symple to hym," and that his purchasing "myghte nat been infect."[2] Fee simple is not a precise concept, but it typically referred to a sort of possession that was unrestricted by conditions or entailments, and particularly by those that might prevent the possessor from selling their title. The Man of Law is able to cut through such traditional, familial obligations to alienate land because of his ability to "endite and make a thyng" of such quality that no being could "pynch at his writing" (I.325–6) – which is to say he knew how to find and exploit procedural loopholes, and to block off his opponents from doing the same.[3] More to the point, the Man of Law is able to accomplish this writing through his knowledge of "caas and doomes alle | That from the tyme of Kyng William were falle," which is to say the recorded precedent of cases and judgments going back to King William the Conqueror (1066–87 CE).

30   Chaucer's Problem of Prose

In her influential reading of *MLI*, Maura Nolan has written about how the "insoluble textual problems" that surround the Man of Law are "structured by a legalistic relation between empirical fact – the textual difficulty, the legal evidence – and a transcendental abstraction, a final form, for *The Canterbury Tales*, 'the law.'"[4] Given that citable common law precedent only extends back to 1189 CE, the "caas and doomes" of King William most useful to the Man of Law would have been the Domesday book, which was indeed cited by purchasers in the fourteenth century to establish "ancient demesne" and so free up land for exchange.[5] Hence Nolan's "empirical fact" and "final form" are situated in this passage between the embodied archive of early English history, which attested the sorts of entailments and precedents that limited or allowed purchasing, and an ideal law where all land is imagined to be fully alienable "fee simple" – which is to say the conditions most favourable to the processes of settler-colonial dispossession described by Coulthard. The contradiction witnessed in this tension between material precedent and aspirational form will be an important one for this study, and so it merits a brief discussion before we move on to describe how the Man of Law fits into it.

Though Domesday book is often cited as a watershed moment in the history of institutional literacy, not only in England but in Europe as a whole,[6] the use of written records in England predated William by centuries. Several of the records that survive make a telling distinction between an alienable form of title called "bocland" – introduced, it seems, by the church[7] – and a form called "folcland," which is rarely evoked, poorly described, but is nonetheless consistently contrasted in legal documents with bocland.[8] For our present purposes, I will set aside the historical question of what these forms of title actually entailed in early English law, and simply note that the terms' very existence suggests that at least some transactional agents in the pre-Domesday period were concerned to protect community (i.e., "folk") identity and ownership from the novelties of written records (i.e., "books"). We should always be skeptical about such divisions of "old" from "new": nostalgic constructions of history are just as likely to encourage novel arrangements as they are to preserve old ones, for the simple reason that it is easier to gain popular support for new practices and frameworks if you can pretend that you are reviving old ones, and so exploit the vague but powerful feelings about shared pasts that attend the experience of political identity. Indeed, given that change is an ontological fact of being in time, continuity requires constant innovation if it is to be maintained, and so innovation can always be framed as an effort to foster continuity. In the case of early English law, the contrast between the terms

The Problem of Prose in Fragments II and VII   31

"folcland" and "bocland" opposes a fantasy of primitive, unmediated, irreducibly communal form of title with an innovative, mediated, and irreducibly alienable alternative, which framing therefore makes both forms seem desirable: it is good to have strong community ties and a sense of one's place in history, and it is good to have personal freedom to pursue wealth. There is, in this sense, plenty of precedent for the Man of Law's professional practice of carefully studying recorded precedent so that he can then help his clients do whatever they want. The rules of engagement in the fourteenth century have changed significantly from those of the ninth and tenth, but the conceptual oppositions at play are not only persistent but have served as a primary mechanism of institutional persistence itself.

Nor is the construction of such oppositions unique to medieval English law. Twentieth-century scholars of orality and media did not invent the narrative that imagines new communications technologies to have regularized the idiosyncratic local traditions they encountered, so that previously unmediated social relations would become mediated by things: the scholars themselves commonly trace the trope back to Plato.[9] Similar narratives of primitive simplicity and growing complexity are attested in the terminology, anecdotes, and myths witnessed by our earliest written English documents, which have helped to validate English cultural anxieties about ongoing institutional changes for the entirety of recorded English history. The crucial point here is that even though such narratives commonly lament the changes they describe, they nonetheless commonly lead to policies that either reify novel complexities or introduce additional ones. For reasons I will explain below, the "problem of prose" I identify in the cracks and fissures of *The Canterbury Tales* constitutes an attempt to represent this phenomenon both formally and thematically from within the confines of a text that is itself a manifestation of it. Is there a way to "get back to basics" that does not in fact result in greater complexity? Is it possible to at least represent this paradoxical dynamic of reform, to engender greater understanding of how it works? My argument in this chapter is that Chaucer's efforts to meet this challenge informed the insoluble textual problems that have clustered around the Man of Law's fragment II.

In the Man of Law's portrait, his introduction, and (as we shall discuss in chapter 5) his tale, he acts consistently as an agent of institutional innovation and the consolidation of imperial power,[10] in a manner consistent with the larger trend whereby "purchasours" asserted the courts' authority to invalidate and thereby transmute (nominally older) forms of constrained, traditional land ownership into (nominally newer) forms that afford owners more freedom,

32   Chaucer's Problem of Prose

which was accomplished by applying their expert knowledge of the very archived documents whose original intentions they blatantly subverted. The implicit contrasts between the Man of Law and the Monk, discussed fully in chapters 4 and 5, demonstrates how these processes are intimately bound up in Chaucer's self-representation as an author of verse, and hence in his decision to include two prose tales. In chapter 2 I will provide some additional historical context that helps to explain why I make this connection between "purchasing," prose, and specifically monastic land, before then turning in chapter 3 to the text/gloss contradiction in the dialogue between the Friar and the Summoner, which will serve as a useful heuristic for describing the similar conflict between the Man of Law and the Monk. In the present chapter, I will make a second beginning of this study with the second beginning to *The Canterbury Tales*, the *MLI*, wherein both the Man of Law and the "problem of prose" are introduced to the collection.[11]

Mediality and Time in *The Man of Law's Introduction*

MLI starts with a strong temporal marker identifying the date of its events as the 18th of April – the mediating "messager to May" (II.6) – and the time as 10:00 a.m., exactly one quarter-length of the day, at the precise moment when the sun was at a 45 degree angle to the ground and so when the length of the shadows cast by every object were precisely equal in height to the objects that cast them (II.7–15) – an occurrence rare enough in the calendar that Chaucer may well have chosen to set his frame narrative in April, rather than his usual May, to allow for this specific scene.[12] As the shadows suggest, this moment of equilibrium on this "messenger" day is also a moment of perfect representational transparency, wherein the shadows justly represented the precise dimensions of the objects they imitate.

The symbolically fleeting perfection of these shadows' representations of the objects they reflect is itself a representation of how the circulation of media objects ("messages") can undermine even the most perfect instances of transparent mediality. Even when an artist perfectly captures their subject, time will change both the subject and the context of the artwork's reception, and so the representation will become a distortion. The same problem adheres to legal documents that attempt to capture the value of a parcel of property or the intentions of the parties to an agreement. Domesday book is a perfect example of the issues at stake: even if this survey of English wealth

The Problem of Prose in Fragments II and VII   33

was indeed a perfect shadow of the estates that it recorded at the time of its assembly, this representation changed with the passage of time, until it could be cited by the Man of Law to justify transactions that William himself might not have dreamed possible, much less have approved of. For all that "ancient demesne" attempted to capture something of the spirit of demesne as William experienced it in "ancient" times, it was a thoroughly modern category of ownership, rendered such by the legal context within which the Man of Law used it.

The Host's own words for expressing anxiety about the changes in representational shadows are as follows:

> Lordynges, the tyme wasteth nyght and day,
> And steleth from us, what pryvely slepynge,
> And what thurh necligence in oure wakynge,
> As dooth the streem that turneth nevere agayn,
> Descendynge fro the montaigne into playn.
> Wel kan Senec and many a philosophre
> Biwaillen tyme moore than golde in cofre;
> For "Los of catel may recovered be,
> But los of tyme shendeth us," quod he.   (II.20–8)

The Host observes that the precise representation of objects accomplished by their shadows at the moment he speaks is made possible by a confluence of events that can never be precisely repeated, any more than the mountain stream will outlast the end of that winter's thaw. Transparent, immediate representation is stolen from us by time's passage, in the same way that the movement of the sun changes the shape of our shadows and distorts them. This sentiment is then followed by a quotation from Seneca, which accomplishes two things. First, it concretizes the general anxiety of the earlier lines through a specific worry about the damage time does to one's money and fungible "catel," which also – as David Wallace observes – suggests that the pilgrims' "debt" in the competition is in some sense usurious.[13] Second, the quotation instantiates the ways in which authoritative texts may resist these processes, since of course the words of Seneca were written down a long time ago but survive to profit us. And as we shall discuss below, the Host's specific analogy between lost time and the lost virginity of a woman (II.31) ties this second question of authorial immortality to two persistent tendencies in Chaucer's work: first, to objectify

34   Chaucer's Problem of Prose

women, and second to feminize himself while representing himself as an author of text.[14]

As many readers of *MLI* have observed, the Host's address to the Man of Law frames the tale-telling contest in highly legalistic terms as a formal contract:[15]

> Ye been submytted, thurgh youre free assent,
> To stonden in this cas at my juggement.
> Acquiteth yow now of youre biheeste;
> Than have ye do youre devoir atte leeste. (II.35–8)

These lines pick up the same "assent" / "juggement" lines from the *GP* (I.817–18), which enshrined the host as their "governoure, | And of oure tales juge and reportour" (I.812–13). The reoccurrence of the terms here frames *MLT* as a fulfillment of a sworn oath, both to deliver testimony before the Host (acting as a judge) and to provide a contracted service. Essentially, the Man of Law has been asked to go on the record and so to speak formally and professionally in anticipation of the future that matters of record always anticipate, when other lawyers will hunt through them for evidence or ambiguities that will help their claims. And as his portrait in *GP* led us to expect, the Man of Law's own exercise of his expert counsel will not require him to honour the original arrangement but on the contrary will help him to get himself out of it.

The Man of Law begins his response to the Host's request as follows:

> "Hooste," quod he, "Depardieux, ich assente;
> To breke forward is nat myn entente.
> Biheste is dette, and I wole holde fayn
> Al my biheste, I kan no bettre sayn.
> For swich lawe as a man yeveth another wight,
> He sholde hymselves usen it, by right;
> Thus wole oure text. But nathelees, certeyn,
> I kan right now no thrifty tale seyn" (II.39–46)

The end of the passage constitutes a remarkable reversal of the statements at its beginning. Again, the Host has asked the Man of Law to "telle us a tale" (II.34). The Man of Law replies by saying that he assents, insofar as he does not *generally* wish to break his contracts and agrees *in principle* that promises are binding. Nonetheless, *right now*, he cannot tell a tale. The sentence then proceeds to a discursus on Chaucer's poetry that concludes with a promise to "speke in prose" instead (II.96).

The Man of Law's reversal of his earlier oath pivots around the crucial distinction between the principles articulated in "oure text" (II.45) and the contexts of their reception and application. The original contract of the *GP* has no provisions to address the (pointedly metafictional) problem that confronts the Man of Law, that Chaucer has already told all of his tales in other books and so there are none left for the Man of Law to tell here – as certainly may have been a real problem for Chaucer, given the breadth of his corpus and the extraordinary number of tales that *GP* promised (I.792–5). The Man of Law's situation therefore precisely instantiates the problem of time and text illustrated by the image of the proportionate shadows: even good faith attempts to uphold the just principles of earlier laws may be thwarted by the distortionary pressures of later contexts, wherein factors may arise that the original authors of the contract did not anticipate. The agreement of the participants in the Canterbury pilgrimage is no exception to this unfortunate truth.

The specific evocation of Chaucer in the Man of Law's speech marks these relatively legal-procedural concerns as central to the larger question of the collection's organizing principles and purpose.[16] The Man of Law's list refers to Chaucer's paraphrase of Ceys and Alcione that begins his *Book of the Duchess* and *Legend of Good Women* (*LGW*), before going on to summarize the latter work (II.57–76). Meanwhile *LGW* includes its own summary of Chaucer's earlier works, which appears in the course of an introductory debate about whether or not Chaucer has represented women poorly (*LGW* G.246–316). In *MLI*, too, the Man of Law is concerned particularly to identify Chaucer's thrifty tales about "wifhod" (II.76).[17] This sudden concern for the representation of women calls back to the Host's aside about lost virginity, cited above, and it anticipates the representation of women in the tales discussed in this book's later chapters. Before I proceed, then, I will paraphrase the working interpretation of the oft-discussed theme of "women's virtue" in Chaucer's poetry that will inform this study.

In her influential study of Chaucer's alleged feminism, Elaine Tuttle Hansen begins with an insight she had about *LGW*, to the effect that it "was best thought of as a poem about men, not women."[18] Proceeding from Richard Firth Green's argument in *Poets and Princepleasers* that Chaucer's "women" are typically figures for his own disempowerment as a court poet, Hansen goes on to conclusively demonstrate that Chaucer's representation of women is not so much proto-feminist as it is provocatively incoherent, as he projects onto his women anxieties about masculinity, power, and authorship that are made all the

36   Chaucer's Problem of Prose

more inscrutable by the obvious intelligence, wit, and self-awareness he brings to bear expressing them.[19]

Continuing this work in her influential *Chaucer's Sexual Poetics*, Carolyn Dinshaw identifies a "gendered structure" in Chaucer's poetry:

> [it is] a structure that associates acts of writing and related acts of signifying – allegorizing, interpreting, glossing, translating – with the masculine and that identifies the surfaces on which these acts are performed, or from which these acts depart, or which these acts reveal – the page, the text, the literal sense, or even the hidden meaning – with the feminine.[20]

Gender and sexuality are in these terms a symbolic vocabulary for thinking about authority and mediation in poetry more generally. Continuing in this vein, Carissa Harris has argued compellingly that the male narrators in fragment I of *The Canterbury Tales* "dehumanize women to bond intimately with one another, to compete viciously with one another, and to authorize violence against women and aggression towards men," in this sense reducing women to a medium of communication and exchange between men.[21] In all of these readings, then, we see that Chaucer's representations of women are only concerned indirectly with the material conditions of embodied femininity, and so they are only concerned indirectly with the forms of violence and suffering endemic to those conditions. Far more central to Chaucer's representations of women (and meditations thereon) are the symbolic affordances of the feminine experience as they pertain to the condition of mediation, which makes them useful for representing the contradictions and anxieties that attend the affordances and strictures of the technology of writing as a mode of (masculine) self-expression.

It bears emphasizing that Chaucer's exploitation of women's experiences to represent the embodiment of textual media is itself misogynist even when it is sympathetic to those experiences, for the simple fact that it reduces the suffering of real women to mere discourse. More to the point, as Susan Nakley has argued in continuation of a point made by Kathleen Davis, women in *The Canterbury Tales* "bear their communities' collective ethnic and religious identities," and so their dehumanization directly figures the imperial ambitions that attended the development of English identity in Chaucer's milieu.[22] Nor did the modern scholarly criticism of Chaucer adequately address the problematic aspects of the texts' representations of women before quite recently. Though recent discoveries have complicated the long-standing thesis that Geoffrey Chaucer was formally accused of raping Cecily Chaumpagne,[23] the new historical details only underscore how transparently

The Problem of Prose in Fragments II and VII 37

earlier scholars have projected their own investments onto the evidence in ways that exposed their sympathies with medieval rape culture.[24] Here I will argue that in *The Canterbury Tales* the horrors of patriarchal abuse and sexual assault are consistently trivialized by Chaucer to figure the vagaries of textual circulation and use, in a way that is itself a useful example of both the dehumanization of women in the fourteenth century and the dehumanization of women at the time of this writing. Chaucer's problematic figuration of women's suffering reminds us how his poetry ought not to be read as the wisdom of a clever and neutral observer, who has somehow managed to poke his head above the clouds of emergent patriarchal-settler-colonial ideology to glimpse its most productive possible futures. On the contrary, Chaucer gives us every indication that he was an active participant in the ongoing structural violence of his time and place, and he deserves to be read as such. Though I do believe *The Canterbury Tales* expresses a productive self-critical awareness of the contradictions in its own project, the methods used by the text to address and incorporate those contradictions were only partially successful at best, and the failures are highly illuminating.

The Man of Law's evocation of Chaucer's women is precisely such an illuminating failure. Again, the Host had just used an analogy to a woman who has lost her virginity to figure the passage of time and its impact on the truth of embodied representations (II.30–1). Shadows that are precise, accurate reflections of the objects that create them become increasingly distorted as the sun continues to move, and the analogy between this process and the imagined transformation of women after they enjoy their sexual maturity plays off of misogynistic assumptions to figure the passage of time negatively, as the loss of something beautiful and pure. The Man of Law then deploys his own sexual analogy to refigure the passage of time as a good thing, by evoking the taboo against incest (II.77–89).[25] Incestuous reproduction resists the passage of time to perpetuate unnatural sameness, and it especially did so in the political institutions of medieval Europe, which commonly required the marriage of close relatives to ensure institutional continuity. The Man of Law's unprompted rejection of incest narratives therefore accomplishes two things: first, it trivializes the rape in his examples; second, it rejects the Host's desire for pure, unmediated transparency in representation.

There is, then, considerable thematic consistency in the dialogue between the Host and the Man of Law in the *MLI*. Where the Host wishes for time to stand still, for agreements to be honoured, and for women to keep their virginity, the Man of Law wishes for time to move

38 Chaucer's Problem of Prose

forward, for agreements to evolve to fit the new circumstances, and for women to seek sexual gratification outside of their families in a way that will break the lines of inheritance and enable property transfer. In place of the "tale" he could have told on the model of Chaucer's lives of historical women, the Man of Law provocatively states: "I recche night a bene | though I come after [Chaucer] with a hawebake. | I speke in prose, and lat him rymes make" (II.94–6). Even if Chaucer's *LGW* presented a filling meal and the Man of Law offers only a handful of berries, the Man of Law still prefers his own offering, because at least it will be new and not bound to the mere repetition of the same old classical poetic authorities that characterize the many examples of Chaucer's works he has cited. In contrast to Chaucer the traditionalist, the Man of Law places himself on the avant garde and names prose as the fitting vehicle for his novelties.

As I have stated in the introduction, there is no surviving ordering of the collection where the Man of Law then goes on to tell a tale in prose. There is a well-established consensus among readers of the tale surmising that *Mel* may have been assigned to the Man of Law in some earlier draft. Given also that *Mel* is followed by *MkP* and *MkT*, this would imply that the tales may be ordered *MLI*, *MLP*, *Mel*, *MkP*, *MkT* on the basis of internal evidence, and so that the Man of Law and Monk can be placed in direct dialogue with each other. Again, this ordering is not attested in any surviving collection, but it does follow the internal logic of the text itself: *MLI* promises a tale in prose, which suggests *Mel*; *MLP* follows *MLI* in the manuscripts, and its connection to *MLT* is tenuous at best; *MkP* begins with the Host's reaction to *Mel*, which sets off a series of musings that leads him to turn to address the Monk.[26]

Of course there is no particular reason to privilege this possible ordering as a draft or a plan, or even to say that it was consciously considered by Chaucer at all. Ultimately the present study is not concerned with these unanswerable textual-critical questions.[27] It does not matter if Chaucer or his scribes ever intended to highlight the dialogue between the Man of Law and the Monk that may be inferred from reading across the texts, or if it is simply an accidental consequence of the text's unfinished state when it went into circulation. The dialogue is nonetheless discernible in the internal logic of the text's reconfigurable fragments, and the unexpected continuity between seemingly disparate sections of the text merits investigation as an unexplored forking path in the garden of the collection. In the next and final section I will engage with the reading by Eleanor Johnson – one of the most recent to proceed from the assumption that the Man of Law's "prose" refers to the tale of

The Problem of Prose in Fragments II and VII   39

Custaunce – before then proceeding to consider the implications of the sequence *MLP – Mel – MkP* for the larger collection.[28]

Disordering Fragment II: "Prose" and Prologue

Johnson proceeds from the assumption that the Man of Law confuses formal categories in her introduction as part of "the programmatic cultivation of juridical assent in his audience, so as eventually to elicit a desired verdict from them on the guilt or innocence of an accused party" – in this instance, the Man of Law himself, who wished "to exonerate himself from any blame in the kinds of legal corruption that motivated the dizzying array of antilegal sentiment in the late Middle Ages."[29] Johnson argues that the Man of Law evokes the "imaginary and idealized deep history" of the tale's setting because he wishes to find in that history an origin for his own legal practices that might evade charges of novelty and corruption.[30] The Man of Law's claim to "prose" may be imagined in these terms more precisely as a claim to artlessness and by implication transparency – as she puts it, prose "is a designation of truth, rather than a promise of composition in continuous, unversified lines of writing."[31]

My own reading departs from Johnson's not to contradict it, but rather to put it in productive tension with the alternative possibility that the internal narratives of the fragments also suggest and that indeed adheres to even the most obvious linkages between tales. *The Canterbury Tales* was certainly unfinished. Editors intervened at some early stage to create the orderings that currently survive, and so it is irreducibly possible that not only some but *all* the linkages between tales in the various prologues and epilogues might have been added by some later editor or scribe.[32] The Host's anxiety about time is clearly a perceptive one. The shadows did in fact move.

There is an important homology between Johnson's description of the Man of Law, who wishes to apply a veneer of antiquity to the forms of novel legal systems, and the way Chaucer similarly combines the subject matter of classical antiquity with the forms of novel English poetry. It is quite striking that Johnson's reading of fragment II – whose conclusion, *The Man of Law's Epilogue* (*MLE*), is called by Helen Cooper "the greatest textual dilemma posed by the whole work"[33] – sees its texts connected by a concern for transparent historical accuracy as a guarantor of justice and a bulwark against corruption, expressed through a figure whose own deep knowledge of historical precedent is the precise reason that he expects the other pilgrims not to trust him. If the Man of Law promises to tell a tale in straightforward, unaffected

40   Chaucer's Problem of Prose

prose because he wishes to distance himself from the arcane subtleties of legal proceduralism that were the subject of popular complaint, then his promise is then necessarily ironized by the fact that his "prose" is in rhyme royal verse.

In other words, the multiple possible theories about the ordering of the collection ultimately reinforce the same reading of the Man of Law. If one believed that Johnson were wrong to infer authorial intent from the juxtaposition of "prose" with the tale of Custaunce, then one could nonetheless tease out a thematic thread in Chaucer's recurrent concern for the relationship between individual self-interests and the interests of the institutions that employ them, as the institutions govern the evolution and preservation of texts and histories in ways that may or may not contribute to the larger social good. If, on the other hand, one agreed that Johnson is right in her account of the apparent discrepancy around "prose," then it might seem striking indeed that Chaucer's efforts to engage with the themes of transparency in writing would produce a fragment of the collection that contained so many logical leaps and apparent inconsistencies that generations of scholars would assume a scribe must be responsible for them. Either way, the Man of Law's use of the word "prose" here raises a problem about form and history that the author and scribes of *The Canterbury Tales* never managed to satisfactorily contain, but which sits at a structurally important moment in the larger collection's narrative no matter how that structure is envisioned. The text either accidentally exemplifies or intentionally models the disorderings of the Chaucerian archive at the time of his death, and either way this disorder has had a profound impact on the meaning of *The Canterbury Tales*.

I take this moment to engage with Johnson's reading to emphasize a key point about my methodology in the study that follows. Again, I am unconcerned with the task of reconstructing a "real" order through *The Canterbury Tales*, or with establishing which bits of the text might date to early in his composition process, late, or might originate in the editorial efforts of his scribes. The multiplicity of tale orderings across the manuscript witnesses of *The Canterbury Tales* is a key element of the text's structure as it has been received, and a *Canterbury Tales* that proceeded clearly from start to finish according to a single discernible authorial or scribal plan would not be our *Canterbury Tales*. My particular focus on the connection between fragments II and VII suggested by the possibility that *Mel* was originally assigned to the Man of Law does not privilege this particular path through the collection, but rather it demonstrates the larger principle that the surviving manuscripts do not exhaust the multiplicity of orderings that readings of the text can sustain, and that

The Problem of Prose in Fragments II and VII   41

all of these implicit paths merit exploration and description. When the text suggests that A precedes B and that B precedes C, then A-B-C is a textually authorized ordering of the narrative in conversation with other orderings, whose multiplicity either accidentally or intentionally refuses the final imposition of a singular narrative structure.

A final fork in the garden that must be addressed before I can continue to the next chapter is the brief *MLP*. This homiletic aside has a powerfully ambiguous relationship to the texts that surround it in all possible orderings.[34] As I have observed above, the *MLI* ends with the statement that the following tale will be in prose, and it is thought that this might be a reference to *Mel*. Since Alfred David, the rhyme royal meter of *MLP* has led scholars to assume it was intended to preface the tale of Custaunce, written in the same meter.[35] And yet the thematic connections between *MLP* and *MLT* are murky at best, raising in many cases more questions than they answer. As I will show, *MLP* fits at least as well with *Mel* as it does with *MLT*, if not better. More to the point, the connections between *MLP*, *Mel*, and *MkP* are concerned with the problems of history and media that contextualize the problem of prose.

MLP begins with an adaptation to English verse of Innocent III's *De miseria*, which transforms the original passage's lament for the condition of poverty into a celebration of wealth.[36] In a telling passage that marks it as a deliberate secularization of Innocent's themes, the Man of Law concludes by addressing an imagined audience of merchants as follows:

> Ye seken lond and see for yowre wynnynges;
> As wise folk ye knowen all th'estaat
> Of regnes; ye been fadres of tidynges
> And tales, bothe of pees and of debaat.
> I were right now of tales desolaat,
> Nere that a marchant, goon is many a yeere,
> Me taught a tale, which that ye shal heere.   (II.127–33)

Merchants seek to use their wealth to purchase "lond and see," and this desire for traditional sorts of ownership and dominion leads them to know all of the "estaat" of kings – which is to say not only the experience of wealth, but also the respect due to the king's rank generally and the king's legal rights to title and property specifically. Because merchants are constantly seeking out and trading this knowledge, they are the fathers of tidings and tales, about both peace and conflict. The Man of Law concludes by asserting that the tale he is about to tell comes from one such merchant, and so we may infer that it is a story about

42 Chaucer's Problem of Prose

peace and debate which moreover records information concerning the estate(s) of kings. Hence while the beginning of the prologue suggests that the tale will be a work of conventional morality (and indeed it is one), the ending suggests rather that the tale will record a highly instrumental set of information that is useful for the enrichment of merchants. This is all consistent with *Mel*, which is the story of a woman Prudence who spends the whole text in a "debaat" with her "myghty and riche" (VII.967) husband, as she instrumentalizes statements of conventional morality to convince him of a truth that kings would do well to know, that "pees" is more profitable than war.

As a continuation of *MLI*, *MLP*'s framing of *Mel* further concretizes the implicit connections I have teased out above, where the problem of being a Chaucerian poet and the problem of swearing trustworthy oaths are both individual expressions of a shared, overarching problem of recording past events in such a way that they remain undistorted at future moments. In *MLP*, we find a solution to all of these problems in the publication and circulation of tales, "both of pees and of debaat," which creates a shared memory and knowledge that is more difficult for individual malicious actors to support. The fact that circulation is itself a major mechanism of distortion references the similar contradiction we saw in the Man of Law's portrait. Again, his knowledge of the cases and judgments back to King William is not cultivated so that he may honour earlier agreements and the traditional practices of ownership they perpetuate, but so that he may end those old agreements and subvert those practices of ownership to alienate the land as fee simple. The merchants of *MLP* are precisely the sorts of purchasers whose interests the Man of Law would have represented in such transactions.

For reasons I will explain in the chapters ahead, *MLI* and *MLP* reveal how *Mel* can be read as a provocation that the Monk is forced to redress. And as I will demonstrate in the next chapter, the problems of poetry and historical writing in English are connected by the archives of early English history, which preserved English-language legal documents that were largely discursive and quasi-poetic. In *MLI* the Man of Law, who in his profession uses his knowledge of legal precedent (i.e., Domesday book) to invalidate earlier agreements and do as he wishes, uses his knowledge of literary precedent (i.e., Chaucer's many poems) to invalidate his own agreement to tell a tale in verse. Meanwhile, a prose tale that the Man of Law may have been intended to tell inspires the Host to turn to the Monk and lament the consequences of the Monk's own earlier agreements (i.e., his vows of poverty and chastity). In the ordering *MLI*, *MLP*, *Mel*, *MkP*, the Man of Law and the Monk are in direct dialogue, and the discussion yokes the vagaries of

The Problem of Prose in Fragments II and VII   43

historical memory to wealth, poverty, and the danger of moving from the former state to the latter. Meanwhile in the dominant ordering of the manuscripts, the Man of Law instead tells a story set in conversion-era England whose thematic and symbolic parallels to the Monk's tale of Cenobia have led many readers to juxtapose the two in their analyses of Chaucer's investments in imperialism. In the chapters that follow I will both describe and account for the patterns that emerge when we read across these alternative orderings of the tales. But before I may do so in chapters 4 and 5, I must first contextualize my claims in history (as I will do in chapter 2) and in relation to the rest of *The Canterbury Tales* (as I will do in chapter 3).

Chapter Two

Saxon Script and Chaucerian Verse in London BL Add. MS 14848

In this chapter, I will step back from *The Canterbury Tales* to establish the historical context for the overarching supposition of this book, that it is reasonable to read Chaucer's work in juxtaposition with the Old English archive of laws and documents which was contested ground in the ongoing struggles between local, traditional (monastic) administration and its centralized, emergent (mercantile and common law) replacement. My efforts to uncover a dialogue between the Man of Law and the Monk about the uses of historical media presupposes that Chaucer knew about the importance of specifically English language laws and documents to the monastic historiographic project, and that he was familiar enough with the vagaries of the conflicts to recognize the operations of the politics of recognition within them. And though the charter manuscript I will focus on below postdates Chaucer's death by some decades, its connection to Lydgate places it proximate enough to Chaucer's milieu that its evidence may serve to ground this supposition about not only Chaucer but about his anticipated audience.

The manuscript in question is London BL Additional MS 14848, a fifteenth-century register of Bury St. Edmunds assembled by the abbot Richard Curteys that contains a series of foundational charters in Latin and/or Old English paired with rhyme royal Middle English translations, attributed by modern scholars to John Lydgate.[1] This meter – also called "the *Troilus*-measure" or "*Troilus*-stanza" – was popularized by Chaucer, who used it especially in his moral and philosophical works like *MLT* and the Boethian lyrics.[2] As Frank Stenton observes, "any medieval text which claims to be a copy of an ancient charter represents in itself an elaborate framework of local circumstance."[3] The juxtaposition of Old English text and moral verse in Add. 14848 suggests, first, that Old English charter-texts was considered to be an archaic, quasi-English

"Saxon";[4] and second, that rhyme royal poetry is more appropriate for translating legal documents written in this other language than Middle English prose would be. Below, I will argue that Add. 14848 does not so much witness the emergence of a new *historical* literacy as it does the coalescent new phase of an evolving *formal* one, whose concerns were just as resolutely presentist and political in the fifteenth century as they would be in the twentieth and had been in the tenth.[5] The problem of prose in *The Canterbury Tales* serves precisely to both articulate and manage the constraints and affordances of literacy's ever-evolving formal configurations, which contextualized his own efforts both to enact his plan for the collection and to represent that plan within it.

As Charles Insley has written, the long and ornate "proems" of pre-Conquest charters likely played "a very real role in the development and dissemination of English royal political and ideological agendas," as these documents were used not only to record the facts of transactions but to shape the meaning of those facts for posterity.[6] The Curteys register Add. 14848 shows how later readers of these documents recognized the importance of such literary and rhetorical forms to historical and legal claims and so took pains to translate not only the contents but the forms of early texts. In the first section of this chapter below, I will unpack the implications of these poems' juxtaposition with imitations of Old English insular letterforms. I will then proceed in the second section to Lydgate, whose charter poems recognize the thematic similarity between the charters and Chaucer's moral lyric and on this basis use the latter as an authorizing form.[7] In the chapters that follow I will argue that the tension witnessed between historical and formal literacies witnessed in the register is discernible also in the cracks and fissures in the structure of *The Canterbury Tales* as it presently survives, as Chaucer's text responds to the same pressures that shaped the charter-poems. This will demonstrate the basic shape of the conundrum that faces *The Canterbury Tales*. For all that it may strive towards a direct, unmediated representation of the state of the English nation which its estates satire genre attempts to depict, its poetic forms place it in a well-established media ecology of English language writing that will shape the way Chaucer's poetry is received in ways that contradict its stated purposes. The problem of prose in *The Canterbury Tales* expresses a structuring awareness of and wish to redress this conundrum in the collection.

Historical Formalism and Saxon Scripts

This chapter will focus especially on the two pre-Conquest documents initiating this series of charters in Add. 14848: the Latin, Old English,

46   Chaucer's Problem of Prose

and Middle English versions of Cnut charter S 980 (ff. 243v.–246v.),[8] and the Latin and Middle English versions of the Harthacnut charter S 995 (ff. 246v.–247v.).[9] The Middle English poems are attributed to Lydgate because of their obvious similarities to works like *The Lives of Ss. Edmund and Fremund*, which similarly use the examples of pre-Conquest English royalty to model how a virtuous king might preserve the franchise and liberty of monasteries like Bury St. Edmunds.[10] The primary difference between the charters and the saints' lives is that the former are not merely discursive, but represent royal virtue as part of an authorizing procedure confirming the contents of specific legal documents that were preserved to protect Bury's liberties from encroachment.[11] Thus they are particularly explicit examples of what John Ganim calls a "poetics of exemption" in Lydgate's works, which – broadly conceived – is indeed widely attested in English monastic literature back to the age of Bede.[12] Below, I will read this "poetics of exemption" as one among many manifestations of the medieval politics of recognition impacting communal life in exempt monasteries.

In Lydgate's lifetime, as now, early English history was recorded primarily in monastic historical sources, emerging from the twelfth-century upsurge in historiography discussed in the introduction that attempted to preserve pre-existing land rights in the wake of the Norman Conquest.[13] Monasteries relied both on the incompleteness of the record as a whole and on the vagueness of the surviving documents to claim forms of autonomy that were, by this late period, extraordinary.[14] The fragmentary informality of their earliest legal records generated obvious concerns, but nonetheless these features of the archive had to be preserved, if the unusually favourable arrangements were to persist in the new legal and political contexts of later centuries. The privileges in question were atypical and so they needed atypical documents to justify them, and this need created problems because the authority of documents generally rests on their conformity to type. Thus the antiquity of early royal charters was a double-edged weapon. The outdated forms of the oldest charters established long precedent by the fact of their very existence, at the same time that they invited counterclaims of obsolescence. The older the document was, the more compelling both of these contrary claims became, and so the more pressure there was on the scribes, archivists, and historians at monastic institutions to devise novel ways of renovating their old documents to highlight their genuine antiquity while downplaying their informality. This pressure was one of the ways that the politics of recognition drove monastic communities to organize themselves around their claims and uses of their territory.

Add. MS 14848 is a particularly striking example of this evolution, because of its conjunction of two interrelated renovation strategies: first, the rhyme-royal form of Lydgate's verse translations; second, self-conscious imitations of insular miniscule in the Old English charter texts themselves. Among the key features of the Old English script in this manuscript are the insular letterforms "g" (ᵹ), "r" (ꞃ), and "s" (ſ), single-compartment "a," ash (æ), eth (ð), and wynn (ƿ), and wedged ascenders.[15] These features are derived from letterforms first brought into England in the conversion era by Irish missionaries, who had in turn developed their own insular scripts from the Roman uncial bookhands.[16] During the English Benedictine Reform of the tenth century the continental Caroline miniscule script, developed during similar reforms on the continent, was adopted in England for Latin writing. Insular remained standard for Old English, and the two were even directly juxtaposed in those pre-Conquest charters containing vernacular boundary clauses.[17] Hence by the fifteenth century, insular letterforms had been coded as English and vernacular for centuries, and this coding surely played a role in their use in Add. 14848.

As I have said, the works of Lydgate that most closely resemble the charter poems are his *Lives of Ss. Edmund and Fremund*. Most of the recent scholarship on these saints' lives has been focused on their manuscripts, whose features indicate that they were the products of a sophisticated book trade that anticipates "early-modern" "print culture" more fully than traditional period divisions typically allow.[18] And though a full consideration of the question is beyond the scope of the present study, it is worth acknowledging at the outset that there is an obvious analogy between the Old English charters in the Curteys register and the most famous "archaizing" European script in this century, which is the so-called Roman letterforms of continental "humanist" scripts that are in fact based on Caroline miniscule.[19] As James Wardrop observes, the progenitors of humanist script Coluccio Salutati, Niccolo Niccoli, and Poggio Bracciolini "made that choice not so much because the Caroline miniscule was beautiful, as because it was old."[20] A similar combination of aesthetic and historical judgments appears to be at play in the contemporary developments in English monastic copies of Old English documents. The parallel to Add. 14848 is made especially compelling by the juxtaposition of archaic scripts with the poetry of John Lydgate, since of course Lydgate was so profoundly influenced by the Italian poetry produced in the immediate circle of these authors.

It is a noteworthy feature of the surviving evidence that the best examples of "archaizing," insular scripts in English manuscripts tend to be dated quite late in the medieval period.[21] Other examples besides

48 Chaucer's Problem of Prose

Add. 14848 include the fifteenth-century single-sheet Cotton Augustus ii 8 (S 980) and the Bury registers London BL Add. 14850 (S 1219, f. 85r.) and Add. 45951 (S 1527, f. 1r.).[22] Each of these manuscripts reproduces Old English charter texts in what Kathryn Lowe calls "a semi-imitative way."[23] Nor are scribal semi-imitations of Anglo-Saxon scripts and letterforms unique to fifteenth-century Bury. Most famously, imitative copies of Old English letterforms may be found in the Hyde Abbey cartulary BL Additional 82931 (see f. 21r.) and in Thomas Elmham's *Speculum Augustinianum* (*Cambridge, Trinity Hall MS 1*; see ff. 21v. and 22r.).[24] Both of these manuscripts are large, ornate registers where the scribes make sustained, formal efforts to use insular script when they write Old English.[25] Julia Crick has observed that the existence of such manuscripts resists those traditional accounts of the so-called modernity that would attach archaism to the emergence of what may be called an "historical literacy."[26] This chapter builds on her work and on the work of other early English legal historians – in particular Kathryn Lowe, cited above – to situate this new literacy in relation to the developments in Middle English poetry that contextualize the poetic translations that are juxtaposed with these "archaizing" scripts.

In her important study of Matthew Parker's editorial practices and their political context, Emily Butler re-assesses his first printed edition of Old English texts in relation both to its immediate sixteenth-century political context and to the tradition of post-Conquest Old English, and in particular the manuscripts glossed or written by the Tremulous Hand of Worcester.[27] Parker was the archbishop of Canterbury during the transition to the Reformation, and his edition of Ælfric's homilies famously makes these texts seem as if they anticipate the Anglican doctrine of consubstantiation. It seems, then, that both he and his contemporaries studied Old English in order to ground historically their claim that the English church and the Roman papacy not only were but *had been* historically distinct entities.[28] And as Butler observes, Parker's activities did not arise in a vacuum, as for example the evidence that he and his fellow antiquarians relied on the Tremulous Hand's glosses suggest that readers of Old English between the thirteenth and sixteenth centuries may be placed into a single (though diachronic) "textual community."[29]

One of Parker's more intriguing projects was his commission of a typeface based on Anglo-Saxon insular letterforms, which he used to print a Latin life of King Alfred.[30] For Parker, "Old English is a language defined almost as much by its proper script as by its linguistic features, meaning that even Anglo-Latin texts may be brought into the graphemic fold of Anglo-Saxon textuality."[31] Butler observes that these editions are not, in any modern sense, facsimiles – there is no particular effort to imitate the letterforms of any one manuscript – but rather that they exhibit what may be called after Siân Echard an "impulse to facsimile."[32] In other words, we see the scribes using letterforms and techniques that seem unconventional in comparison to similarly dated and situated manuscripts, but which also resemble in some way the conventional features of earlier scripts.

What is striking about the similar impulse discernible a century earlier in the manuscript Add. 14848 is that it occurs after an apparent waning of scribal imitations of Old English scripts over the course the thirteenth century. Indeed, to my current knowledge, Old English scripts are unattested in fourteenth-century cartularies and registers, and only reappear in my fifteenth-century examples cited above. It is by now well established that the Norman Conquest was not the major event in the history of English literacy that modern scholarship has often imagined, and especially in monastic archives there is very little evidence for upheaval.[33] Though of course a considerable body of pre-Conquest documentation was lost in this period (as archivists in Ramsey and Worcester complained) and there was a corresponding explosion in document production, it is nonetheless the case that charters dated before William's arrival were often copied after his arrival in the same communities that produced and stored the originals.[34] So also are there many twelfth-century examples of insular miniscule in English literary writing, as its forms appear, for example, in the twelfth-century copies of Ælfric's homilies found in Oxford, Bodleian Library, Bodley 343.[35] Similarly copies of pre-Conquest legal documents continue to use insular letterforms for Old English up to about 1250.[36] This practice then appears to be interrupted by the enormous explosion of documentary and literary output in the thirteenth century, which occasioned the reforms and standardizations in English scripts that culminated in the bookhand Parkes called "Anglicana."[37] After this occurred, the scribes who copied Old English documents typically made little to no effort to distinguish Old English from the Latin text surrounding it, and the few insular features that survive appear to be accidental.

This, at least, is the narrative suggested by the evidence of surviving Old English charters. The Electronic Sawyer website (cited above) lists 81 manuscripts of charter texts dated to the fourteenth century and 66 dated to the fifteenth. There are documents tagged as containing "English" in 34 (42%) of the fourteenth-century and in 29 (44%) of the fifteenth-century manuscripts listed, either because the documents are wills or writs written in Old English or because they contain Old English boundary clauses, brief interpolated statements, and translations.

50 Chaucer's Problem of Prose

Generally speaking, the Old English text in these manuscripts tends to be quite brief (varying between a single line and half a page in length), to be more or less intelligible to later English speakers (as they mostly list place-names or recognizable privileges like "sake and soke"), and to be written in a script identical to that used to copy the Latin, though the letter "þ" is commonly used (as it is in Middle English manuscripts dating to this period).

Less commonly used, but still discernible, are forms of the uncial "g" (ʒ) and of eth (ð).[38] There are also many instances of the runic wynn (p) being mistaken for either thorn, "y," or "p," though such occurrences often occur alongside words where "w" has been substituted and so they typically appear, at least, to be errors and not archaizing gestures.[39] But though such features remind us that the line dividing deliberate archaism from scribal confusion is blurry at best, it nonetheless seems from my investigations that few if any cartularies dated c. 1250–1400 demonstrate an "impulse towards facsimile" to "Saxon" script comparable to that discernible in Add. 14848 and the other fifteenth-century manuscripts listed above.

At Bury, Curteys drew on the long tradition of historical writing and record-keeping, and indeed the Bury archive still has one of the most robust and complex archives of any English monastery founded before the Conquest.[40] The existence of this archive may be traced back to the twelfth-century abbot, Samson, whose struggles to reform the convent's administrative procedures are detailed in the Bury chronicle written by Jocelin of Brakelond.[41] It appears that Bury's earlier abbot, Baldwin, must have decided in the eleventh century that Old English translations were typical features of Anglo-Saxon charters, and so it is typically assumed that many of these translations of Bury's charters preserved by Samson are forgeries.[42] Given, then, that the sorts of financial crises that inspired Baldwin and Samson to copy and/or manufacture their charters continued to beset monasteries like Bury until the Reformation, it is unsurprising that the Old English texts in legal documents were studied and copied continuously in monastic contexts throughout the medieval period.

One particularly pertinent example of a cartulary for our present discussion is London BL Harley 743, a fourteenth-century manuscript produced in Bury St. Edmunds by John Lakenheath. This manuscript witnesses copies of the Cnut charter S 980 (ff. 57r.–v.), the Harthacnut charter S 995 (ff. 57v.–59r.), and the Edward charter S 1045 (f. 59r.; in its Latin version), and so it is a helpful point of reference. Lakenheath comments in his brief introduction to Harley 743 (f. 3v.) that he assembled his calendar from the various registers to make sure that the abbey's documented agreements might be available to posterity in a response to the destruction of the archive by Bury's tenants in 1327.[43] Lakenheath likely undertook this project with the awareness that it was an extremely political endeavour, and indeed his archival work may well be a reason that his life was taken during the 1381 Uprising.[44] Hence it seems reasonable to infer that the script of the documents Lakenheath must have seemed incidental to his specific political purpose of shoring up the abbey's legal rights, and so incidental to the task of establishing the charter-texts' authority.

The question, then, is what changed in the half-century that elapsed between Lakenheath's registry and Curteys' that made insular letterforms seem worth reviving, even though it meant making the text incomprehensible and so needing of a second English translation. As I have stated above, Lydgate's poems provide an important clue, as his direct debts to Petrarch and Boccaccio place him in the ambit of the reforms to script developed in Italy during precisely this period.[45] Though the concerns of an abbot Curteys were clearly quite different from the concerns of a Salutati or Bracciolini, it remains true that in both cases, (historio)graphic and (formal) poetic forms worked together to reinforce each other's authority.

In the next section, I will identify the productive parallel between the resistances offered by these fifteenth-century copies of tenth-century documents to the narratives that would read the popularization of the printing press as an epistemic shift, which among other things led to the development of modern "historical literacy."[46] As his critics cited above have long since established, Lydgate's charter poems and his saints' lives present a *formal* challenge to modern periodizations, as formatting decisions about book production that have long been treated as the consequences of the printing press, secular modernity, and capitalism appear in manuscripts produced by one of England's oldest monasteries, for the purpose of continuing their traditional and local governing practices. More to the point, the specific point of connection between present and past is Lydgate's famously Chaucerian verse, which demonstrates how at least one privileged early reader of Chaucer made the connection proposed in this volume between the forms of *The Canterbury Tales* and the remembrance of early English historical media.

Historical Formalism and English Verse

The charters of monastic institutions were not the only Old English texts continuously copied into the fifteenth century. Somewhat more prominent are *Caedmon's Hymn* and *Bede's Death Song*, which

52 Chaucer's Problem of Prose

circulated as part of Bede's *Historia ecclesiastica gentis Anglorum* and the *Epistola Cuthberti de obitu Bedae* respectively.[47] There are three copies of the Old English *Caedmon's Hymn* in manuscripts dated to the fourteenth century or later, and ten of *Bede's Death Song*. Dobbie identifies a single hand in two late fourteenth-century manuscripts of the latter – Oxford, Bodleian MS Fairfax 6 (ff. 220r.–v.) and Bodleian Laud Misc. 700 (ff. 27v.–29r.) – that offers what he calls "a very good imitation of Anglo-Saxon script."[48] Outside of this single scribe's contributions, there is little evidence for archaizing hands in the late medieval copies of these poems. The witnesses of both poems in the fourteenth-century copy of the poem in Cambridge, Trinity College MS R 5 22 are exemplary of the larger pattern. In *Caedmon's Hymn* (f. 32v.), the scribe makes no visible effort to adopt Old English script beyond his copying of runic wynn for "W," though even here his wynns resemble his "P" and so this may be a transcription error.[49] In the copy of *Bede's Death Song* (f. 44r.–v.), meanwhile, eth ("ð") appears.[50] Confusion about wynn also appears in the copy of *Caedmon's Hymn* appearing as a marginal gloss in the fifteenth-century manuscript San Marino, Huntingdon MS HM 35300 (f. 82r.), which is particularly relevant to the present discussion because it was once located at Bury St. Edmunds.[51] In any event most copies of the poems are similar to the copies of Old English in the cartularies of this same period, in that the appearance of archaic letters is more commonly suggestive of scribal confusion about exemplars than it is about scribal efforts to archaize the script.

Be that as it may, there is considerably more evidence outside of these manuscripts for a popular awareness of Bede's Old English poems than there is for knowledge of Bury's Old English writs and charters. In John Trevisa's *Dialogue Between a Lord and a Clerk*, the Lord cites the legend of Caedmon of Whitby from Bede's *Historia ecclesiastica* and a putative translation by Bede of the Gospel of John, along with King Alfred's translations of the Psalms, to argue that there is considerable precedent for English translations of sacred texts.[52] Bede's *Historia* was also cited in Wycliffite texts to justify their translation of the Bible – a circumstance that I will return to in my discussion of the Parson's "Lollardy" in chapter 6.[53]

Such allusions to Old English anticipate Parker's efforts to politicize the corpus in the service of debates about the place of English in the liturgy, and for this reason they offer a possible explanation for the reappearance of archaic "Saxon" letterforms in the fifteenth century. Insular scripts mark "Old" English monastic charters as *not* English, in a time when distracting controversies about the appropriate uses of translation might have undermined the authority of important foundational documents. There may be a similar strategy at play in Curteys' inclusion of a contemporary English translation of the charters alongside their "Saxon" text: if Lydgate's poem is the "English" version, then the Old English version is simply the old version, which mutely but visibly demonstrates that there is ample precedent for the charter's claims.

But while this reframing of the Old English translations may explain why Curteys chose to append a Middle English version of the charters in his register, it does not explain what was accomplished by rendering this version in verse. To understand the implications of this decision, we must return to the genre of the Anglo-Saxon royal charter itself. The "poetic," "literary" quality of Anglo-Saxon charters has been observed more than once,[54] and indeed these texts are too discursive to fit comfortably in the formal category of the royal land grant as it existed in the fifteenth century. Anglo-Saxon charters were far more homiletic documents than their successors, and it was not uncommon for them to expend the majority of their length describing the piety of a royal benefactor and the spiritual motives of his gift, sketching only briefly the actual rights and privileges conferred.[55] The focus of these documents on the moral rectitude of donations over their terms and limitations was precisely the reason that such early grants were so valuable to institutions like Bury, since they granted a vague, broad autonomy that was otherwise unheard of in later eras.

The literary quality of early English documents appears to have influenced "documentary poetics" in the late medieval period, most commonly discussed in relation to symbolic, devotional "charters" like *The Charter of Christ* and *The Charter of the Abbey of the Holy Ghost*, though there are more explicitly local and institutional examples as well.[56] One such example is the inscription of a brief Middle English rhyming poem on the side of Cooling Castle, formalized as a charter with the image of a seal carved beneath it.[57] Another is a (probably wholly fabricated) Middle English charter-poem of King Athelstan in two medieval copies, one of which is a single-sheet charter.[58] This evidence suggests that Curteys' decision to append poetic translations of these documents was not an idiosyncratic one, but was based in a popular and well-founded perception that these documents were quasi-poetic texts.

The charter-poems in Add. 14848 are particularly useful for assessing the broader implications of using verse to translate charters, because they invite a comparison between the forms of these early

54 Chaucer's Problem of Prose

English documents – with their elaborate proems, unparalleled in documents from later eras – and the poetic idiom of the poet Lydgate. A passage from the Harthacnut charter will demonstrate more clearly how strikingly well suited these documents are for Lydgate's authorial voice:

> In many a place of devyne scripture
> It is remembryd by ful contemplatyf,
> Al worldly thyngis be variable and unsure,
> Ful of trouble, of myschef, sorwe, and stryf,
> The stormy cours here of this present lyf
> Gothe lyk a whele in mevyng and unstable,
> Lowe in a vale of wepynges lamentable.
> For who that lokyth with his inward sighte
> This worldly chaunges ful of doubylnesse,
> Sholde he gret cause of conscience hy ryghte,
> Upward to hevene his herte al hool to dresse,
> For ther may be no verray sykyrnesse,
> Nor no felicite nor no perfyt glorye
> In worldly thynges, that bene aye transitorye.   (246v.–247r.)

This passage is a relatively straightforward translation of the Latin text.[59] At the same time, and for this very reason, it reads like a thoroughly Lydgatian pastiche of Chaucer's many Boethian passages, which also allude to the unstable Wheel of Fortune (*Book of the Duchess* 353) and the stormy course of life (*Troilus and Creseyde* [TC] 2.778).

Boethius' *Consolation of Philosophy* was translated into Middle English by Chaucer and into Old English by King Alfred.[60] It was also a major influence on the political philosophies articulated in early English chronicles and the proems of early English charters, in conventional passages that cited the vagaries of Fortune to justify both the documentation of gifts (which might otherwise be forgotten) and the gifts themselves (which prepare the souls of the grantors for death). And as scholars of Chaucer have known for decades, the themes of fate and fortune are highly prevalent in all of Chaucer's poetry.[61] One clue that they are particularly pertinent to the dialogue between the Monk and the Man of Law is the fact that the tales of both figures draw from the writings of the Dominican friar Nicholas Trevet. Trevet's commentary on *Consolation* is also the likely source for the Monk's definition of tragedy in *MkP*,[62] and Trevet is also the original author of the story of Constance witnessed by *MLT*.[63]

Saxon Script and Chaucerian Verse in London BL Add. MS 14848   55

Lydgate's charter poem, meanwhile, can be productively compared to Creseyde's speech in Chaucer's *TC*, book 3, which contains the only appearance of the word "transitorie" in Chaucer's poetry:[64]

"O brotel wele of mannes joie unstable!
With what wight so thow be, or how thow pleye,
Either he woot that thow, joie, art muable,
Or woot it noght; it mot ben oon of tweye.
Now if he woot it nought, how may he seye
That he hath verray joie and selynesse,
That is of ignoraunce ay in darknesse?
Now if he woot that joie is transitorie,
As every joye of worldly thyng mot flee,
Than every tyme he that hath in memorie,
The drede of lesyng maketh him that he
May in no perfit selynesse be."   (*TC* 3.820–31)

As in the charter-poem, the word "transitorie" describes an attribute of "worldly thyng[es]," which is an obstacle to "joye" for Chaucer and "felicite" for Lydgate. There is one parallel between Lydgate's general statement about the "doubylness" of "worldly chaunges" and Cresey-de's similarly doubled observation that a man either "woot that thow, joie, are muable, | or woot it nought; it mot ben oon of tweye," and another between Chaucer's man who "hath in memorie | the drede of lesyng" and Lydgate's man "that lokyth with his inward sighte" on the fact of worldly change. Finally, the "brotel wele" alluded to by Creseyde is almost certainly the "fragile wealth" and not the "mutable wheel" of man's unstable joy, but the latter reading would provide yet another echo of Chaucer's poem discernible in Lydgate's translation of Har-thacnut's charter.

It bears emphasizing that my claim is not that *TC* directly influenced Lydgate's translation, especially when so many of Lydgate's choices listed above may be explained with reference to the Latin charter. On the contrary, my claim is that both the Harthacnut charter and Cresey-de's speech deploy the same Boethian tropes to make the same conventional arguments about the fickleness of fate and the transitory nature of worldly things, which find many parallels throughout both the corpus of early English charters and the corpus of late medieval moral lyric. Given that the works of Lydgate, Chaucer, and their continental influences make very similar observations about great men and Fortune to those that we see in the earliest English legal documents, it was

56 Chaucer's Problem of Prose

therefore a short leap for Lydgate to adapt his Chaucerian poetic idiom to reinforce the legal, political claims grounded in Harthacnut's charter. Both sets of claims are based in the same Christian wisdom, about the transitory nature of worldly wealth and the strategies that the nobility should adopt to address this problem. One premise of this book, then, is that Chaucer himself recognized the same homology between his engagements with Boethian convention and the engagements in early English documentary precedents, and he found that homology troubling.

This context for the poems and the transcriptions also helps us to frame and resolve the problem of understanding the redundancies in Add. 14848's multiple versions of the same charters. For now, I will posit that the editorial decisions that shaped Add. 14848 respond to the very particular language politics of England in the era of the so-called Lollards. Bury's choice to use recognizably "Saxon" letterforms in copying the Old English passages allows these texts to confirm the antiquity of Bury's claims to franchise and hence their validity while also sidestepping any uncomfortable questions about their use of English. Unfortunately, this decision came at the expense of the texts' intelligibility. The example of the Harthacnut charter demonstrates how the Middle English poems serve not only to supplement this loss, but to reinforce the claims to the moral authority of antiquity, through the classicizing medium of vernacular lyric verse. In the Curteys register's juxtaposition of Old English charter texts and Middle English poems, then, we see the co-emergence of the same opposed but mutually supportive impulses that would characterize early modern humanism: first, to carefully study and imitate the textual remnants of the antique past, and second to write creative works in one's own spoken language and from one's own experience, as the antiques themselves did.

The clearest evidence for this complimentary bifurcation in Add. 14848 may be found in the unique text of the series to juxtapose Latin, Old English, and Middle English versions: the Cnut charter S 980. The Latin text of the Cnut charter S 980 begins with an extended "proem," of a sort that is common in especially late Anglo-Saxon charters.[65] Julia Barrow has noted that such proems are more common in forgeries than they are in authentic documents, and so there is evidence from the early period that the literary and poetic qualities of the texts were probative in the sense that they made the documents seem authentic.[66] The Old English and the Middle English texts treat this section of the Latin document very differently, in a manner which is telling about their combined effect.

The Old English translation of S 980 eliminates the proem of the title almost entirely, reducing the first 100 words or so to begin simply "On aelmihtiges drihtnes naman ic cnut ... (in the name of Almighty Lord, I Cnut ...)" (Add. 14848 f. 244r.). In contrast, the Middle English poem not only imitates the homiletic floridity of the Latin proem but revels in it, expanding 100 words into six rhyme royal stanzas. This expansion is not mere ornament, but deploys the literary authority of Middle English verse in the service of the charter text. The Latin text begins "in nomine poliarchis Iesu Christi saluatore mundi totiusque creaturae creatoris (in the name of Jesus Christ, saviour and polyarch of the entire world and creator of creatures)," and this beginning is rendered in verse: "In name of hym whiche that is monarke | Of hevene and erthe, mankyndes savyour | Of clerkes callys sovereyn polyarke ...." Line 3 of this stanza is the unique occurrence of the word "polyarke" in Middle English, and its unusual difficulty is signalled by the translation's statement that it is a word used by "clerkes."[67] Alfred Hiatt has pointed out how Lydgate's translation "mediates the term's somewhat arcane technicality by the specification of its location in clerkly vocabulary."[68] In fact this mediation is only part of what the passage accomplishes. Just as important, if not more so, is the echo of Chaucer's conventional allusions to the authority of "clerkes," witnessed for example in *TC* 3.814. The difficult Latin word becomes the occasion for incorporating the voice of a Chaucerian speaker, who will make an aside to explain difficult words and concepts when he deems it necessary.

For most of the poem this speaker uses the first-person voice of Cnut, who is the speaker in the original Latin charter. Then in the signatures section of the document, the first-person speaker changes twice. First, in the twenty-third stanza, Cnut's first-person signature is followed without transition by his queen Ælgifu's own statement "and I, Algyfa, in hope the bet to spede, | fully conferme it." Second, in the twenty-fifth stanza, a new narrator intervenes to say that he finds the signatures of "xij abbotys which that I can nevene." This last speaker is clearly not Cnut nor Ælgifu but the poet, who narrates his consulting and paraphrasing of his source text. The key implication of the lines cited here is that they reveal the true "speaker" of the poem to be the voice of the translating poet, who performs an historical authority derived from the voices of poets like Chaucer, Petrarch, and Boccaccio who frequently skip past information that they see in their source text but deem impertinent to their purpose – as for example Chaucer claims to condense a letter from Creseyde whose text is found in his sources (*TC* 2.1564–6, 1595–6). Like speeches in poetry, the first person statements by Cnut and Ælgifu may be understood to be quotations from historical figures

58 Chaucer's Problem of Prose

adapted from source texts into verse by a poet-compiler who – here as in *TC* and *Il Filostrato* – speaks in the voice of a reader and archivist who reads books from the past and makes their contents comprehensible to a contemporary audience.

Kathryn Lowe has suggested that the cartularies and registers produced at Bury during Curteys' career respond to Richard Ullerston's 1408 *Petitiones quoad reformationis ecclesiae militantis*, written at the request of the Bishop of Salisbury, which called for the elimination of privileges like Bury's.[69] If we follow Lowe's connection, we see a telling contrast between the cited evidence for maintaining such privileges and the suggested justification for eliminating them. The historical questions addressed by Add. 14848, of whether or not actual kings granted these particular privileges to Bury, have very little bearing at all on Ullerston's point that Pseudo-Dionysius the Areopagite places abbots below subdeacons in his *Ecclesiastical Hierarchy*.[70] Arguably the poems provide a more direct refutation of this more theological argument than do the authentic Old English texts, because the poems perform the moral rectitude of the kings who made the grant and so place their authority *as authors* in conversation with Pseudo-Dionysius'. In other words, it is insufficient to read the relationship between the Man of Law's prose and Chaucer's poetry as a mere analogy. At the cusp of the fifteenth century the formalisms of law and poetry co-habited the same continuum, and this relationship was especially visible in the early English documents that were also often poems. The limitations and affordances of this continuum for Chaucer's artistic ambitions is the "problem of prose" whose implications are traced by this study.

In chapters 4 and 5 below I will place the Man of Law and the Monk on either side of this debate, with the Man of Law occupying the position of those who would profit from Ullerston's *petitiones* and the Monk on the side of those who would lose. I will argue that Chaucer appears to define these opposing positions by their relation to the historical media of the evidence supporting their contrasting claims. The novel methods used by Curteys' register seem nevertheless to represent the charter texts themselves, and so they imply his investment in the contents of those texts, which he wishes his audience to adhere to. In contrast, Ullerston cites an abstract principle from another text as a gloss on these documents, claiming that they are invalid on the basis of their inconsistency with other, external principles. In the next chapter, I will demonstrate how precisely this same contradiction in critical practices may be found in the debate between the Summoner and the Friar in fragment III of *The Canterbury Tales*, as these figures personify the pitfalls of, first, legalistic adherence to the letter of the text and, second, glossating practices that feel free to infer and even invent underlying principles on the text's basis. Though these rivals have contradictory approaches to their shared task of exploiting institutional authority for personal ends, they both place the use of authoritative texts at the centre of their strategies, in a way that explains the curiously balanced equality between their anti-clerical satires. They each serve each other's purposes, and work together to drive both not only the growth of literate bureaucracy but also its secularization and eventual co-optation by the apparatus of settler-colonial empire.

Chapter Three

The Text, the Gloss, and Fragment III

The conflict between the Friar and the Summoner begins near the end of *The Wife of Bath's Prologue* (*WBP*) with the Friar's comment: "'Now dame,' quod he, 'so have I joye or blis, | This is a long preamble of a tale!'" (III.830–1). The Summoner takes offense on the Wife's behalf that the Friar, of all people, would make this complaint, and he expresses his anger as follows:

> A frere wol entremette hym everemo.
> Lo, goode men, a flye and eek a frere
> Wol falle in every dyssh and eek mateere.
> What spekestow of preambulacioun?
> What! Amble, or trotte, or pees, or go sit doun!
> Thou lettest oure disport in this manere. (III.833–9)

The Summoner makes two related complaints here. First, he claims that Friars will insert themselves into every matter, asserting authority where they have none – a complaint whose connections to anti-fraternal invective have often been noted.[1] Second, he criticizes the hypocrisy of a Friar accusing anyone else of "preambulacioun," playing on the two senses of this word – first, the sense of "preamble" (as the Friar himself used it), and second the sense of walking the boundaries of a territory as a ritual of either renewing or transferring ownership.[2] This second sense is then transformed by wordplay into the "amble" of a horse's pace, with the implicit suggestion that the Friar may continue travelling with the company at any pace he desires, so long as he does not *per-ambulate* and thereby "entremette" himself and take illegal ownership of someone else's property.[3]

This wordplay is noteworthy for the way it neatly encapsulates several themes from the widespread anti-fraternal discourse of the

The Text, the Gloss, and Fragment III   61

period, which compared the friars to the Biblical exile Cain because of their unregulated preaching in pre-established ecclesiastical districts.[4] And as Amanda Walling has demonstrated, this fraternal capacity for "wandering" is clearly connected to that conventional association of friars with the gloss or "glose," so central to the Summoner's depiction of Friar John in his tale and linked by satirists to Biblical injunctions against the scribes and Pharisees.[5] The throughline that connects these abuses together is their origins in the technology of material, embodied text, which defined and delineated both the orthodox interpretations of scripture and the boundaries of ecclesiastical jurisdictions.

It is obviously ironic that the Summoner, of all pilgrims, should be the one to publicly call out the Friar for his simony, and also that the Friar should be the one to call out the Summoner. Jill Mann suggests that this irony is deployed here to figure anger. She argues: "what these stories show us about the 'irous' man is that he insists on enforcing his own version of reality; or, to put it another way, he imposes himself on the world even in the teeth of the world's resistance."[6] In this chapter I will build on Mann's reading to argue that the tales are focused especially on how anger animates the institutions that governed the production, storage, and use of authoritative texts, whose authority was martialled by friars and summoners alike to undercut the world's resistance to the ordering of reality that they would aggressively impose. As I will discuss in further detail in chapter 6, anger in *The Canterbury Tales* is a sin associated particularly with the frustration of communication.[7] Here, the structural parallels between the two tales – for example their mirrored interruptions (III.1332, III.1761) – frame their failed communication as a sort of recursive process for generating further failures, wherein the Summoner's critique of the Friar reflects the Friar's own critique of the Summoner in a closed system that promises to go on generating further text even as it offers no hope for reform or improvement. The Friar and the Summoner make no defenses of their own positions, only attacks against the other, and so the debate does not so much move towards an Aristotelian balance between the two extremes as it spirals increasingly out of control. The obvious implication of this satire is that the ecclesiastical bureaucracy was a closed and inescapable system of text and gloss, wherein the critique each position offers of its obverse does nothing to mitigate injustice but does serve to justify its own self-perpetuation.

In his prehistory of the "media concept" in English thought, John Guillory has observed that "whether communication fails ... or is deliberately frustrated ..., the effect is to bring the medium into greater visibility."[8] Below I will demonstrate how these tales' use of the well-known

62 Chaucer's Problem of Prose

text/gloss dichotomy to represent the failure and/or deliberate frustration of these two mediators of divine will makes the medium of the manuscript more visible, both as a communications technology with its own constrained affordances and as a tool for the creation and maintenance of ecclesiastical wealth and influence. Here and in the chapters that follow, allegiance to the "text" means using strategies of reading that (at least claim to) fixate on the precise wordings of authoritative texts and documents and resist any efforts to contextualize or otherwise undermine their strict authority. Allegiance to the "gloss," in contrast, means using strategies of reading that attempt to account for the context of authoritative texts and documents, as they (at least claim to) endeavour to learn about the likely intentions of a text's authors or the unspoken assumptions when it was produced, and to think about how the text's strictures might be adapted or updated. Both strategies are flawed, and indeed they are not very different. Nonetheless, the distinction animates the conflict between the Friar and the Summoner.

Below, I will argue that fragment III stages conflicts between text and gloss as a way of figuring the self-perpetuating dynamism of clerical corruption, which attended the production and circulation of written texts not despite but *precisely because of* the efforts of ecclesiastical reform movements. Benjamin Saltzman has explained how the dialogue between the Friar and the Summoner is "subtly governed by a logic of mutual cancellation."[9] My own reading will build upon this insight to observe how this logic of cancellation is paradoxically an engine for the proliferation and continuation of texts and glosses, in a way that figures the ways in which attempts to refine, consolidate, or otherwise cancel textual precedent always ends up generating more of the very complexities they set out to reduce.

Useful for understanding this conflict's engagement with the medieval tradition of debate and dialogue is Nicolette Zeeman's important recent study of allegory in *Piers Plowman*, which calls allegory in its title an "art of disruption."[10] In one key chapter about Middle English debate poetry, Zeeman argues that the well-known tendency of the major texts of this genre towards irresolution in their conclusions reflects how "personification debate is not a model for disengaged intellectual exchange, nor a combat in which the winner takes all, but rather a dramatic representation of the ways that opposition, relation, and contradiction are at the heart of the struggle for meaning."[11] The insight of Zeeman's study that bears emphasis here is that a particularly useful affordance of medieval allegorical debate is its ability to represent the embodied nuances of opposition, relation, and contradiction undergirding the sorts of social problems that we would now call "structural." Certainly

The Text, the Gloss, and Fragment III   63

the oppositionality, disjuncture, and dissonance in her example *Piers Plowman* is thematically concerned with structural problems like (in the debate between Mede and Conscience) "how does the self-interested pursuit of reward fit into public life" and (in Piers' administration of his half-acre) "how do you motivate people to work without starving them." But where Langland's debates present different approaches to genuinely difficult and perhaps even insoluble social ills, the debate represented in fragment III of *The Canterbury Tales* demonstrates how the method of debate can itself be endemic to the very structures of harm that the Friar and Summoner hypocritically claim to critique. In brief, the truly disquieting problem in fragment III is not that the Friar and the Summoner are sinners – a basic premise of the Bible is that the world is full of sinners and will be until the Final Judgment – but rather that their trenchant and informed critiques of each others' limitations emerge from and contribute to the same overarching system of harm.

The chapter below has four sections. The first two will demonstrate how precisely the text/gloss dichotomy is manifest in the conflict between these characters. On the one hand, friars are commonly associated with "glosing" in Middle English, and certainly the association carries over into *The Summoner's Tale (SumT)*.[12] On the other, the Summoner is a creature of the ecclesiastical court system, who will be criticized by *The Friar's Tale (FrT)* for his abuses of the procedural "text," exemplified for instance in the "feyned mandement" (III.1360) forged by the Friar's summoner to extort a bribe. As I will explain in chapters 4 and 5, this pattern maps onto the implicit dialogue between the Monk and Man of Law applying the formal terms of the text/gloss contrast to the historical conditions of the specific archives of early English history. Because the Friar's association with the problematic freedom of the gloss is more explicitly named in *SumT* than the Summoner's association with the problematic strictures of the text is named in *FrT*, I will begin with *SumT* in section one, and then return to *FrT* for section two.

The third section of this chapter then reads across both tales, to show how both of their narrators implicitly and unselfconsciously model the flaws described in the contrary pilgrim's critique. *FrT* does indeed instantiate the tendency of friars towards gloss in its long discursus about Hell, and *SumT* demonstrates the tendency of summoners towards reductive legalism in its consideration of how to divide a fart. Ultimately, the formal distinction between their principles of textual criticism and use serves only to obscure the true problem, that methodological consistency in reading practices does not typically serve the actual intentions of a text or document's creators as well as it serves the interests of the readers who developed the method.

64 Chaucer's Problem of Prose

The fourth and final section of this chapter will return to the beginning of their dialogue, to look at the relationship of these two figures to the Wife of Bath whom they interrupt. In the chapter on the Wife of Bath that is the heart of *Chaucer and the Subject of History*, Lee Patterson observes that "the Wife's analogy between her 'joly body' and the corpus of her text invokes a powerful medieval connection between sexuality and reading."[13] I will argue that this powerful connection to text also connects the Wife to the Friar and the Summoner who interrupt her, through the conjoined themes of textuality, sexual violence, wealth, and territoriality in her tale. As Carolyn Dinshaw has noted, the counterpart to the Wife's embodied "text" is Jankyn, who can "glose" her body so successfully.[14] Indeed the (ambivalent, deeply problematic) "happy" ending of both her prologue and tale is a positive spin on the "marriage" of the (glossing, womanizing) Friar and the (text-adhering, gender-noncomforming) Summoner, who also find themselves in a relationship where neither has mastery over the other.

Patterson frames *FrT* and *SumT* as a sort of retreat from the "brilliantly innovative" *WBP* and *The Wife of Bath's Tale* (*WBT*), "constructed from highly traditional materials that while, again, are brilliantly reaccented, nonetheless remain comfortably within the settled structures of medieval social ideology."[15] This framing of the tales as a sort of retreat into conservatism considerably undersells the complex ambivalence of fragment III. I agree with Patterson's argument that the Wife's optimistic, secularizing, bourgeois individualism marks her as a prototype for the figure of the modern subject that would dominate both English literature and English ideology in the centuries that followed her creation. My reading in this chapter explores how the Friar and the Summoner anticipate later critiques of the material conditions that underpin this modern subjectivity, by demonstrating that the novel forms of power she represents are not so much new as they are newly secular and so more overtly imperial. In the next two chapters I will show how the dialogue between the Man of Law and the Monk express ambivalence about the secularization of institutional literacy embodied by the Wife, which contributed not only to individualism but also and simultaneously to the crown's centralization of power towards the achievement of imperial ambitions, at the expense of local power centres like England's many exempt monasteries. It may just be a coincidence that the Wife's home city of Bath was the site of an abbey dating back to the seventh century whose Latin and Old English muniments are preserved in the late twelfth-century cartulary Cambridge, Corpus Christi College 111, parts of which were once bound with the abbey's gospel book.[16] If so, it is a coincidence that underscores how many of these institutions

The Text, the Gloss, and Fragment III   65

and documents there were in Chaucer's England, and so how surprisingly proximate the post-Conquest memorials of Old English writing would have been to the debates about ecclesiastical bureaucracy and wealth raised by the conversation between the Wife of Bath and her two interlocutors.

The Friar's Glossing in *The Summoner's Tale*

SumT begins with the conventional complaint that in their preaching and begging, friars deprive the established church of their funding sources. The Summoner summarizes his friar's preaching as follows:

> Excited he the peple in his prechyng
> To trentals, and to yeve, for Goddes sake,
> Wherwith men myghte hooly houses make,
> Ther as divine servyce is honoured,
> Nat ther as it is wasted and devoured,
> Ne ther it nedeth nat for to be yive,
> As to possessioners, that mowen lyve,
> Thanked be to God, in wele and habundaunce.   (III.1716–23)

This friar distinguishes his order's own "hooly houses" from two alternatives: first, places where their donations might be "wasted and devoured," and second places where "it nedeth nat for to be yive" because the pre-existing possessions of the institutions in question are sufficient to maintain their services. The obvious irony here is that fraternal houses did indeed "devour" wealth, and often held possessions and endowments that provided them with financial support. This friar, in other words, is making a distinction without a difference to justify a redundancy in the ecclesiastical structure that benefits himself.

In the action of the tale that follows, the friar works especially through the mechanism of flattery. As Walling writes, "flattery is precisely the form of language tailored to the pursuit of material gain, so that when the friar's mendicancy supercedes his mission as a spiritual counsellor, he naturally becomes a flatterer as well."[17] Beyond just being a flatterer, the Summoner's friar is indifferent to the obvious discord between the language he uses to frame his statements and the content of the statements themselves. When he is asked if he is hungry, his polite refusal quickly reverses itself into a request for an entire pig's head and a set of other delicacies (III.1837–45). The sudden shift in this speech from polite blandishment to naked greed exemplifies the basic rhetorical move of this friar: he first says what is necessary to satisfy the basic

66   Chaucer's Problem of Prose

requirement of etiquette, before he then goes on to reverse himself to get what he actually wants. The early and unusual allusion in *SumT* to this friar's use of wax tablets for writing (III.1741) underscores the point: everything he says is impermanent and subject to erasure.[18]

This abuse of language is framed as "glosing" in a pointed, ironic speech, made by the Summoner's friar to his donor Thomas in a description of his services:

> Nat al after the text of hooly writ,
> For it is hard to yow, as I suppose,
> And therfore wol I teche how al the glose.
> Glosynge is a glorious thyng, certeyn,
> For lettre sleeth, so as we clerkes seyn –
> There have I taught hem to be charitable,
> And spende hir good ther it is resonable   (III.1790–6)

That this passage's praise for "glose" is playing off of the negative connotations of this word has been recognized since Robertson at least.[19] The brief quotation from 2 Corinthians 3:6 demonstrates both the danger of the gloss and the complexity of the problem. On the one hand, Paul's original statement that "the letter slays but the Spirit gives life" clearly did not mean in context that Paul thought preachers may say anything they wish whether it conforms to the gospel or not. On the other, Paul is actually referring to the vexed question of how Christ's "new" law relates to the Mosaic "old law" of the Hebrew scriptures, given especially that Christ so pointedly flouted Mosaic law in his own ministry. This friar's claim that his preaching has "taught hem to be charitable" applies the formative terminology of St. Augustine's *de doctrina Christiana*, which clarified Paul's vague gesture towards "Spirit" by suggesting that all Christian exegesis directs readers towards *caritas* and away from *cupiditas*.[20] In this passage, then, the Summoner's friar claims that his "glosing" directs his listeners towards charity and so it technically accords with Augustine's recommendations, even though of course the specific "charity" in question will only feed his own gluttony.

The dominant, conventional view in studies of medieval historiography holds that there is a tension in medieval chronicles between truth-claims derived from the Augustinian ethic of reading paraphrased above and truth-claims derived from documented historical facts, so that medieval historians will find themselves torn between the letter of their sources and the spirit of moral *exempla*. In contrast to these historians, Friar John transparently exploits the freedom of

The Text, the Gloss, and Fragment III   67

interpretation granted by Augustinian reading practices to cover for the howlers in his preaching that result from his laziness and ignorance about history. Most crucially for our present reading, Friar John's "glosing" of scripture enables his departures from more secular "texts:" first, the historical record writ large, and second his own contractual obligations.

John's departure from the historical record is exemplified by his brief statement that the Biblical prophets Elijah and Elisha, who lived in the ninth century BCE, "Han freres been – that fynde I of record" (III.2117–18). Though it is correct that in the "record" there are some Carmelites who claim these prophets as the mythical founders of their order, even these sources do not quite go so far as to suggest what Friar John says here, that these prophets were literally friars two thousand years before the career of St. Francis.[21] This absurd misreading of historical sources – made even less forgivable by the fact that Friar John has a master's degree (III.2185–6) – marks how the Summoner imagines Friar John's glosing as fundamentally ahistorical, freely rewriting recorded "facts" to fit the rhetorical needs of the present.

The allusion to these figures is also ironic for the way it draws attention to John's inability to meet his own contractual obligations to his supporters. If the Friar's prayers were as effective as he claims (III.1865–80), then he should have predicted or even prevented the death of Thomas' child (III.1852–3). Meanwhile, in I Kings 17, Elijah is fed by a mother as John is fed by Thomas' wife, and as payment for her kindness he later restores her son to health. If we set aside historical accuracy and accept the premise that John and Elijah share the same profession, this only raises the question of why John cannot deliver the same services Elijah delivered in exchange for the same fee Elijah received.

Thomas' questions along these lines (III.1948–53) are the occasion for the sermon on anger that takes up a considerable portion of the tale. Jill Mann has noted that the obvious dramatic irony of the sermon – that the friar's warning to Thomas against the pitfalls of anger is itself so obviously infuriating – is itself a play on an anti-fraternal motif about the anger of friars, most famously witnessed in the figure of Wrath from *Piers Plowman*.[22] I would add that it is also a "glosing" departure from another, more local historical text, of the various promises John has made to Thomas without ever delivering on them. Hence while theologically grounded complaints about friars and their illicit preaching certainly inform the anti-fraternalism of *SumT*, the critique seems primarily concerned with the friars' lack of professionalism: in brief, the main problem with friars is that they don't keep promises very well because they don't pay much attention to detail.

68   Chaucer's Problem of Prose

Thomas' notorious decision to express his anger in the form of a fart draws attention to the fact that the "text" from which Friar John departs is a form of embodied media. It has been argued that the famous passage from *The House of Fame*, in which the eagle explains that "Soun ys noght but eyry broken" (765), implicitly suggests that there is no meaningful material distinction between the substance of human speech "lowd or pryvee, foul or fair" (767) and the substance of "breaking wind."[23] Whether this point holds true of all human speech in Chaucer's dream vision, it is certainly true of Friar John's words summarized above, which deliberately abandon the persistent solidity of material text and context to pursue ends whose selfish offensiveness is fart-like in this regard. Thomas' "broken wind" is precisely equivalent to John's own media-without-message, and so an appropriate repayment for what he has received.

The Summoner's Literalism in *The Friar's Tale*

The association of the Summoner with the legalistic "text" in *FrT* is not quite as easily identified as the association between friars and gloss in *SumT*, but only because the "texts" in question take so many forms. *FrT* begins by enumerating some of these:

> Whilom ther was dewllynge in my contree
> An erchedeken, a man of heigh degree,
> That boldely dide execucioun
> In punysshynge of fornicacioun,
> Of wicchecraft, and eeek of bawderye,
> Of diffamacioun, and avowtrye,
> Of chirche rives, and of testamentz,
> Of contractes adn of lakke of sacramentz,
> Of usure, and of symonye also.   (III.1301–9)

As this list emphasizes, the archdeacon and the ecclesiastical system of law he administrates has particularly jurisdiction over contracts: between testators of a will and the beneficiaries, husbands and wives, lenders and borrowers, and of course between God and his creation.[24] As Dan Kline notes, the problem of oaths in *FrT* is a problem that signifies across economic, legal, and theological discourses.[25] And as Eric Weiskott has demonstrated in his reading of the devil from the story as a forester, the archdeaconal administration of territory is the particular target of the Friar's scrutiny in the story that follows.[26]

The Text, the Gloss, and Fragment III   69

Consistently throughout *FrT*, we see a much truer representation of the principle the Summoner sarcastically cites in his own tale, that the letter "slays" while the spirit gives life: oaths, records, and other fixed texts are consistently figured as violent tools of extortion and death. We see this for example when the old woman asks the Friar's summoner if she can see the physical "libel" or copy of her summons, and if she will have a "procuratour" to defend her (III.1595).[27] The Friar's summoner replies "yes," but then proceeds to ignore her request for the libel and to address only the request for an advocate, in his claim that he can acquit her in exchange for the arbitrary sum of twelve pence (III.1598–9). In this scene we see that for all that this summoner's power depends on the *idea* of the letter, his actions have only a nominal relationship to the actual contents of any actual written documents, and this is mirrored by the Friar's own exploitation of the "spirit" that has only a nominal relationship to the actual meanings of the various texts he preaches from.

Perhaps the most provocative illustration of this summoner's flaws appears in his remarkable decision to keep his word and remain friends with the Devil after he learns his true identity: "My trouthe wol I holde as in this cas" (III.1525). This moment is widely acknowledged to be the crux of the tale, as it subverts the moral message common to stories of this kind in folk traditions and Biblical literature, where a character is cursed by an oath or wish because they have not fully thought through the implications of its supernatural terms. In a noteworthy reversal of this folk motif, the supernatural "trickster" of *FrT* is concerned only to hold people to their oaths when they are made with intention and full knowledge of their ramifications (III.1555), and he even coaxes the old widow to give the Summoner an opportunity to repent before he agrees to uphold the terms of her curse (III.1624–6).

Indeed, the entire premise of the tale is arguably an elaborate pun on the title "summoner": the main character's administrative "summoning" of folks to appear before the archdeacon and his magical "summoning" of a demon to undo him are presented by the tale as related negative consequences of the same rigid proceduralism. No one is responsible for the summoner's fate but the summoner himself; the demon functions only as a medium for transmitting the summoner's self-inflicted harm back upon himself. And though it is an obvious irony that the summoner of the tale is less ethically nuanced in his thinking and behaviour than an actual demon, this framing implicitly amounts to a condemnation of procedural consistency as itself an intrinsically demonic apparatus for maximizing harm in all its forms. Where

70   Chaucer's Problem of Prose

Thomas' fart in *SumT* is the emblem of the gloss that encapsulates its fundamental repugnance, so also is the demon in *FrT* the emblem of the text, as his calm, steady proceduralism leads inevitably to him bringing the Friar's summoner (and, absurdly, the widow's pan) with him down into Hell (III.1635).

Glossing in *The Friar's Tale*, the Text in *The Summoner's Tale*

The Summoner's angry response to *FrT*, with its infamous description of where the friars are kept in Hell, begins:

> This Frere bosteth that he knowed helle,
> And God it woot, that it is litel wonder;
> Freres and feendes been but lyte asonder.   (III.1672–4)

With this statement, the Summoner draws attention to the second and more subtle element of Chaucer's anti-clerical satire in these tales, that each of these pilgrims exhibits in his own tale the negative qualities attributed to him by his opponent in the other. The Summoner is alluding specifically to the overlong passage of *FrT* running from lines 1456–1522, wherein the Summoner asks the Devil questions about Hell and the Devil replies. This long digression, packed with Biblical allusions, sets up the joke at the end of the story, where the Devil comforts the summoner: "thou shalt knowen of our privetee | Moore than a maister of dyvynytee" (III.1637–8).

This throwaway aspersion of the knowledge gained in a master's degree – framing an advanced degree as an imperfect substitution for the experience of going to Hell – anticipates the throwaway reference to Friar John's own master's degree in *SumT*, cited above (III.2185–6). In both cases, the point seems to be that a desire for theological learning can lead one away from moral truths. This point is reinforced further in the following exchange:

> "Yet tel me," quod the sumonour, "faithfully,
> Make ye yow newe bodies thus always
> Of elementz?" The feend answered, "Nay.
> Somtyme we feyne, and somtyme we aryse
> With dede bodyes, in ful sondry wyse,
> And speke as renably as faire and wel
> As to the Phitonissa died Samuel.
> (And yet wol som men seye it was nat he;
> I do no fors of youre dyvynytee.)   (III.1504–12)

The Text, the Gloss, and Fragment III   71

This passage has no obvious connection to the overarching satire of the Summoner. Instead, it seems that the Friar is concerned to make the fiction of his tale believable to an imagined audience of theologians, who might ask the obvious questions raised by the premise of this tale: "how is it possible for this insubstantial demon to appear in human form and also carry a pan?" Line 1510 couches the question through a reference to an Old Testament prophet, which is parallel in this sense to Friar John's evocation of Elijah and Elisha: in 1 Samuel 28.7–20, a witch of Endor summons the ghost of Samuel to prophesy for Saul, and the demon cites this event as a helpful counterpoint to his own appearance.[28] Unfortunately, this reference raises more questions than it answers and so undercuts the rhetorical force of what the Friar is trying to say. Though I Samuel 28 is interpreted many different ways by theologians from St. Augustine to Tertullian to Origen to Aquinas,[29] the Friar's demon simply abandons the issue as soon as he has raised it, claiming that he does not care enough about human "dyvynytee" to be able to say if the ghost were really Samuel – though, again, he is himself an immortal demon who speaks through corpses from time to time, and so one would expect him to know what really happened. In this inconclusive and distracting theological digression and gloss on the tale in which he appears, the demon in the Friar's tale displays one of the precise traits of friars writ large that is satirized by the Summoner, which is their "glosing" tendency to digress from their main arguments and "perambulate" fruitlessly among the minutiae.

Meanwhile, the conclusion of *SumT* also demonstrates the veracity of the Friar's critique of the Summoner for being both legalistic and unconcerned with intent. As I have written above, there is an obvious irony in the friar's excessive anger at Thomas' fart, especially when he had just lectured at length about the dangers of anger. And certainly the final scene, with its famous conclusion that the Friar should use a wagon wheel to divide a fart among his convent, serves the narrative function of teasing Friar John and making him even angrier.[30] At the same time, it appears to be a moment parallel to the discursus on hell in *FrT*, where we see the narrator giving free rein to his own worst impulses as a legalistic literalist and so losing the thread of his own argument.

In *FrT*, the summoner urges the demon to take the haycart of a carter on the grounds that in a moment of frustration the carter had said "the devel have al, bothe hors and cart and hey!" (III.1547). The demon tells the summoner that the offer is not binding because it was not the carter's true "entente" (III.1556). Similarly, Friar John's complaint about "this false blasphemour" Thomas assumes without evidence

72 Chaucer's Problem of Prose

that Thomas truly intended him "to parte that wol nat departed be |
To every man yliche" (III.2213–15), when of course it is just as likely
that Thomas simply said whatever was necessary to trick John so that
he could then fart into his hand. Meanwhile the lord's brief musing
that the challenge came not from Thomas but from the devil (III.2221)
underscores the parallel between the Friar's summoner and the narratorial voice of *SumT*. To the denizens of this tale, it is easier to imagine
that the devil possessed Thomas in order to vex the assembly with a
riddle of fart-division than it is to imagine that Friar John might have no
real contractual obligation to divide the fart in question, as would likely
be the judgment of the devil in *FrT*, who holds that such obligations can
only be upheld when the intentions of the oath-taker have been con-
firmed. Hence while the Summoner's joke is clearly intended to be at
the expense of his Friar John, it is in the end at his own expense as well,
when his narration becomes as caught up in the contractual niceties of
fart distribution as the Friar's narration was caught up in the theological question of how his demon could carry a frying pan. Outside of the
discursive contexts of the tale-teller's professions, both of these questions are literally immaterial to the stories where they appear.

Fiona Somerset has written about the "layward progression" of
the *SumT*, wherein the secular authority of the lord and lady's court
"draws on the scholastic mathematical authorities Euclid and Ptol-
emy to validate the squire as a *clerical* speaker, and even goes so far
as to transform the churl Thomas into a subtly *clerical* thinker."[31] I
would add that this transformation completes the Gordian knot of
text-based injustice that binds the Friar to the Summoner in these
tales. *SumT* seeks not only to humiliate and demean its friar, but also
to triumph over the destabilizing force of the fraternal gloss, dividing and delineating its "hot air" according to a rigid and legalistic
procedure for fart distribution. Similarly, *FrT* did not only seek to
humiliate its Summoner, but also to imagine a perfect knowledge of
the realm of Hell and hence of the whole genre of scholastic theological knowledge in which discussions of Hell occur, as the summoner
will finally learn how immaterial demons can take on material bodies. The fact that both a perfectly divided fart and an eternity in
Hell are intrinsically unpleasant experiences underscores how thoroughly self-defeating are both of these figures' relationships to textual authority, and how deeply undesirable are both alternatives.
Further, the oft-noted parallels between the fart-division scene and
the Penecost drive home how the impasse between text and gloss
is nothing new, as it has always attended the troubled, difficult-to-
parse relationships between the historical institution governed by

the apostles' successors and the theological institution governed by the Holy Spirit.[32] The fact that the devil finds himself blowing theological hot air and the fart finds itself subject to legalistic subdivision exposes how in the end their distinction is without a difference, as every gloss proceeds from a text and every text requires a gloss, and neither text nor gloss produces anything meaningful to the lived experience of Christian believers.

Given the larger themes of this volume, it is worth observing before I conclude this reading that in the course of his theological speech about Hell, the devil casually alludes to the Benedictine Reform English saint Dunstan of Canterbury (III.1502), who founded Canterbury's own monastic cathedral chapter and who also wrote the first known coronation oath in English history, used in the second coronation of King Edgar at Bath Abbey in 973 CE.[33] Dunstan appears here in an allusion to the legend that he tortured the Devil, by either pulling his nose with blacksmith's tongs or by putting horseshoes on his demonic hooves.[34] The devil's casual observation that he and other demons had been the "servant" of St. Dunstan marks him as a personification of the literate, institutional church of England that this famous archbishop of Canterbury shaped so indelibly, which moreover emphasizes the particular role played by this church in secular governance through its influence over England's kings. In the chapters that follow I will situate this reference to an important pre-Conquest English churchman in relation to the Monk's mourning for Edward the Confessor and to the Man of Law's legend of England's first conversion in the Age of Bede. By framing Dunstan as a master of devils, this passage is one among many where Chaucer's ambivalent anti-clericalism – which seems less concerned with the theological aspects of ecclesiastical abuses than it is with the procedural aspects that secularization cannot correct – is expressed with reference to the English church and to English historical figures.

In the next section, I will return to *WBP* and *WBT*, where the debate between the Friar and the Summoner began. In a famous passage from *WBP*, the Wife observes of her clerk husband that "therwithal so wel koude he me glose | Whan that he wolde han my *bele chose*" (III.509–10). In her chapter on the Wife of Bath that takes its title from these lines, Carolyn Dinshaw argues that "glosing" religious texts here and throughout the *WBP* is associated with masculine imposition of authority over women's bodies, complicated by the irony that the Wife is an expert exegete herself.[35] I will build on this reading by observing that the embodied "text" in question is coded specifically as a legal document by her use of the French word *chose* to refer to her "thing": *chose*

74   Chaucer's Problem of Prose

is derived from Latin *causa* and maintains its senses of action of legal judgment in Anglo-Norman "Law French."[36] A similar pun appears earlier when she calls both her own and her husbands' genitals by the term "instrument" (III.132, 149), whose connotation "legal document" is emphasized by both passages' attention to the specifically contractual dimension of their sexual relations.[37] In other words, the problem of "wo in marriage" (III.3) that is the subject of *WBP* and *WBT* may be framed as a problem of formalizing and interpreting contracts that is such a central theme in *FrT* and *SumT*, where a summoner and a friar respectively are punished by contractual obligations that they cannot get out of. In the next and final section of this chapter, I will elaborate on this reading, with particular attention to the historical claims implicit in *WBT*'s Arthurian setting.

Historical Writing and the Wife of Bath

The strongest hint we are given for reading the relationship of the Wife of Bath to the debate that follows her tale appears in an important passage near the beginning of *WBT*, where the Wife contrasts the faeries of Arthur's time with her own era when the fraternal orders have driven them extinct:

> For now the grete charitee and prayeres
> of lymytours and othere hooly freres
> that serchen every lond and every streem,
> As thikke as motes in the sonne-beem,
> Blessynge halles, chambres, kichenes boures...
> This maketh that ther ben no fayeryes.   (III.865–72)

The Wife suggests here that the actions of "lymytour" friars who "bless" and take ownership of territories at the moment of their sale or settlement has led to the genocide of the faeries.[38] Thus the quasi-historical Arthurian setting of the tale is cast by the Wife as an historical period that was brought to an end specifically by the territorial ambitions of ecclesiastical institutions.

Patricia Ingham has written about how Arthurian romance served to model and think through contestations over identity and sovereignty in England, and particularly about the intersections between "Englishness" and "Britishness."[39] The same was true of Arthurian "history." As Walter Ullmann has demonstrated, Geoffrey's *Historia regum Brittaniae* was treated as a genuine historical source in the medieval period despite its obviously legendary content, to the degree that parts of it ended up in the articles on London in the Magna Carta.[40] Geoffrey's legendary history was commonly instrumentalized in the service of specifically secular territorial rights, developed in dialogue with the overlapping territorial rights of ecclesiastical institutions whose monastic institutional histories typically began where Geoffrey's history ends. Even by Chaucer's lifetime, such quasi-historical claims were often tied to the expansionist imperial tendencies of the English crown, in its struggle against the expansionist imperial tendency of the Roman papacy. King Edward I, for example, cited Geoffrey's history in a letter he wrote to the pope attempting (unsuccessfully) to gain recognition for his claim to Scotland.[41] Hence while the Wife's history frames the friars as settlers and the faeries as displaced Indigenous peoples, she is also contributing to that use of Arthurian literature to historically justify and mythologize England's own imperial ambitions.

This context is important for assessing the implicit rape apology in the *WBT*'s notorious ending, which is a crucial occurrence of the woman-as-media trope in *WBP* and *The Canterbury Tales* as a whole discussed in chapter 1.[42] The Rapist Knight makes three arguments for why he does not wish to marry the Loathly Lady: "thou art so loothly, and so oold also, | And therto comen of so lough a kynde" (III.1100–1): which is to say that he finds her ugly, old, and lowborn. The Lady famously allows him to choose if he prefers her to be "yong and fair" (III.1223), and so correct the first two of these deficiencies; but the question of changing her "kynde" is not raised. Instead, the Lady sidesteps the importance of class in her own description of her trick:

> And but I be to-morn as faire to seene
> As any lady, emperice, or queene,
> That is betwixte the est and eke the west,
> Dooth with my lyf and deth right as yow lest. (III.1245–8)

When the Rapist Knight then looks, he sees "that she so fair was, and so yong thereto" (1251) – which is to say, that she was precisely equivalent in fairness and youth to any given lady, empress, or queen in the known world. Given that ladies, empresses, and queens have always varied in their beauty and youth, the phrasing therefore implies that the Loathly Lady does not so much change her actual embodied self as she changes the knight's perception of her. As Susan Nakley writes: "Once the Knight accepts his wife's sovereignty, English institutions, particularly marriage, the law, and the knighthood (which languish throughout the preceding tales), regain strength and health – and she gains youth and beauty."[43] Perhaps the "miracle" is

76   Chaucer's Problem of Prose

that his perspective has been swayed by her argument, so that he has become indifferent to her "kynde" and so able to change his experience of her youth and beauty. In any event the concern for appearances that would motivate the Friar's flattery and the Summoner's gossip has disappeared, and in their place is a mutual recognition of true, immediate relation.

My own reading of this ending proceeds from the unspoken fact that the Loathly Lady's actual "kynde" is apparently "faerie." By implication, the Rapist Knight's antagonism towards this "kynde" places him on the side of the friars in the tale's opening lines, a connection that is reinforced by the Wife's comparison of friars to the incubus (III.880) and by the intimations of rape in the *GP* descriptions of the Friar's relations to women (I.208–69).[44] Meanwhile, the obvious parallels between the Wife's account of her marriage to Jankyn (III.634–825) and the story of the *WBT* identify the Wife with the Loathly Lady and Jankyn with the Rapist Knight. It bears emphasizing that the Wife's conflict with her "glossator" Jankyn is among other things a drama of attempted dispossession, where Jankyn is a would-be invading friar and the Wife a would-be displaced faerie. Jankyn "holds in fee" (III.630) the Wife's property during the period of their marriage where he reads to her from his book, she accuses him of murdering her for her land when he strikes her (III.800–1), and he relinquishes both his rights to ownership and his right to speak as part of their reconciliation (III.813–15). Hence we may identify a recurring binary opposition in *WBP* and *WBT* where in one column we have Jankyn, the Rapist Knight, and the settler friars and in the other we have the Wife herself, the Loathly Lady, and the Indigenous faeries.

The appearance of the friars in this binary allows us to extend it to the gloss/text dichotomy of *FrT* and *SumT*. The implicit gendering of gloss and text contextualizes the oft-discussed queerness of the Summoner in the *GP*, who joins in with the Pardoner to sing "Com hider, love, to me!" (I.672–3), and also the Wife-like proclivity of summoners towards gossip in the *FrT* passage cited above.[45] Such feminizations of the Summoner underscore how the twinned reconciliations of Wife and Jankyn, Loathly Lady and Rapist Knight are parallel fantasies of an ideal balance between the Summoner's authority of the text and the Friar's authority of the gloss, which are moreover framed as explicitly secular and secularizing by the genre of Arthurian legend. More to the point, the Wife's discursus on the friars and the faeries marks the conflict between these positions yet again as explicitly territorial, and so also reveals the ideal balance between them to be an expression of the same fantasy of (assaulting) occupiers and (assaulted) occupied

The Text, the Gloss, and Fragment III   77

living together in harmony that is quite precisely the fantasy critiqued by Coulthard in his account of the colonial politics of recognition.

Lisa Lowe's study *Four Intimacies*, discussed in the introduction of this book, applies Ann Laura Stoler's notion of the "intimacies of empire" in her analysis.[46] One key idea from Stoler that animates Lowe's study is the point that the "ideal of intimacy – sexual and affective intimacy within the private sphere of the bourgeois household" must be situated "within the material conditions of colonial relations."[47] This point is a helpful one for naming the confluence of themes I have identified in fragment III of *The Canterbury Tales*. When Chaucer's bourgeois Wife of Bath shares her embodied experiences of marriage and the conversation shifts immediately to a debate between a friar and a summoner about the best ways of conceptualizing contractual obligations, the text accomplishes precisely Stoler's shift from a consideration of sexual and affective intimacy to a consideration of the material conditions of imperial Christianity, which in Chaucer's era of Crusades and Iberian "Reconquista" was well on its way to laying the foundations for later colonial relations. The Wife's identification with the faeries may seem to critique the ecclesiastical order whose divisions of England into fungible territory effaced the pre-existing networks of social relationships and alternative epistemologies of her forebears. In the end, however, her fantasy of *troth*, reconciliation, and recognition turns her tale into a claim of ownership over both the past and the territories of England, in which she fantasizes about exerting power within a secular aristocratic political sphere that had already begun to venture into new territories "as thikke as motes in the sonne-beem" (III.868), imposing novel forms of ownership on local populations. That such fantasies lead the Wife of Bath specifically to her famous notion of her own personal agency points towards the forms that Christian "Englishness" would assume in the centuries after *The Canterbury Tales* was completed.

Above, I have argued that the remarkable dialogue between the Friar and the Summoner is both one of the most openly anti-clerical sections of the entire *Canterbury Tales* and also the most extended meditation on the misguidedness of reform-minded anti-clericalism, for the way it reveals how the worst problems adhere not in any particular ecclesiastical power centre but the structures of the imperial bureaucracy that pit those power centres against each other. The formal question posed by the debate between the Friar and Summoner of whether we should return to the literal reading of the official text (as the Summoner would have us do) or to open it up to reasoned consideration and adaptation (as the Friar would have us do) distracts us from the true situation in late medieval England, which is that the ecclesiastical systems of literate

78 Chaucer's Problem of Prose

administration developed on Roman models inevitably recapitulated Roman imperial violence and rape culture, in a way that was not only impervious to reform but that was enabled precisely by the ideology of reformism itself (as the Wife of Bath's fantasies suggest). In next two chapters, I will apply this model of text and gloss to unpack the implicit dialogue between the Monk and the Man of Law, where we see Chaucer grappling with the specific implications of this truth for England in the fourteenth century.

Chapter Four

Tragedy and the Law of Edward in
The Monk's Tale

After the Host asks the Monk to tell a tale in *MkP*, the Monk replies:

> I wol doon al my diligence,
> As fer as sowneth into honestee,
> To telle yow a tale, or two, or three.
> And if yow list to herkne hyderward,
> I wol yow seyn the lyf of Seinte Edward;
> Or ellis, first, tragedies wol I telle,
> Of which I have an hundred in my celle. (VII.1966–72)

Unlike the Man of Law, who in *MLI* could not identify a single tale to tell in verse that would not be a redundancy, the Monk enthusiastically promises to tell a hundred familiar tragedies, beginning with the oft-told life of "Saint Edward." This is almost certainly King Edward the Confessor.[1] Edward was venerated by Richard II and appears in the Wilton Diptych,[2] he is the subject of many vitae,[3] he is cited in *Piers Plowman* as an example of charity just before a fantasy about monastic disendowment,[4] and he is an important figure in late medieval memories of early medieval institutional history and of pre-Conquest property rights in particular.[5] Following Paul Olston, Juliet Dor argues that the Monk's focus on kings and emperors in his tragedies signals that he "is not aware of the pitfalls faced by his estate at the time" and that "[r]eligion is not his central concern."[6] Below, I will argue that the Monk's plan to tell a life of this particular king, still today buried at Westminster, demonstrates that in fact the Monk focuses on the pragmatic, legal challenges that face his "religion."[7] In the symbolic economy of text and gloss, the Monk exercises the same stubborn adherence to the text of early monastic charters that is more generally personified by the Summoner, and together they differ from the Man of Law, who shares the Friar's openness to the free

80 Chaucer's Problem of Prose

play of the gloss in his own interpretations of documented title. In this chapter and the next I will elaborate on these claims through close readings of first *MkP* and *MkT* and then *MLT*.

One ready-to-hand example of Edward's importance to monastic history is "St. Edmund's Liberty," which is to say the section of modern Suffolk County governed by Bury that was granted by documents recorded in the Curteys cartulary described in chapter 2.[8] Edward granted to the abbey the same control over this territory that his mother had held, which is to say that he gave the abbot the right to administer the courts himself and to have his own ministers and bailiffs in charge. In a chronicle account of the donation, Edward warns the Bury abbot Baldwin that protecting this grant will be a "great and continual labour" (*grandem et continuum laborem*).[9] This statement is indeed prescient about the ways that the politics of recognition would shape the careers of Baldwin, Samson, Lakenheath, Curteys, and Lydgate surveyed in chapter 2, as Bury was required to constantly confirm and renew Edward's original grant in the face of neighbours and royal officials who subjected it to constant, continuous challenge. The Monk's obsession with Boethian tragedy and his corresponding indifference to the strictures of his monastic rule work together to mark the toll of this labour on monastic communities more generally.

In this chapter I will focus my discussion on the most-discussed tragedy in *MkT*, that of Zenobia (or, as Chaucer's scribes spell it, "Cenobia"). The Monk makes several choices in his representation of Cenobia that participate in the trope of the "virago" or woman who transgresses gender boundaries, typically in conjunction with orientalist tropes about the ambiguous gendering of Eastern subjects.[10] My own reading of her tragedy will build in particular on Susan Nakley's readings of these women as "ethnic others whose extraordinary language skills as well as their femininity contribute to their dangerousness."[11] Nakley's study focuses on the ways in which these figures are evoked and then excommunicated for the purpose of constructing an English national identity. I will build on this argument to argue that the particular focus on language skills she notes is a sign of the connection between Chaucer's viragos and the overarching trope of woman-as-text in Chaucer's work, discussed in chapters 1 and 3.[12]

In *MkT* (and, as I will discuss in chapter 5, *MLT*) I will argue that the trope of woman-as-text extends into the gender category of the "virago" to figure these woman as representations of the documentary categories of "reconstruction" and/or "forgery," which similarly conform to and depart from conventional expectation to exercise troubling and often illegitimate power. The processes of excommunication

Tragedy and the Law of Edward in *The Monk's Tale* 81

identified by Nakley in their narratives may then be read as processes of invalidation, which evaluate the traditional claims to sovereignty these women embody and find them to lack the qualities that would authorize the modes of power they encode. To my knowledge, no one has ever commented on the fact that Cenobia, Donegild, and Custaunce are given names by Chaucer's scribes that not only depart from the spellings in their closest analogues (Zenobia, Domild, and Constance), but also suggest terms from the profession of the tales' tellers (*cenobia, geld, customs*). In the remainder of this study, I will proceed from the assumption that with these renamings, Chaucer is toying with the same practice of ambiguous allegorization that I have identified elsewhere as a key part of his representation of "Prudence" and "Sophie" in *Mel*.[13] In each case, Chaucer's suggestion of an allegorical interpretation grants readers a sort of critical distance from the texts, which represents in them thematically the larger structural problem of textual mediation for *The Canterbury Tales*.

Useful again is the definition of allegory advanced by Nicolette Zeeman's study of how medieval personification allegory is an "art of disruption." In chapter 3, I applied her framing of allegorical relation in terms of opposition and negation to explain how Chaucer uses allegory to address what we would now call structural critiques of social ills.[14] In the debate between the Friar and the Summoner in fragment III, Chaucer deploys debate allegory not only to articulate a structural critique, but also to name the role of structural critique as itself a harmful aspect of the structure that he is critiquing. The Friar has a compelling case to make about the wickedness of the ecclesiastical courts, just as the Summoner has a compelling case to make about the hypocrisy of the fraternal reforms, and the implication is that compelling critiques do not necessarily accomplish much by themselves and may indeed lead to the perpetuation of underlying imperial systems of harm. Similarly, the allegorical names of the women listed here each suggest that their stories may be a form of structural critique. "Cenobia" sounds like an allegorization of cenobial life or law; "Custaunce," of royal customs; "Donegild," of the imperative to pay taxes (*"dona geld"*); "Prudence" and "Sophie," of different forms of wisdom. By extension, the fates of these women in the tales where they appear suggest allegorical statements about the laws and imperatives that the women may personify.

Be that as it may, Chaucer's subtle changes to the names of these characters merely opens the door to readings that rely on personification allegory, in a manner far more circumspect than, say, the straightforward signal to readers that Lady "Mede" in *Piers Plowman* is a personification of "reward." Rather, the allegorical women's names present

82   Chaucer's Problem of Prose

readers with a choice that does more to disrupt the meaning of the text
than it does to bring clarity to it. As my argument in the next two chapters will demonstrate, readings that tease out the allegorical implications of the tales on the basis of these names formulate those tales as a
debate about the imperial politics of recognition between the Monk and
Man of Law, which as I have already explained can be easily ignored
by a critical reader who chooses to treat the allegorical namings as the
accidental and not particularly noteworthy choices of scribes writing
in a manner broadly consistent with the widely divergent spellings of
proper names in particular that readers of Middle English will commonly encounter. Once again, the allegorical names catch readers in the
larger structural tension in *The Canterbury Tales* as we have it, between
a Chaucer whose intention is operating imperfectly in the text but who
presents a general outline that can be reconstructed (e.g., the Man of
Law was at one time in dialogue with the Monk and the allegorical
names preserve the substance of that earlier, abandoned dialogue) and
a Chaucer whose intention is unreconstructable because of the choices
of scribes (e.g., it is an unfortunate coincidence that these unrelated
tales all have characters whose names happened to be rendered with
allegorical-seeming spellings). While it is also undecidable whether this
undecidable tension was itself an intended aspect of the text, it is certainly the case that it falls into Chaucer's consistent pattern of authoritatively abdicating authority in his poetry at the level of discourse, and so
the quasi-allegorization of the characters listed above is an irreducibly
noteworthy aspect of the larger problem of prose that *The Canterbury
Tales* poses to its critical readers.[15]

In *MkT*, the name "Cenobia" marks her as an idealized personification of ideal "cenobial" law, so that her conflict with Rome allegorizes
the conflict between monastic institutions and the centralized authorities that would erode monastic rights to self-governance. In particular,
Cenobia is a figure for Edward the Confessor, whose feminization and
racialization causes her to embody not only the more formal contradictions of the archive figured by the Wife of Bath, but also the specific
contradictions that pertain to the archival records of English history –
in this instance, the uncomfortable truth that the vast majority of surviving early English charters attributed to Edward are almost certainly
forgeries.[16] To establish that this is the case, however, I will have to start
at the beginning to explain why I ascribe so much significance to the
Monk's brief allusion to Edward.

As I have written in chapter 1, the Monk is asked to tell his tale
immediately after the end of *Mel*. Since *Mel* is a likely candidate for the
"prose" tale that the Man of Law promised to tell, this juxtaposition is

Tragedy and the Law of Edward in *The Monk's Tale* 83

an important circumstance for my claim that there is an implicit dialogue between these two pilgrims. Another circumstance is the Monk's use of the word "prose" in his prologue, in the only attested appearance outside of *MLI, Thopas-Melibee Link,* and *The Parson's Prologue (ParsP).* In the next section, I will pick up the thread of this suggested connection, to demonstrate how the Monk's dialogue with the Host picks up the themes of poverty, wealth, and ecclesiastical power raised by the Man of Law's ironic reframing of Innocent's sermon in *MLP*, to frame his tragedies as expressions of his perspective on the politics of recognition that would ultimately destroy whichever monastery he inhabited, and that had already moved his community away from the Benedictine values upon which it was founded.

The Monk and the Problem of Prose

The Monk defines tragedy as follows:

> Tragedie is to seyn a certeyn storie,
> As olde bookes maken us memorie,
> Of hym that stood in greet prosperitee,
> And is yfallen out of heigh degree
> Into myserie, and endeth wrecchedly.
> And they ben versified communely
> Of six feet, which men clepen exametron.
> In prose eek been endited many oon,
> And eek in meetre in many a sondry wyse.   (VII.1973–81)

Many readers of *MkT* have observed that the Monk's subsequent mixture of ancient, modern, mythological, and Biblical tragedies flatten and so disorder its temporality.[17] Paul Strohm argues about the tale's *de casibus* genre generally: "the constancy of the genre's appeal rests in the unfixed and highly adaptable nature of its exemplarity."[18] Nonetheless, as Lee Patterson observes, the Monk's description of tragedy as "a certeyn storie" marks it specifically as a *history*, with all of the claims to veracity, precedent, and narrativization with reference to datable texts and artifacts that this category entails.[19] L.O. Aranye Fradenburg observes, "our understanding of tragedy depends on techniques of storage and transmission"; the *MkT* is a collection of tragedies where the institutional dependency on these techniques is a source of anxiety.[20]

Amanda Gerber has connected the passage from fragment VII cited above to the important role of monasteries in the "cultural processes of literary production," which reflects the truism of medieval studies that

84 Chaucer's Problem of Prose

monastic libraries and scriptoria are the most important centres of book production and storage in the early medieval period, which by Chaucer's time were still not fully supplanted by their secular alternatives.[21] By implication, the authority of these early texts does not derive from their rigorously consistent formal qualities, in prose or in hexameter, but from the age of the material books witnessing the texts and of the archives that have held them in one place for so long. And as the scholars of early English diplomatics know well, the lack of formality in early English charters is compelling evidence for a text's age, for the obvious reasons that the authorities drafting the document were inventing new bureaucratic processes and so were likely to have started simple. Meanwhile the most common sign that ostensibly early documents have been changed is the presence of later formulae, though also it is incorrect to call such documents "forgeries," when there is every reason to believe that the modifications to the text may in some cases have helped to authorize the document before a literate authority who was only looking to check the boxes on their imagined list of authenticating features, and so who might have rejected the actual text of the original document for its informality. There is, then, a problematic interrelationship between historicity and form in monastic archives, which the similar problems in the Monk's tragedies serve to figure.

As I have already said, the Monk's reference to "prose" in his definition of tragedy is the only occurrence of this word in *The Canterbury Tales* that does not appear in a metafictional comment to the reader signalling that the poem's heroic couplets are about to be abandoned for a new form. The most obvious explanation for the word's appearance here is that the Monk is reflecting on the importance of form in response to the prose *Mel*, whose conclusion is signalled in the very first line of the *MkP*, and so his tragedies are in some sense a rejection of or response to this earlier tale. Where the form of the "proverbes" in Chaucer's second tale is explicitly linked to prose by its narrator (VII.936–58), the Monk's tragedies can be written in verse or not in verse, it does not matter either way.

The Monk's performative indifference to metrical form is made even more striking by the so-called Monk's Tale stanza of the tale that follows. This is recognized not only as one of Chaucer's most unusual and elaborate metrical forms, but also as a major inspiration for the Spenserian stanza that remains one of the most floridly unique meters in all of English letters.[22] Hence even though the Monk does not tell a tale in prose, he is nonetheless a key figure for the problem of prose in *The Canterbury Tales*, and this connection appears to be linked to the problematic interrelationship in his tale between literary and legal formalism

Tragedy and the Law of Edward in *The Monk's Tale* 85

and historicity that was so directly pertinent to the institutional health of the oldest late medieval monasteries.

In chapter 1, I suggested that *MLP* could be read as a possible preface to *Mel*, which in this capacity would call attention to *Mel*'s comments on poverty. The word *poverte* occurs ten times in *The Canterbury Tales*, including its appearance in the first line of *MLP* (II.99). Six of these occurrences are in *Mel*, and they are concentrated in a passage where Prudence tells her husband that just because he is wealthier than his enemies does not mean that he should go to war with them (VII.1547–75). The passage even contains a direct citation from the same homily by Innocent III that *MLP* paraphrases (VII.1568–70).

This connection between *MLP* and *Mel* reframes the former, so that the condition of "poverty" it laments may be reframed as a condition of "conflict." *MLP* makes the first connection between poverty and violence when it calls poverty a wound that cannot be wrapped (II.102–3). The image anticipates the central events in *Mel*, whose dialogue is precisely concerned with the five wounds suffered by Melibee and Prudence's daughter Sophie and the question of how they should respond to them (VII.970). Where Melibee laments these wounds and wishes to avenge his daughter, Prudence admonishes him that the wounds will heal on their own (VII.981), and in this sense they are unlike the wounds of poverty in *MLP*. Later in the tale, Prudence allegorizes her daughter's wounds as psychic injuries to Melibee's own five senses, in a departure from Chaucer's sources.[23] We may extend this allegory with reference to *MLP*'s analogy. If poverty is a psychic wound that does not heal and if, moreover, war is a practice that causes poverty (as Prudence suggests), then by implication Melibee's efforts to use war to heal his daughter's five wounds will not only fail but will indeed make it impossible to heal his own psychic wounds, as the conflict will necessarily squander the wealth that maintains Melibee's socioeconomic status and also guarantees an inheritance that might secure Sophie's future "health."

This framing of conflict as a cause of poverty is important context for the Host's famous misreading of the tale at the beginning of *MkP*. Even by the standards of the Host, there is a remarkably abrupt transition between his unfavourable comparison of his own wife to Prudence (VII.1891–1922) and his teasing of the Monk for his abstinence (VII.1932–64).[24] The connection of poverty to violence helps us to follow the Host's train of thought, as follows.

The Host begins *MkP* by citing not only the vindictiveness of his own wife Goodelief, but also her physical strength: "she is byg in armes, by my faith" (VII.1921), implying both that she is sturdy in warfare and that she has powerful arms – traits that mark her as a cause of conflict

86 Chaucer's Problem of Prose

and so of poverty, as is certainly consistent with the well-worn misogynistic tropes about the impact of marriage on a husband's finances. The Host then juxtaposes Goodelief's sturdiness with his description of the Monk's own physical form, in which he exclaims that "of brawnes and of bones" the Monk was "a wel farynge persone for the nones" (VII.1941–2). By implication the Monk, too, is well-prepared for conflict, and so by further implication he too is in danger of conflict's impoverishing effects.

Taken together, then, we may see in the progression *MLP* to *Mel* to *MkP* how the general principle "conflict causes poverty" applies to the specific case of English monasteries. Monasteries are founded as retreats from the world, where monks can live in poverty; they end up pursuing and hoarding wealth despite these starting premises; this pursuit puts them in conflict with their neighbours and the crown, as they prosecute and defend themselves from lawsuit after lawsuit; and in the end this conflict impoverishes them, ironically fulfilling their original vow. As I will unpack below, this theme of conflict and poverty in the *MLP – Mel – MkP* progression neatly expresses the double-bind that faced monasteries because of the medieval politics of recognition, which indeed impoverished communities by putting them into conflicts over wealth and land that then threatened to transform those communities by mandating them to set aside their own values to instead seek profit and stability within a system designed to prevent them from achieving either.

More locally, this theme contextualizes the logical leap that leads to the Host's importunate meditation on the many children that the Monk would have had if he had not been celibate (VII.1946–8), culminating in his extraordinary claim that the loss of good men to religion has depleted the genetic stock of all humanity (VII.1957–8). If the discussion of conflict brought up the vow of poverty, the Host is now turning his attention to the vow of chastity. It is clear from *GP* that the Monk's administrative duties make him indistinguishable from any other secular official or country baron, except that his office is not hereditary and his property is communally held by his monastery.[25] If, however, his monastery were in fact just another country estate, then the Monk would pass on his administrative role and its benefits to his children like everyone else. And if the monastic estates were no longer exceptional, their owners would no longer be constantly tied up in court, and the Monk would not have to waste his capacity for violence on conflicts he is doomed to lose. Thus the Host's fantasy of the Monk's many children is also a fantasy of the total assimilation of monastic wealth into the secular state, abandoning both the rule and the administrative

Tragedy and the Law of Edward in *The Monk's Tale* 87

exemptions that make their community unique, and leaving behind the oaths of poverty and chastity to concentrate on the oath of obedience. In this way, the Host's teasing of the Monk expresses the precise pressures put on monastic institutions by the assimilative politics of recognition, in a way that prompts him in his tale to present his own monastic perspective on those pressures.

My reading of the Monk therefore expands on David Berndt's comments on the Monk's *acedia*,[26] and on L.O. Aranye Fradenburg's reading of *MkT* in *Sacrifice Your Love*, worth quoting at length:

> If *The Monk's Tale* is stupefying, that is partly because it is sentimental about nothing. It seeks neither to ennoble nor to defame the human "spirit" and its experience of misfortune. It shows that the tragedy of Fortune exhibits the workings of the law. It shows the arbitrariness of that law, the law of our befallenness – we can be taken from without – and its inessential relation, its exteriority, to human "character." ... And it shows that the deadness of the law (its inanimacy, insensibility, mechanicity) informs signifying forms, like the tragedy of fortune, that refuse life and maintain what they can of indifference by constructing groupified (generalized, codified, uniformed, but also groupified temporally, that is, repeated) representations in which the death drive can seek refuge from the torments of aliveness and desire.[27]

In effect, my argument below simply adds historical and political context to this perceptive account of the Monk's affect in his tale. The "law" here is not only the Lacanian construct, but more precisely the inanimate, insensible, mechanical apparatus of literate administration whose tendency towards generalization, codification, uniformity, and repetition mindlessly furthers its imperial goals of self-perpetuation, consolidation, and dispossession. During the reign of Edward the Confessor, the monasteries in England like Bury St. Edmunds were still the beneficiaries of these processes, and they were established precisely to assist in the task of bringing order and uniformity to England. But by the time of Chaucer's Canterbury pilgrimage they were perceived as outmoded, and the processes of standardization and assimilation that would culminate in the Dissolution were already underway. The old, "dead" law of early England that these processes worked so assiduously to undermine both supports and constrains the Monk, as it forces him to imitate the Summoner's rigid adherence to the text in contrast to the Man of Law's Friar-like openness to the free play of the gloss. Hence my reading below will put Fradenburg's reading in context, to show how the Monk's stupefaction of his

88   Chaucer's Problem of Prose

readers is operating in relation to the larger structural anxieties of *The Canterbury Tales* as a whole.

Below, I will proceed from Fradenburg's comments on "signifying forms" to argue the Monk combines his wish to remember the virtuous life of Edward the Confessor with an apparent belief that the distinction between the forms of prose and verse is not a meaningful one, at least when it comes to tragedy. Again, in *MLI*, the Man of Law rejects Chaucer's *LGW* – whose structure and intent clearly resembles the Monk's "tragic," *de casibus* series of tales – as a model for his own tale when he chooses prose instead (II.45–96). Thus where the Man of Law is concerned to choose the exact right form for the message he wants to give, the Monk is willing to try any form at all, as long as the tragic content remains in place. And indeed, this yes/and approach to signifying forms and authorizing narratives corresponds to the multiple contrasting formalizations of the repetitive early English charters recorded in the Bury St. Edmunds register Add. 14848 discussed in chapter 2. In both cases there is a reasonable principle at work: when one attempts to convey the historicity of an old text that seems formless by contemporary standards, one might as well impose as many applicable contemporary forms as one can think of in one's representation of that text, since one cannot know ahead of time which form is most likely to convince the authority that will evaluate it, and the effect of the different forms may be additive even when they logically contradict each other.

The example of the Bury register also provides important context for the primary claim of this chapter, that the Monk's consideration and rejection of Edward the Confessor as a subject for his tale contends with a tension in written English related to its long history as a language of monastic administration. Chaucer's project of elevating the status of English into a literary and philosophical language on the model of Boccaccio's and Petrarch's Italian had to contend with the inconvenient existence of those exceedingly local, neither literary nor philosophical Old English charters whose survival was almost entirely thanks to the libraries of Benedictine monasteries like Worcester priory, Bury St. Edmunds, Bath Abbey, Christ Church Canterbury, Westminster, and especially St. Albans – the last of which is directly alluded to in *MkP* when the Host guesses that the Monk's name might be "Aubin."[28] In the next section I will first look more broadly at the legacy of Edward the Confessor in fourteenth-century historiography, before focusing in particular on his relationship to both Westminster and Rochester, also explicitly alluded to by the Host in *MkP*.

Edward the Confessor in *The Monk's Prologue*

In *GP*, the narrator describes the Monk's antipathy to the authority of the text clearly and unambiguously:

> The reule of Seint Maure or of Seint Beneit –
> By cause that it was old and somdel streit
> This ilke Monk leet olde thynges pace,
> And heeld after the newe world the space.
> He yaf nat of that text a pulled hen
> ...
> And I seyde his opinion was good.
> What sholde he studie and make hymselven wood,
> Upon a book in cloystre alwey to poure,
> Or swynken with his handes, and laboure,
> As Austyn bit? How shal the world be served? (I.173–87)

There is an obvious contradiction between the Monk's view of monastic rules and his membership in the so-called regular clergy, whose membership in their communities is predicated on their oaths to follow the rules of those communities. In the passage cited above, he is specifically resistant to monastic rules. To the Monk, such books are "olde thynges," and so contrary to the "newe world" of action that he would prefer to inhabit.

Like the Summoner, the Monk's indifference to the theoretical law of rules and principles is matched by a pragmatic loyalty to the way the law is actually practiced. The Monk's basic question in I.187 is actually a rather good one: how, indeed, would the world be served if he personally adhered better to the text of his monastic rule? The Host speculates at some length about how the Monk must occupy an administrative office of the sort that touched on such secular matters (VII.1935–42). If this were the case, then would not his correct conduct in exercising the enormous administrative power that came with his monastery's independence be much more important than whether he goes hunting in his free time? The rights of both monks and nobles to govern (and hunt upon) their vast estates was explicitly granted in exchange for administrative service, which might include for example the administration of the king's justice and the collection and payment of the king's taxes. If this particular Monk were to devote his time and effort to study and contemplation, as the Benedictine rule would have him do, this would interfere with his ability to conscientiously do the work associated with the rights and responsibilities that his community had assigned to his

90   Chaucer's Problem of Prose

office. Would it not be better for the world, then, if he focused his attention on his worldly job?

One indication that the Host believes the Monk to be an officer of a large, powerful convent is his unprompted observation that Rochester is close by (VII.1926).[29] Rochester was the second-oldest diocese in England after Canterbury and it was refounded as a cathedral priory in 1080 CE. The Host is perhaps alluding also to the bishop of Rochester Thomas Brinton (d. 1389 CE), whose sermon about "the belling of the cat" was preached to the Good Parliament and is the likely inspiration for the famous passage in the prologues of *Piers Plowman*.[30] Rochester also happens to be the home of the important *Textus Roffensis* manuscript of Old English and pre-Conquest law, which witnesses the laws of Athelberht that are the oldest dated Old English text on any subject.[31] While there is little reason to believe that Chaucer or the Host would have known about this particular manuscript, its name does come from a gloss written in the book in a fourteenth-century hand, and there are two manuscripts from Rochester today that witness fourteenth-century copies of pre-Conquest charters.[32] Someone, at least, was still reading and copying Old English at Rochester within decades of the Canterbury pilgrimage, as they were in so many other monastic contexts.

There are many valences, then, to the Monk's wish to tell a life of Edward the Confessor. According to his biographies, Edward chose not to have any children, and according to the records of early English charters, he was extraordinarily generous to monastic institutions. The earliest of these biographies was a *prosimetrum* written for his widow Edith of Wilton, whose hexameter poems are woven together out of classical references.[33] Westminster Abbey was originally endowed by Edward, and its cathedral was made the traditional site of English coronations in the reign of his successor William, whose explicit vow to uphold the laws of the Confessor remained a part of coronation formulae into Chaucer's own lifetime.[34] Finally, Edward is the namesake of King Edward I, and hence also of the king Edward III who reigned in Chaucer's own lifetime.

Unsurprisingly, Edward's foundation of Westminster is a major topic of later historical accounts of his life, and the abbey was and remains the home of his relics.[35] There are also many documents attributed to Edward in the Westminster muniments room, including some written in Old English "Saxon." Not unrelatedly, post-Conquest Westminster has a reputation among modern historians as a particularly notorious factory of forgery production.[36] One example of a Westminster document attributed to Edward is the Old English writ S 1119,[37] declaring that the monks are to have the land and wharf which Ulf the portreeve and his wife Cynegyth gave to Westminster.[38] This document survives in two manuscripts. The first is the thirteenth-century manuscript London, British Library, Cotton Faustina A.III (f. 11r.–v.), and the second is the fourteenth-century London, Westminster Abbey, WA Muniment Book 11 (f. 506r.–v.).[39] The main reason to copy a charter is to use it, and the main way to use a charter is to present it to an official in order to protect the rights it guarantees, whether these be specific rights to something like a wharf or a general principle of royal patronage that Edward's successors should uphold.

Beyond Westminster, Edward had long served as a model for restraint in royal dealings with autonomous local powers, whose (incorrectly attributed) law code *Leges Edwardi* has been described by its modern editor as "rather straightforward reflections of the aspirations of the English clergy in the early twelfth century towards peace and cooperation with the king."[40] More proximate to *The Canterbury Tales*, the Law of Edward was evoked as such by the holy blissful martyr Thomas a Beckett's supporters to resist the Constitutions of Clarendon, and it was also used by Andrew Horn as part of his efforts to secure a favourable charter for the city of London (discussed in the next chapter).[41] In other words, the prerogative to uphold the "laws of Edward" referred symbolically to a prerogative by the crown to observe checks on its power, to which the recognition of long-standing monastic autonomy and exemption were a form of lip service. The Monk, then, is not only lamenting the slow disintegration of England's large and wealthy monasteries, but also the consolidation of sovereign power in the institution of the crown, which made the institution less dependent on tradition or the consent of the governed. Part of the tragedy is that even the figure of Edward the Confessor that the Monk uses to symbolize an alternative to novel royal power is himself a figure whose symbolic uses already served to facilitate the consolidation of that novel power.

To briefly recap, then, the subtext of the Host's point is that it would be better for not only the Monk but for his land's tenants if the Monk had children, who could ensure continuity of stewardship and avoid impoverishing conflict. The Monk then responds by citing the example of Edward the Confessor, who on the one hand failed to have children but who on the other bestowed important wealth and privilege on to monastic cathedral chapters. The monk then quickly abandons the example to turn his attention to tragedy. On the one hand, Edward's importance as a lawgiver revered by English monarchs made him an important historical reference point to the defenders of English monasticism who followed in his wake, as is represented by the many law codes and charters that were either falsely attributed to him or forged in

92 Chaucer's Problem of Prose

his name.[42] But on the other, Edward's failure to procreate led to a Conquest that had extreme consequences for monastic institutions, and that laid the foundation for the politics of recognition that would destroy their ways of life, as litigators like the Man of Law would use William's Domesday book to convert Edward's gifts into fee simple.

After abandoning Edward, the Monk proceeds to the documented downfalls of great men, chosen and organized according to no discernible order. Perhaps Edward the Confessor was not the potent symbol of monastic autonomy he had once been, and the Monk imagines that a broader appeal to Boethian historical principle in many nations might work better to make his point to an authority with imperial aspirations. But while the Monk's stories of men losing their property may have once served to inspire the wealthy to donate land to ecclesiastical institutions while they have it, the Knight and the Host are bored by the predictability of a literary genre whose familiar repetitiveness and remoteness from contemporary political realities have made it ineffective. In the next section, we will demonstrate some of the ways in which the Monk's use of tragedy continues the theme of futurity and consistency that was brought up by his exchange with the Host.

Tragedy and Disendowment in *The Monk's Tale*

Boethius' *Consolation of Philosophy* is a major intertext of *MkT*, as for example it is the direct and the indirect source respectively (via the *Roman de la Rose*) for the tragedies of Hercules and Nero.[43] As I discussed in chapter 2, the *Consolation* is also a major intertext for the corpus of early English charters and legal documents, which consistently discuss worldly transience in great detail. In this section I will argue that the Monk's Boethian tragedies evoke the authorizing forms of these monastic documents to express similar anxieties about the difficulty of protecting wealth and power from encroachment.

MkT begins as follows:

> I wol biwaille in manere of tragedye
> The harm of hem that stoode in heigh degree,
> And fillen so that ther nas no remedie
> To brynge hem out of hir adversitee.
> For certain, whan that Fortune list to flee,
> Ther may no man the cours of hire withholde.
> Lat no man truste on blynd prosperitee;
> Be war by thise ensamples trewe and olde.

Tragedy and the Law of Edward in *The Monk's Tale* 93

There is a long history of debate over whether or not the Monk's use of Boethian Fortune in his tragedies is successfully "instructive" for his audience.[44] In his approach to this question, Siegfried Wenzel demonstrates that the Boethian language and themes are wholly conventional to medieval appropriations of the *Consolation*, and hence he suggests that that the occasion for this critical doubt is occasioned primarily by the Monk's apparent inattention to antiquarian, historiographic concerns.[45]

Modern critics are correct to note that the Monk pays little attention to the historical contexts within which the men who stand in high degree fall into inescapable adversity. In place of such context, the Monk emphasizes (or, when necessary, imposes) a consistent moral pattern that attributes events not to local contingencies but to the structures of the universe. Jodi Grimes has argued that *MkT* emphasizes the limits of human knowledge and hence the impossibility of human action in the face of Fortune's destructive forces.[46] In these terms, *MkT* is *anti*-historical in conception, or at least it is philosophically opposed to that common motivation of historical inquiry, which is to learn what happened in the past so that one might prepare for the future. In the Monk's hands, tragedy is a genre that demonstrates the uselessness of such preparations. In the passage quoted above the Monk emphasizes the impossibility of human action in the face of Fortune – "ther may no man the cours of hire withholde" – and he suggests that this impotence is the only valuable lesson from "thise ensamples trewe and olde." It is in this sense that early critics were correct to question the Monk's "instructiveness": the only course of action his vision of history permits is passive forbearance, and it does not affect the outcome if one heeds the lesson or not.

The first sign that the *MkT* tragedies evoke the specific rhetoric of charters may be found in the Monk's strange, oft-discussed decision to begin the series with Satan:

> For though Fortune may noon angel dere,
> From heigh degree yet fel he for his synne
> Doun into helle, where he yet is inne.
> O Lucifer, brightest of angels alle,
> Now artow Sathanas, that mayst nat twynne
> Out of miserie, in which that thou art falle.   (VII.2001–6)

There are two obvious points to make about this beginning. First, Satan is not an especially sympathetic figure, and so a strange choice to serve as the subject of a tragedy. Second, as the Monk acknowledges, the

94 Chaucer's Problem of Prose

Satan of conventional medieval Christian theology is hardly a victim of Fortune. As an angel, his downfall is a direct consequence of his own informed choices.

I would read Satan's appearance here as a sign of the generic analogy between the Monk's tragedies and the texts of early English charters, which commonly evoke Satan in sanction clauses that cite him as a recorded precedent of a criminal who tried to alienate territory from his sovereign without permission and experienced damnation as a consequence.[47] This framing of trespass as a specifically Satanic crime also appears in several Old English representations of Satan in Old English literature. Perhaps the most fascinating instance appears at the end of the Junius 11 poem *Christ and Satan*.[48] Satan is forced by Christ to measure the size of hell with his hands as punishment for tempting him in the desert with dominion over the Earth.[49] Jill Fitzgerald argues that Satan's task echoes the Rogationtide ceremony of so-called *gangdagas*, where parishioners trace the boundaries of their parish to drive out the demons from its confines.[50] It also resembles the procedures for defining and protecting territorial boundaries. For example, in the charter S 1441, the parties agree to confirm their settled agreement about a disputed territory by sending representatives to ride together around its boundaries together, so that no one can say later that they did not know where the boundaries were.[51]

Similarly, the Old English poem *Genesis A* shares an unusual image with a passage about the fall of the angels in the important charter S 745, documenting Edgar's refoundation of the New Minster at Winchester.[52] The charter has been attributed to St. Æthelwold, contemporary of St. Dunstan and architect of the Benedictine Reform, and it seems likely that it was written as a general justification for the many other activities of that reform, which generally involved replacing Augustinian canons and secular chapters with Benedictine monks. Both the charter and the poem contain an account of the fall of the Angels, which claims that humans were created to occupy the thrones in heaven that the fallen angels left vacant. In the charter, the story is then explicitly cited as an instructive parallel for understanding the administrative overhaul of the New Minster, undertaken because the canons did not profit the king. Like the figure of Satan in *Christ and Satan*, the fallen angels in *Genesis A* are grasping figures who attempt to leverage their personal power to overturn or ignore pre-existing agreements, and who find themselves alienated as a result. More to the point, the example of Satan – God's first angel – drives home the principle that ownership is stewardship, derived not from who one *is* but what one *does* with the responsibilities conferred on one as part of a given grant of title.

Tragedy and the Law of Edward in *The Monk's Tale*   95

The same principle is emphasized in the tragedy of Adam directly following Satan in *MkT*. The Monk specifies, strangely, that Adam was "nat bigeten of mannes sperme unclene" (VII.2009). This attention to biological particularity is best explained as a way of emphasizing the point that Adam cannot be imagined to have inherited his title as a beneficiary of primogeniture, since he had no biological father. Rather, Adam's right to Paradise was contingent on his service to it. Like Satan and the fallen angels of *Genesis A* and S 745, Adam then loses his endowment because of his failure in his service:

> Hadde nevere worldly man so heigh degree
> As Adam, til he for mysgovernaunce
> Was dryven out of hys hye prosperitee
> To labour, and to helle, and to meschaunce.   (VII.2011–14)

Adam's original terms of property ownership carried with them responsibilities for governing, and his failure to fulfill those responsibilities led to his alienation. Precedent in and of itself is not probative: no one disputes that Satan was born the chief of angels, nor that Adam was given dominion over all of creation. These title-holders simply failed to respect the asymmetrical relationship between themselves and God's divine imperium, and they did not put enough effort into the grand and continual labour that was necessary to maintain their rights.

But while figures like Satan and Adam would have seemed in the Old English poems and early English charters to allegorize uneducated aristocrats and secular clergy, in fourteenth-century England they appear rather to allegorize the Monk himself, as the ability of monasteries to properly govern their land was a matter of intense public debate. Certainly the Monk's tragedies are poorly received by both the Host – who baldly tells the Monk: "Youre tale anoyeth al this compaignye. | Swich talkyng is nat worth a boterflye" (VII.2789–90) – and by the Knight, whose stated distaste for the entire premise of Boethian tragedy did not bode well for the future of monastic donations.[53] If we read between *The Knight's Tale* (*KnT*) and MkT, we can see indications that the differences between the Monk and the Knight on the question of tragedy come down to their differing views on sex and procreation. This is discernible in their conflicting representations of Hercules, whose portrait by the Monk may be productively contrasted with his depiction in *KnT* (beginning I.1943).

Hercules appears in *KnT* in a list of famous lovers represented in the temple of Venus, followed by a summary statement about human

96 Chaucer's Problem of Prose

impotence that resembles the Monk's main theme, except the overbearing power driving human fate in this instance is not Fortune but Love:

> Thus may ye seen that wysdom ne richesse,
> Beautee ne sleighte, strengthe ne hardynesse,
> Ne may with Venus holde champartie,
> For as hir list the world than may she gye. (I.1947–50)

In *KnT*, this power of Venus to control men is ultimately connected to future prosperity, by the simple fact that Palamon's prayer to Venus contributes to a series of events that leaves him "lyvynge in blisse, in richesse, and in heele" (I.3102) at the end of the tale. This framing gives sex and procreation the same positive valence that the Host gives it in *MkP*, when he is teasing the Monk for his celibacy.

In *MkT*, the narrator also follows Boethius to draw explicit attention to Hercules' service to love, but he calls it another form of misgovernance that leaves him with neither bliss, nor wealth, nor health. As the Monk explains, the "sovereyn conqueror" (VII.2095) Hercules lived an extremely dangerous and violent life, and yet he was killed by the gift of a poisoned shirt by his beloved. From this the Monk extrapolates the following lesson:

> Beth war, for whan that Fortune list to glose,
> Thanne wayteth she her man to overthrowe
> By swich a wey as he wulde leest suppose. (VII.2140–3)

This passage suggests that Fortune's tendency to "glose" or deceive means that Hercules' service to love and marriage occasioned his downfall. The passage's word choice also aligns Fortune with the glosing Friar, and so with the Man of Law whose "purchasing" is the material manifestation of unknowable, threatening contingency. In contrast, the Monk strives constantly for the rigid predictability of his source text, even though it means alienating his audience in the process.

In the next section, I will turn to the most striking and important figure in *MkT*, Cenobia. Cenobia's feminized embodiment of the laws and charters of Edward are marked by her dark skin, by her name's evocation of Latin *cenobium*, and by her decidedly monastic mode of martial virtue. Lindeboom has argued already that she is a "role model" for the Monk.[54] Here, I will argue that her subjugation by the emperor Aurelius is a fantasy of the eventual erasure of monastic autonomy, in the face of emerging English imperialism.

Cenobia and Edward

Cenobia is figured as a racialized warrior queen in her first description:

> So worthy was in armes and so keene
> That no wight passed hire in hardynesse,
> Ne in lynage, ne in oother gentillesse.
> Of kynges blood of Perce is she descended.
> I seye nat that she hadde moos fairnesse,
> But of hir shap she myghte nat been amended. (VII.2249–54)

First, we are told that she is an excellent warrior, who moreover is descended from the kings of Persia. Then, in marked contrast to the other descriptions of Zenobia that emphasize her legendary beauty, the narrator makes a wry comment in line 2253 that ironically understates the fact that she is a dark and not fair-skinned beauty.[55]

As Susan Nakley observes in her reading of this passage, the Monk plays on the multiple meanings of "fair" to imply that she is not only dark but also unattractive, and so he "naturalizes and propagates the English language's bias against dark beauty."[56] Among the implications of this gesture is its participation in the trope, most famously attested in the personal letters of Abelard and Heloise, of connecting the black skin of the Ethiopian queen in the Song of Songs to the black robes worn by Benedictine "black monks" and nuns.[57] "Blackness" is figured by Abelard as a visible consequence of worldly existence, which necessarily mark the body of the monastic who must live on Earth.[58] Black clothing serves as a sort of armour that keeps the harmful effects of worldliness on the surface and protects the "white" soul within.

Similarly, Cenobia's blackness marks her as a figure who struggles to maintain monastic virtue – or, more specifically, the Monk's own particularly secular, martial-heroic version of that virtue – despite the vagaries of the secular world. She loved hunting, and (if the Host is correct) "kepte hir maydenhod" for as long as was possible (VII.2269), giving it up only for the sake of procreation (VII.2282–6). Critics have identified the same combination of traits in the Monk, whose love of hunting is the subject of his portrait in the *GP* and whose vows of chastity are the subject of the Host's teasing in the passage discussed above.[59] But the same combination of traits also apply to Edward, who went hunting every day after attending church,[60] and whose chastity was a major theme of his hagiography.[61] The awkwardness of the Monk's assertions that Cenobia had children despite her wish to remain celibate only underscores

98 Chaucer's Problem of Prose

how Cenobia is cast as a sort of Edward figure, as reflects the moral pattern of history rather than the attested facts.

Hamaguchi has argued that "Chaucer's assignment of the story of Zenobia to the Monk functions as Chaucer's own ironic criticism of the Monk himself: the Monk's violation of monastic codes, including Augustinian and Benedictine rules, parallels Zenobia's neglect of codes defined for her gender."[62] I depart from this reading to observe that the Monk appears to have carefully selected Cenobia as rather a justification for precisely his violations of the abstract rule to adhere to the rule he actually practiced in his powerful fourteenth-century monastery, in his administration and enjoyment of monastic property. Edward, too, neglected the abstract codes of conduct for kingship when he refused to procreate, as the Host's teasing of the Monk reminds us. But like Cenobia, Edward's violations of his gendered duties are admirable and so their negative consequences are framed as tragic.

We see this framing most clearly in the Monk's most remarked-upon change, which "moves Zenobia from the Orient to the West in order to punish her."[63] Her public humiliation is made particularly pointed by the golden chains around her neck, put there by an emperor "Aurelius" whose name literally means "golden" (VII.2364): Cenobia is both a victim of the wealth and power of empire and is herself objectified and adorned as an example of that wealth and power. Dor's reading of this scene is worth quoting at length:

> the end of this tragedy must be read as the humiliation inflicted on the heroine for sinning against gender as well as for decolonising (and then colonising anew under her own rule) the eastern Roman territories.... The Roman Emperor restored order by regaining the land and ostentatiously submitting her to her female condition; moving her to the West and making her a Roman slave similarly mark the return of a rebellious Oriental nation to the Roman yoke.[64]

My own reading aims to supplement this insight by adding a more local layer to its symbolic significance. I agree that Aurelius and Rome signify the secular, fiscal authority of the English crown, which by this period was well on its way towards the articulation and even preliminary achievement of imperial aspirations. So also do I agree that Cenobia is a figure for the eventual targets of this colonization, who prefigures in particular the racialization of the colonized and enslaved peoples that would accompany and justify genocidal capitalism. I would only add that at the same time and by means of the same symbolism, the Monk identifies himself and his profession with Cenobia, and in this way he positions monks as targets of English imperial oppression who may be productively compared in this way to the eastern Roman territories. This is clearly signalled by Cenobia's similarities to Edward the Confessor, by the identity of the tale's author, and by the allegorical spelling of her name "Cenobia." Aurelius the Roman emperor who subjects and constrains her to his normative sexuality signifies both the crown and the papacy, whose politics of recognition traced their historical origins back to William the Conqueror and the Domesday Book, which in turn arose as a direct consequence of Edward the Confessor's (tragic) failure to have any children, and which created the structural conditions of asymmetrical recognition that underlie the constant conflict between monasteries and their neighbours satirized by the Host.

With this established, we may now turn finally to *MLT*, which similarly tells the story of another allegorical woman (Custaunce, or "customs") who is similarly assimilated and effaced by the centralizing authority of Rome. The parallelism between the sultan of Syria and the English king Alla of Northumbria expresses the same curious association we see in the parallelism between Cenobia, the Syrian queen, and the English king Edward the Confessor. As we shall see, I will identify in this tale too a connection between the highly visible themes of emergent imperialist ideology as it applies to racial Others, and the less visible but more historically germane themes about the politics of asymmetrical recognition.

Chapter Five

Chronicles and Customary Law: Chaucer's Tale of Custaunce

In chapter 1, I discussed Eleanor Johnson's argument that the Man of Law's claim to tell his tale in prose is part of a larger effort to exploit the "imaginary and idealized deep history" of England in order to evade the common (and rather justified) critiques of his profession's unprecedented novelty.[1] In this chapter, I will build on Johnson's insights to explain how the tale of Custaunce fits into my reading of the problem of prose that links the Monk to the Man of Law.[2] In my reading of *MLT* below, I will aim to articulate the great contradiction of the text, that it parodies and criticizes the blatantly self-interested framings of monastic chroniclers who base their claims to exemption and autonomy on vague gestures towards an imperfectly recorded "time immemorial," though (as Johnson demonstrates) the tale is itself an even vaguer and more self-interested gesture towards an even earlier and more imperfectly memorialized history. But first, I must briefly return to *MLI* to discuss how it relates to the tale of Custaunce that follows it.

My reading of *MLI* in chapter 1 identified a dense knot of anxieties in this text about the persistence of historical media and its tendency to admit distortions over time. The *MLI* begins with a description of how movement of the sun changes the shape of shadows that were previously proportionate to the objects that created them, and this symbol of temporal distortions occasions the Host to address the Man of Law and evoke the forms of the contract that indeed were developed precisely to guard against such slippages in representing the terms of gifts and agreements. The Man of Law's reply to the Host proves the validity of the Host's concern, as he very quickly backs out of his promise to tell a tale. Indeed the Man of Law even goes so far as to figure the Host's very desire for him to keep his promise as itself unnatural and analogous to incest.

Chronicles and Customary Law   101

This dialogue brings together three concerns in *The Canterbury Tales*. First, it demonstrates the political concern to represent the societal impact of documentary proceduralism, in which the formulae and interpretive procedures designed to fix obligations in fact make it easier to revise and subvert them. Second, it demonstrates the recurrent thematic concern in all of Chaucer's poetry, regarding his famously ambivalent ambitions as an author of English verse. Third and finally, the *MLI* instantiates the concern to use women to symbolize text, wherein the impossibility of figuring women's agency in a patriarchal society is used to figure the vagaries of the processes of mediation and textual transmission, wherein the agency of interpretation belongs to readers. In this Chaucerian symbolic economy, agreements recorded as oaths or documents and thoughts recorded as poems or treatises are all like women, in that they have no power over how they are used. The figure of Cenobia in *MkT* is parallel in this regard to the Sultaness, Donegild, and Custaunce of *MLT*, who all figure different models of the recorded "law" writ large, wherein Custaunce's passive travels are contrasted with the far stricter approach to historical consistency preferred by her mothers-in-law. The aimless, improbable voyages of Custaunce nonetheless result in her exact reproduction in the form of her identical son, the Roman emperor Maurice, and this transmission allegorizes a fantasy of the gloss wandering away from the text but still nonetheless arriving at the truth.

As I discussed in this book's introduction, my reading of *MLT* contributes to that recent boom in scholarship that uses the text as an example in studies of medieval English identity formation and medieval global trade networks.[3] Particularly pertinent is Kathy Lavezzo's astute and influential account of the politics of *MLT*, wherein she discusses the vexed relationship between the emergent English nation and its "mother," the Christian Roman empire.[4] Lavezzo draws particular attention to the tale's remarkable and anachronistic depiction of Syria as an Islamic state, whose negative counterpart to conversion-era England facilitates the larger project of bringing the latter into the narrative of continuing imperial hegemony.

In an important refinement of these claims, Susan Nakley has identified the myth of origin in *MLT* more precisely as a myth of sovereignty. As she states, "the nation legitimizes the idea of sovereignty by imagining itself as a pre-existing community that warrants sovereignty as a form of self-determination."[5] The vexed temporality that emerges between cultural nationhood and political sovereignty comes to bear on the mythic history of *MLT*, in which "Chaucer's employment of an impossible past in his narration of national continuity exposes

102   Chaucer's Problem of Prose

the paradox of nationhood, that continuity depends on anachronistic revision and temporal disorder produces cultural disorder."[6] The present chapter expands on Nakley's reading to situate the anachronistic revision and temporal disorder she describes in relation to the earlier anachronistic revisions and temporal disorders of local property relations, and the patchwork of contingent but persistent sovereignties they enabled.

In this chapter's first section below, I will focus in particular on the dialogue between *MLT* and the work of Matthew Paris, the famous St. Albans historian and artist who among other works wrote a verse life of Edward the Confessor.[7] The most pertinent of Matthew's works here is his *Vitae Offarum duorum* ("Lives of Two Offas"), which describes two kings who both lead lives very similar to King Alla's and who authorized the founding of St. Albans Abbey.[8] The comparison between this text and *MLT* highlights how the new myth of national sovereignty described by Nakley and Lavezzo is framed by the Man of Law as a replacement for an older myth of ecclesiastical sovereignty, in a manner that anticipates the dialectic between the gradual disendowment of England's monasteries and the gradual emergence of the English nation-state.

In the second section, I will argue that *MLT* undermines its own historicity, first through the trope of the untrustworthy messenger and second through its suggestion that Northumbrians spoke "corrupt" Latin. The Man of Law implies whenever possible that the story of Custaunce he narrates as faithfully as he can may be a misunderstood or even falsified history, as even the tale itself contains multiple instances of falsified official communications that undermine one's faith in the Northumbrian ability to maintain a faithful historical record. In the third and final section of this chapter I will turn to Chaucer's two largest additions to the tale: the Sultaness' council, and Custaunce's trial, both of which can be placed in productive tension with analogous scenes from Bede's *Ecclesiastical History*.

Matthew Paris and the Man of Law

The most important fourteenth-century copies of pre-Conquest English laws appear in the remarkable set of manuscripts produced by city chamberlain Andrew Horn (c. 1275–1328) and donated to the London Guildhall.[9] Horn's efforts to compile the customs and liberties of the city appear related to the notorious eyre of 1321 CE, when Edward II stripped London of its privileges.[10] Indeed, Horn himself would publicly read Edward III's new charter for the city after Edward II was deposed a few years later, which would return all of those rights and privileges to the city.[11] Among the more noteworthy contents of Horn's compilations are the Latin translations of Old English law codes that retain embedded instances of Old English legal vocabulary.[12] Horn's direct sources for these texts include the Latin compilations and translations of Old English law called the *Leges Anglorum* by modern editors, also compiled by the city of London in the first half of the thirteenth century.[13]

As Ralph Hanna writes, it seems that London civic officials like Horn felt as the chroniclers and administrators at St. Albans and Bury St. Edmunds did, that "the fictive forgery may be the truest form of historical remembering and preserving the liberty that should have been textually instantiated, even if it hadn't been."[14] Like the large, handsomely written and beautifully illuminated chronicles and cartularies of monastic collections, the aesthetic unity of Horn's large, handsomely written and beautifully illuminated *Liber regum* obscures the profound disunity and confusion of the archive it regularizes. Nor were Horn's volumes the only texts deployed to serve the interests of the city's mercantile class that were based on the model of monastic histories and cartularies. The fourteenth-century "London Chronicles," which are among the medieval historical sources Chaucer is most likely to have known first-hand, began with the widely circulated *Flores historiarum* that was in turn an abbreviation of Matthew Paris's *Chronica maiora*.[15] London's civic identity as a literate institution was clearly patterned on the pre-existing literate institutions of nearby monasteries, and they borrowed not only the form but the content monastic histories and records accordingly.

Here, I will argue that the movement of the "accused queen" narrative from the *Vitae Offarum duorum* to the *MLT* models the same pattern of appropriation and revision seen in the Old English law codes and the St. Albans histories. Though of course variations on this conventional story are common throughout medieval Europe and beyond, Nancy Black has observed that they are found in official and institutional histories, and that this circumstance "firmly associates Constance with this genre."[16] These *Vitae Offarum* are among the most historically and temporally adjacent analogues to Trevet's story of Constance, and so they are very likely to have directly inspired his work.[17] Meanwhile Matthew Paris' own text of the *Vitae Offarum* has a number of prominent and far-flung analogues, including the Old English poems *Beowulf* and *Widsith*, which point to a wide circulation of the Offa stories.[18] A particularly striking instance of Offa's popularity is Thomas Walsingham's description of a folk legend of this king that was cited by St. Albans

104   Chaucer's Problem of Prose

tenants participating in the Uprising of 1381.[19] Finally, a letter from Charlemagne to the second king Offa contains the first known mention of the English wool trade, in which Chaucer served as controller of petty custom – yet another reason for Chaucer to know about this figure.[20] My reading will presuppose, then, that Chaucer's adaptation of the Custaunce story to a mercantile context was based in part on his historical knowledge of the Offas and their legends, and so that the tale comments upon the genre of specifically monastic and institutional historiography that the Offa legends exemplify.

The two kings named Offa of the *Vitae*, separated historically by centuries, are firstly the mythical founder of the Anglian line (hereafter, for convenience's sake, "Offa I") and secondly the historical king Offa of Mercia who had been remembered as a founding benefactor of St. Albans for centuries ("Offa II"). All five of the manuscripts recording their parallel lives survive in the archives of St. Albans and the text is sometimes attributed to Matthew Paris, in part because the manuscript British Library Cotton Nero D I witnessing the *vitae* (ff. 2r.–25r.) is illuminated in what appears to be a late version of his signature style.[21] Despite the difficulty of categorizing the *Vitae Offarum* text from a modern standpoint as romance, hagiography, or history, we may infer from the contexts of its survival that the text was considered by the monks to be serviceable enough in this final category, and that it was useful enough in this regard to help confirm the ancient and, indeed, quasi-legendary rights of an institution that claimed to date back to the barely recorded late-Roman era of St. Alban himself.

The legends both parallel *MLT*, but in slightly different configurations. Offa I discovers a nameless woman in the woods, where she was abandoned as punishment for resisting the incestuous advances of her father, a king from York (23–4). Offa marries her, they have children, and then Offa is called up to Northumbria to defend the border against the Scottish (25–8). He sends a message home declaring victory, but the messenger is intercepted by his incestuous father-in-law, who plies the messenger with drink and swaps out his letter for a document saying that the queen and her children should be executed (27–30). As in Trevet, Gower, and Chaucer, the text of the letter is not paraphrased but transcribed: in this instance, the false Offa of the letter blames his loss on his queen, and orders that she be taken with the children back to the wilderness and that all of their hands and feet should be removed (29–30). The soldiers take pity on the queen, but the children are mercilessly dismembered. A passing hermit then prays over the children and they are miraculously reassembled (31–2). Eventually they are reunited with Offa, who promises to found a monastery in honour of the hermit, but

Chronicles and Customary Law   105

does not keep this promise and passes it on to his descendants (35–40). This promise is later kept by Offa II, when he discovers the bones of St. Alban and founds the famous monastery of the same name, after separating from his wicked wife Dreda (Old English "Thryth," perhaps, as in *Beowulf* line 1931) and beginning a life of chastity.[22]

This narrative's analogue to the *MLT* provides a helpful illustration of the political issues at stake for late medieval writers in even legendary representations of the early English past. In this case, the legend of Offa I and his family affirms that St. Albans Abbey exists not only by divine sanction, but also by the sanction of the king and his successors. The miracle further emphasizes that Offa's decision to found the monastery was not only a sign of his holiness but also of his shrewdness as a ruler. Though one may expect the king's relatives to help him secure his bloodline, it is in fact the religious hermit who has the king's interests most at heart, and so the chronicle frames the foundation of a monastery for such men as a good management decision in addition to being an act of devotion. The implicit analogy between clerical skill, clerical piety, and loyal vassalage in this narrative is common throughout the medieval period, as religious institutions sought to maintain the control over the secular administration of written documents that they enjoyed in earlier eras of greater illiteracy.

Another analogue to the *Vitae* that is helpful for framing its relationship to *MLT* is the Middle English romance of *The King of Tars*.[23] In this romance, which has been frequently compared to *MLT*, the Custauncelike Christian queen and her Damascene, non-Christian husband have a child described as "a rond of flesche yschore" (580), which had "noiþer nose no eye" (584).[24] When the child is baptized, he turns into a normal child; the king is then converted and baptized himself, at which point his skin turns from black to white. As Sierra Lamuto observes: "not only does the child represent the illegibility of hybrid bodies prior to his baptism; he also represents the way in which the transformation of hybrid bodies into actors of colonialist domination secures dominant ideologies."[25] More specifically, "the child of a Saracen and Christian is granted the right to life specifically through the erasure of his mixed heritage, a transformation that effectively secures Christian rule over the east."

The most obvious parallel between this romance and the *Vitae Offarum* is suggested by the name itself "Offa," which is not only a commonly attested Old English name for many pre-Conquest kings and earls but is also a Latin word for "lump, piece, or morsel."[26] Certainly Rickert has suggested that this connotation of the name "Offa" explains the striking occurrence in both Offas' lives of the Norse motif of the

106   Chaucer's Problem of Prose

"inglorious youth" or *kol-bitr*, wherein both kings are disabled at birth but are miraculously healed in adulthood.[27] The parallel between these two "lumps" and the child in *The King of Tars* is further suggested by the discrepant accounts of Offa I's father Wærmund or Gotmundus. In some sources, he is a grandson of Odin; in others, he is a "regem Africanorum (king of Africans)" who abandoned his inheritance to adventure across northern Africa, southeast Europe, and southwest Asia.[28] There are, then, some striking parallels between the baby in *The King of Tars* and this mythic English king Offa, whose name means "Lump" and who has a racialized, "heathen" father.[29] More to the point, the parallel reveals how the founding myth of St. Albans stages in miniature the larger drama Lamuto identifies in *The King of Tars*, whereby Christianity establishes itself as a religion for monarchs in a new territory. It is, perhaps, no coincidence that my second Offa is most famous today for "Offa's Dyke" on the Welsh border, which still today divides England from the territory of the "Britons" who would supply the Gospels used in Custaunce's trial (II.666).[30]

John Frankis has observed that in *MLT* Chaucer tends to remove historical detail from Trevet's legend and Gower's retelling of it in *Confessio amantis*, both of which incorporate figures from Bede's account of the conversion of Northumbria.[31] In the *Historia ecclesiastica*, the Roman emperor Mauritius allowed Gregory the Great to send Augustine of Canterbury on his conversion mission, which according to Bede was inspired by a chance meeting between Gregory and a Northumbrian slave whose king was named Ælle of Deira.[32] Though Trevet himself was a Dominican friar, his chronicle's patron was Mary of Woodstock, a daughter of Edward I who was also a Benedictine nun of Amesbury – the site of an abbey since the late tenth century. The tale is therefore in direct conversation with the long tradition of Benedictine historiography described in the previous chapters, as is perhaps most directly signalled by Trevet's claim that he found the story of Constance in "old Saxon chronicles" ("aunciens croniqes des Sessouns"). This statement may well allude to the so-called Anglo-Saxon Chronicle begun in the reign of Alfred but continued until after the Norman Conquest in regional ecclesiastical contexts.[33]

In contrast, the Man of Law claims that he heard the tale from a merchant (II.132). In his influential reading of *MLT*, Jonathan Hsy argues that this indicates how "narrative is, quite literally, the most precious resource that merchants transport," and that this reflects a larger concern for the circulation and transmission of texts in the tale.[34] And as David Wallace has written, Custaunce's boat seem less like the "ship of the Church" than it does like a merchant's ship, in a way that appears to

Chronicles and Customary Law   107

transform the entire story from an allegory for Roman Christian imperium into an allegory for proto-colonial mercantilism – to the extent, at least, that these two historical developments may be productively distinguished from one another.[35] Hence, perhaps, Chaucer's account of the process whereby the Sultan of Syria first decides to marry Custaunce after hearing about her beauty from merchants (II.183–9). After the news is related to him, the Sultan consults his men on the question of whether he should marry her, in a discussion which peters out with the ambivalent assertion that "they kan nat seen in that noon avantage | ne in noon oother way, save mariage" (II.216–17). The Sultan, it seems, has no choice. And given the "diversitee | Bitwene hir bothe lawes," which is to say Christianity and Islam (220–4), the Sultan and his aristocracy must convert, abandon their old ways, and make a payment – "I noot what quantitee" (II.242) – to the church and to the emperor for the privilege of submitting to them.

Hence while the passage may begin with the old romance trope of falling in love with a beautiful woman from the way she is described, it ends with an exchange that we may describe rather precisely as the asymmetrical recognition of the Syrian sultanate by Rome, which begins with the Sultan making concessions because he has no choice and ends with the Syrians having committed atrocities that justify an imperial invasion (II.955–66). Custaunce's complaint that "wommen are born to thraldom and penance, | And to been under mannes governance" (286–7) is ironic, then, in more than one sense. Thralldom and penance do indeed await her, but they also await the people of her betrothed.

But though the tale can be read in hindsight as an allegory for the emergence of a global Christian imperialism that would begin a century after Chaucer's death to extract wealth and consolidate power on an unprecedented scale, its proximity to the monastic analogues and sources surveyed here make it function just as effectively as an allegory for the expansion and regularization of the English crown at the particular expense of exempt monasteries. Either way, Custaunce personifies the imperial law whose adoption would make these processes of dispossession and assimilation possible.

In the next section, I will demonstrate how Chaucer's Northumbria serves in *MLT* as a sort of mythic, virtual space of Christian English origins, which reflects how the tale functions as a *generic* critique of the monastic-historiographic *literary* tradition that extended from Bede into the post-Conquest chroniclers who are Trevet's sources. I will begin with my reading of the tale's deployment of the "untrustworthy messenger" motif. Markus Stock has cited this motif as a key trope for medieval meditations on mediation and its discontents.[36] Here, I will argue

108   Chaucer's Problem of Prose

that the messenger of the *MLT* is not only the deliverer of a forged letter, but also a character appearing in a history that may well itself be forged, or at the very least based on corrupt textual traditions.

Untrustworthy Messenger

In II.470–504, the narrator presents us with a series of reasonable questions.[37] Why did the Sultaness not kill Custaunce at the feast, instead of returning her to her ship? Why was the boat never upset in a storm? What did Custaunce eat and drink during her voyage? The narrator responds to each of these questions with an illustrative example from either scripture or hagiography of a miracle: God saved Daniel from the lion's den; he kept Jonah in the fish's mouth until he was spat up at Nineveh, and he ordered the four angels holding the winds to keep them at bay; and he fed Mary of Egypt while she lived in the desert. The pattern of these examples compares Custaunce to not only a saint, but more specifically a prophet, protected by God not only because of her virtue but because he will use her to send a message.

Custaunce's mediating role is clarified in lines 477–83:

> God liste to shewe his wonderful myracle
> In hire, for we sholde seen his myghty werkis;
> Crist, which that is to every harm triacle,
> By certeine meenes ofte, as knowen clerkis,
> Dooth thyng for certein ende that ful derk is
> To mannes wit, that for oure ignorance
> He konne noght knowe his prudent purveiaunce.

In the context of the urbane and satirical *The Canterbury Tales*, it is very difficult to read this passage without discerning a subtext of narratorial incredulity, which calls attention to the readerly suspension of disbelief necessary to treat this story as a factual, historical account. If Custaunce was a real person and these events truly happened, then the intervention of divine providence is a reasonable explanation for the questions raised above. If, on the other hand, Custaunce is a fictional character and the Man of Law is inventing this story, then the passage makes him appear to be a lazy author, who cannot be bothered to come up with plausible details that might give his narrative coherence. For all that the narratorial speculation here appears designed to address and contain any readerly incredulity, all it does is stoke it, by calling attention to the unfalsifiable opacity of both God's will and of the text that records it. Precisely by claiming that God uses Custaunce to send a miraculous message to Christian believers, the Man of Law invites us to consider how that message might have been distorted, either accidentally over the course of its transmission or intentionally by the Man of Law himself.

The same problem of the story's plausibility is raised more indirectly in the narrator's brief complaint about the easily misled messenger, whose letters to and from King Alla are changed by the wicked queen Donegild.[38] After a letter written by the king to his constable is intercepted, the narrator condemns the messenger as follows, in a passage absent from both Trevet's and John Gower's versions of the Constance story:[39]

> O messager, fulfild of dronkenesse,
> Strong is thy breeth, thy lymes faltren ay,
> And thou biwreyest alle secreenesse.
> Thy mynde is lorn, thou janglest as a jay,
> Thy face is turned in a newe array.
> Ther dronkenesse regneth in any route,
> Ther is no conseil hyd, withouten doute. (II.771–7)

Monastic chronicles like Bede's commonly include transcriptions of many letters, including for example the letters from Gregory to Augustine that he too transcribes with the explicit intention of conferring authority on his historical narrative.[40] The example of this messenger calls into question the authority of all such primary evidence. If a drunken messenger like this one can be put in charge of something as important as delivering royal decrees, what then does that say about quality control in the larger systems of Northumbrian message production and storage from the reign of Alla? What trust can we put in the records kept by the sort of constable who did not even write for confirmation after the king responded to the news of his first child's birth by demanding the exile of the baby and his mother? How are we to trust the accuracy of the information preserved and transmitted by officials capable of mistakes on this scale? And if such information cannot be trusted, then how can we trust narratives like Bede's and Matthew Paris', which quote the letters delivered by messengers like this one as the sources for their historical narratives?

The problem is emphasized in a brief speech by the messenger, when he reads Donegild's second letter:

> "Lord Crist," quod he, "how may this world endure,
> So ful of synne is many a creature?

110   Chaucer's Problem of Prose

O myghty God, if that it be thy wile,
Sith thou art rightful juge, how may it be
That thou wolt suffren innocentz to spille,
And wikked folk regne in prosperitee?
O goode Custaunce, allas, so wo is me
that I moot be thy tormentour, or deye
On shames deeth; there is noon oother weye."   (II.811–19)

There is a considerable irony to the messenger's piety at this moment. After all, it was not God who allowed innocents to suffer and the wicked to prosper in this instance, but the messenger himself who was careless in the execution of his duty. The Boethian platitudes about the vagaries of fate in this passage resemble those appearing in *MkP* and *MkT*, and as I have argued in chapter 2 above, their thematic similarity to early English charters appears to have inspired Lydgate's translation of Bury's charters into Chaucerian rhyme royal verse. Though the messenger is correct to identify the universal constant of change as a condition of Custaunce's suffering, the direct cause of her suffering here is the messenger's own inattention to his job. Perhaps the messenger's contemporaries were similarly inattentive when they wrote their own Boethian platitudes into their early monastic charters, which again are otherwise extremely informal and vague by the standards of late medieval land grants.

In previous chapters, I have suggested that the implicit dialogue between the Monk and the Man of Law may be productively compared to the explicit dialogue between the Summoner and the Friar, with the Summoner and the Monk both figuring an unswerving allegiance to the historical text and the Friar and the Man of Law both figuring an openness to the vagaries of the gloss. One bit of evidence for this parallelism may be seen in a pattern of similarity connecting the messenger of *MLT* from the passage above to the portrait of the Summoner in *GP*. Given the basic overlap in their professions – wherein a summoner is essentially a specialized sort of messenger – these parallels are revealing about not only Chaucer's concept of communications generally, but also how that concept informed his reading of monastic institutional histories.

The key passage from the *GP* is as follows:
And whan that he wel dronken hadde the wyn,
Thanne wolde he speke no word but Latyn.
A fewe termes hadde he, two or thre,
That he had lerned out of som decree –

> No wonder is, he herde it al the day;
> And eek ye knowen wel how that a jay
> Kan clepen "Watte" as wel as kan the pope.
> But whoso koude in oother thyng hym grope,
> Thanne hadde he spente al his philosophie;
> Ay "Questio quid iuris" wolde he crie.   (I.637–46)

Like the messenger, the Summoner finds his language transfigured by drink so that he chatters his words mindlessly. In both cases, the result is equated to the song of a jay that has formal structure but no semantic content.[41] As a consequence, neither figure can be trusted to secure or protect important information. The Summoner's predilection towards gossip, described in chapter 3, is parallel to the messenger's betrayal of "alle secreenesse" (II.773).

As Jill Mann observes, the use of the chattering bird in this passage as a figure for "uncomprehending repetition" is a common one in complaint literature, and indeed Old French "latin" means not only the Roman language but also "the warbling of birds" (def. B.3) and "the language of the clerics, unintelligible to the common people, scholarly language" (def. D.1). [42] In Middle and Modern English, a similar confluence of meanings are found around the word "jargon" (def. 1 and 6 respectively).[43] Chaucer's specific tendency to attribute such birdlike clerical chattering to drunkenness – a theme most fully treated in The Manciple's Prologue (*MancP*) and *The Manciple's Tale* (*MancT*) – is less commonly attested.[44] Like the Manciple, drunkenness makes Alla's messenger and the Summoner mindlessly uncritical in their devotion to institutions of power and tradition, and the meaninglessness of their speech is a result. In the same way that a bird can make a sound that is technically a "word" but has no intention or meaning, so also does the Summoner privilege the form of legal proceedings over their content.

In the case of the messenger, it is also important to note the likely allusion to the common and quite longstanding stereotype of the English that they drink too much. As Elaine Treharne has discussed, this stereotype is already attested in Norman monastic chronicles describing their early English forebears.[45] Perhaps, then, the drunkenness of the Northumbrian messenger is reflective of this larger national failing in Alla's kingdom, and so the indictment for carelessness here is directed not only at this character but at English messengers and archivists in the age of Bede more generally.

And while the specific criticism of the Summoner's poor Latin that might drive this analogy home is not directly attested in the description of the messenger himself, it is arguably applied to Northumbrians

112   Chaucer's Problem of Prose

more generally, in the brief allusion to the so-called corrupt Latin that
Custaunce speaks to be understood when she arrives:

> In her langage mercy [Custaunce] bisoghte,
> The lyf out of hir body for to twynne,
> Hire to delivere of wo that she was inne.
> A maner Latyn corrupt was hir speche,
> But algates therby was she understonde.   (II.516–20)

This passage of *MLT* requires some unpacking, since indeed it may well
be Chaucer's most troubling change to his sources in this text.[46] In Trevet's version, Custaunce speaks "Sessoneis" or Saxon (129–30) – the language of his putative source text – and in Gower's version her ability to
communicate is not explained (736–9). There have been many attempts
to account for Chaucer's version of this event. The phrase might be
borrowed from the categories of Latin defined in Isidore of Seville's
Etymologiæ IX I 6–7, or that it may be an importation into English of Old
French *latin*, referring to speech generally in addition to its derogatory
meanings cited above.[47] More recent suggestions include the idea that
"Latyn corrupt" is a kind of lingua franca, or that Chaucer has obliquely
inserted an occurrence of the miracle of xenoglossia, paralleled in many
saint's lives.[48] In each of these readings, we see evidence reinforcing
Frankis' observation that Chaucer's elimination of details from the text
connecting it to the Anglo-Saxon period has "restored the tale to its
original status as moral romance," as they mark its many romance and
hagiographic motifs as fictional.[49]

My own reading of these lines proceeds from the intrinsic ambiguity
of the pronoun "her"/ "hir," which occurs in lines 516, 517, 518, and
519. In lines 517 and 518, "her" is clearly a singular feminine reference
to Custaunce. In the other two occurrences, "In her langage" and "A
maner Latyn corrupt was hir speche," "her" could also be translated
as "their": "In *their* language she sought mercy," and/or "*their* speech
was a form of corrupt Latin and by means of it she was entirely understood." Certainly "their" is closer to Trevet's syntax in his own version
of this passage ("Et [ele] lui respoundi en Sessoneis, que fu langage
Olda [and she responded to him in Saxon, which was the language of
Olda {i.e., not of her but of "them"}]" [129]). Either way, the ambiguity
illustrates how fundamentally unclear it is which and how many characters are speaking corrupt Latin in Chaucer's line, nor whether this
is their normal speech or something they improvised to communicate
under these extraordinary circumstances. Indeed, it is even possible
that in this garbled version of English history the Old English language

Chronicles and Customary Law   113

does not yet exist when Custaunce arrives, and the corrupt, overly formal and unintelligible *latin* of birds and clerics was the commonly spoken tongue.

This possibility leads me back to the question of the messenger, the Summoner, and the monastic archives of early English history. Again, Alla's messenger is corrupt, and so his message is corrupted. So also is the Summoner corrupt, as is demonstrated both by his mangling of official Latin and by his forgeries of official records. In other words this term "corrupt" suggests both the moral and textual-critical resonances of this term, alongside the merely linguistic ones.[50] Alla's kingdom suffers from an institutional corruption borne of a shared indifference to propriety when it comes to writing and storing authoritative texts, which leads in turn to their corruption as they circulate.

One final resonance of this term speaks to the possibility of Chaucer's direct familiarity with early Anglo-Latin, and perhaps even with Anglo-Latin charters. As the epistolary diplomas cited in chapter 2 exemplify, many early English documents were written in a "hermeneutic" Latin style that has been decried by at least one modern student for its "artificial language employed to the grievous detriment of good sense."[51] So too might Chaucer have thought such texts to be grammatically "corrupt," and to have inferred from them that corrupted Latin would have been easily understood in conversion-era England. Hence, perhaps, Chaucer's change to his source is part of a joke about these primary sources: if one wished to be understood in conversion-era England, one had to sound like Bede's contemporary St. Aldhelm of Malmesbury, whose bombastic, Greek-influenced Latin style clearly influenced the "hermeneutic" charters and was certainly considered corrupt by even eleventh-century medieval English readers.[52] Either way, it is certainly the case that whenever possible, the Man of Law's narration draws attention to the many ways in which the tale of Custaunce could have been corrupted or outright falsified. Only God's "prudent purveiaunce" can be relied upon to ensure that information is transmitted properly, and the only figure protected by God in *MLT* is Custaunce.

In the next and final section of this chapter, I will expand on this final point through a reading of Custaunce and her two mothers-in-law. These women-as-texts embody local traditions to express concerns about the future transmission of those traditions, and the tropes of incest and infanticide express particular concern for rigidity and the failure to evolve. The tragic forbearance of Cenobia, whose gold chains mark her as a martyr to the consolidating forces of imperial wealth, finds its counterpart in the monstrous resistance of the Sultaness and Donegild, whose recirculations of Custaunce do not only fail to exile the imperium

114 Chaucer's Problem of Prose

she symbolizes but indeed facilitate and justify their own dispossessions. I will conclude the section by establishing that the implausibility of the story does not only fail to undermine the mythic history that the story encodes, but serves on the contrary as the very source of its claims to authority, as is demonstrated in the scene of Custaunce's trial.

Asymmetrical Recognition, the Sultaness, and Custaunce's Trial

One of the more commented upon passages of *MLT* is the contradictory but ultimately leering narratorial aside of II.701–14:

> Me list nat of the chaf, ne of the stree,
> Maken so long a tale as of the corn.
> What sholde I tellen of the roialtee
> At mariage, or which cours goth biforn;
> Who bloweth in a trumpe or in an horn?
> The fruyt of every tale is for to seye;
> They ete, and drynke, and daunce, and synge, and pleye.
> They goon to bedde, as it was skile and right;
> For thogh that wyves be ful hooly thynges,
> They moste take in patience at nyght
> Swiche manere necessaries as been plesynges
> To folk that han ywedded hem with rynges,
> And leye a lite hir hoolynesse aside,
> As for the tyme – it may no bet betide.

This passage is only one moment where the tale expresses a general ambivalence about marriage and reproduction, which many readers have connected to the Man of Law's comments on incest in the *MLI*.[53] The passage also strongly resembles the Monk's own leering comments about Cenobia, who similarly "leye a lite hir hoolynesse aside" (II.713) for the purposes of procreation. Once again, anxieties about textual transmission and mediation are expressed through the metaphor of women's sexuality and procreation.

Important context for the Man of Law's aside is provided by the stanza of *occupatio* that proceeds it, which identifies detailed description as "chaf" and compares the length of his tale to the "fruyt" of a stalk of wheat. As Kolve observes, the imagery of wheat and chaff is a ubiquitous one in medieval discussions of poetry and its value, whose twofold association with the Parson (*MLE* at II.1183, *ParsT* at X.35–6) will be discussed in the next chapter.[54] For now, the key point is to note that using grain to figure a text suggests a distinction between useful, meaningful

Chronicles and Customary Law   115

content ("fruyt") and meaningless, excess materiality ("chaf"), which moreover frames the Man of Law's aside about the duties of wives to procreate as an example of the former. In context, the passage expresses yet again the larger discomfort this study traces throughout the entirety of *The Canterbury Tales*, about the underlying tendency of literate institutions to perpetuate empire and institutional violence, often through its ostensible efforts to promote individual and/or local autonomy and freedom. In *MLT* specifically, the illicit continuity of incestuous sex and exact reproduction (i.e., adherence to the text) is contrasted with the somewhat-licit discontinuity of procreation with foreign pagans (i.e., adherence to the gloss), as the Sultaness and Donegild embody the former approach and Custaunce embodies the latter.[55] Like the Monk's noble virago Cenobia, these women embody a continuous, traditional mode of textual circulation that ultimately contributes to the expansion of the empire, whether the individual actors involved attempt to resist that expansion or not.

Also like "Cenobia," the spelling preferred by Chaucer's scribes for the characters' names marks them as allegorical figures. Donegild (vs. the "Domild" of Trevet and Gower) suggests the imperative Latin *dona geld* ("give/pay geld") or even "Danegeld," while Custaunce (vs. the far more straightforwardly allegorical "Constance") suggests not only durative "constancy" but also the term and concept "customs." Gelds are taxes, and the Danegeld was a tax based on property ownership first implemented to pay off Danish raiders in the tenth century but continued into the twelfth.[56] "Customs," meanwhile, has two sets of implications. On the one hand, it suggests a relatively loose and traditional practice emergent from contingent circumstances, not unlike a folklaw (MED def. 4). On the other, it suggests obligatory feudal payments, which had by Chaucer's time evolved into the far more complex set of duties and tolls that replaced the Danegeld, to fund the transformation of royal household into the nascent bureaucracy of the eventual English nation-state (MED def. 6). Hence "customs" may be favourably contrasted with the "Danegeld" for two contradictory reasons. On the one hand, customs are timeless while the Danegeld was an historically specific novelty that arose to deal with the extraordinary circumstance of Norse raiders. On the other, the Danegeld is old-fashioned, since it has been replaced by the far more modern and efficient collection of customs.

In all its senses the term "customs" makes an implicit claim for continuity or "constancy" over time, to the effect that its strictures derive from a shared, cultural knowledge of how things have always been done. The triumph of Custaunce and the death of Donegild may

116   Chaucer's Problem of Prose

therefore be read as a sort of allegory for the core, constitutive features of the English "common law" in contrast to its continental counterpart, that it is a *lex non scripta* or "unwritten law" which derives its theoretical authority from precedent and not from texts like the Domesday book, though of course its practical authority is predicated entirely on the written records of the binding precedents. Custaunce's usurpation of her mother-in-law's place in the governance of Alla (and, by extension, his kingdom) are in these terms legible as another allegorization of the imperial politics of recognition, except the authorial sympathies are with the dispossessors rather than the dispossessed.

Donegild's motive for driving Custaunce out of the kingdom is that she is "so strange a creature" (II.700) – which is to say, because she is both foreign and novel, without genetic precedent in the pre-existing royal line of sovereign descent. As I have already described above, Donegild accomplishes her goal through the manipulation and forgery of official texts and documents, facilitated by the incompetent mismanagement of the Northumbrian messenger. In this section below, I will turn to Custaunce's first mother-in-law, the Sultaness of Syria, whose rejection of her son's marriage is similarly predicated on the perceived threat to traditional continuity. In the first part of this section, I will briefly paraphrase Bede's account of the conversion of King Edwin of Northumbria, described by Bede in book II chapters 9–14 of *Historia ecclesiastica*, which is an important though rarely discussed intertext for the Sultaness' actions. I will then turn to Custaunce's trial. These two public scenes are Chaucer's two most sustained expansions of his sources, and so therefore they are particularly revealing about the way the story is being adapted to fit its context in *The Canterbury Tales*.[57]

In Bede's history as in *MLT*, Christianity first comes to Northumbria through a marriage, when Edwin marries the Æthelburh who was daughter of the king Æthelberht of Kent converted in the original mission of St. Augustine of Canterbury. Edwin, too, sent an embassy to request this marriage, and for he too was confronted by the obstacle that Christian maidens do not marry heathen men. Nonetheless, Edwin manages to strike a rather more favourable deal than the Sultan did, promising only to put no obstacles in the way of the Christian faith and to consider adopting it himself at some later date if his advisors agreed.

When Æthelburh marries Edwin, she brings with her the bishop Paulinus. Some time passes: Edwin is wounded in an assassination attempt, his first daughter with Æthelburh is born, the pope writes to both Edwin and his wife urging haste in conversion. Nevertheless, Edwin remains pagan, until he experiences a miracle. During a period of persecution, a spirit had appeared to Edwin and shown him a hand signal. Sometime

Chronicles and Customary Law 117

later, Paulinus is able to recreate this exact hand signal, and so therefore confirm that the aid that came to Edwin earlier was from the Christian God.

In *Historia ecclesiastica* II.13, Edwin convenes a meeting very like the Sultan's, called a *witan* in Alfred's Old English translation of the text.[58] The first to speak at the meeting is a priest named Coifi, who observes that paganism has never profited him: though he is a priest and so should also be the most greatly favoured by the Gods, in fact there is no tangible sign that this is the case whatsoever. Because Christianity's promises of eternal life and salvation is a much better deal than anything the pagan gods appear capable of offering, it therefore seems to Coifi that they should convert. Once the body assents to this argument, Coifi requests weapons and a stallion, both previously forbidden to priests (who, according to Bede, rode mares), and he rides up to one of the old pagan shrines and desecrates it by casting a spear into it, symbolically reclaiming both his virtue and virility in the action. The scene drives home Bede's message that the conversion of Northumbria was not the decision of an individual king, but an expression of the shared will of the populace, which confirms Gregory's belief that these angelic people were chosen to be saved from the anger of God.

The Sultaness may be productively read as a satire or perversion of the Coifi figure from Bede's narrative, whose gender makes her own parallel assertion of masculine potency unnatural. In her own *witan*, the Sultaness follows the priest to frame the distinction between Christianity and the older religion – in this case, "the hooly lawes of our Alkaron" (332) – in terms of their relative profit to believers in the afterlife. For her, however, this framing leads to very different conclusions:

What sholde us tyden of this newe lawe
But thraldom to oure bodies and penance,
And afterward in helle to be drawe,
For we reneyed Mahoun oure creance? (337–40)

In these terms the Sultaness rejects the asymmetrical recognition offered to Syria by Rome, which she (like Coulthard and, indeed, Fanon) equates to slavery, and which she says constitutes a violation of their own laws, to which they will still be held accountable in the afterlife. The narrator then castigates the Sultaness at length, calling her not only "virago" but a second Semiramis, a serpent (358–61), and also an "instrument" of Satan (II.361–2).

In chapter 3, I noted that the word "instrument" in *WBP* makes a symbolic connection between sexual organs and legal documents. The

118   Chaucer's Problem of Prose

appearance of the term here drives home that this Sultaness is not only Satan's feminized tool, but his own forged document, an image whose resonances are particularly driven home by her fraudulent baptismal oath.[59] The authorization of her fraud by the assent of her gathered assembly therefore parodies the authorizing assent of Edwin's *witan*, and again the implications of the decision are framed as expressions of national identity and destiny. Where Coifi's words demonstrated God's plan to ennoble the English people as a whole, the Sultaness' words demonstrated God's plan to damn the Syrian people as a whole, and so the scene foreshadows their later destruction. More to the point, Coifi's desecration of the "old rites" signals the start of a new, beneficial contract with Rome and the return of his masculine virility, while the Sultaness' desecration of the new rite of baptism breaches the contract with Rome and signals the emasculation of not only her son but her entire nation, whose swift defeat by the Romans points not only to God's anger but also to the disarray one would expect in a nation where the ruler has been murdered by his own mother.

We see the obverse to the fraud and forgery of the Sultaness' *witan* and Donegild's letters in the justice produced by Custaunce's trial.[60] The Man of Law's portrait says that he often served as a justice in assize (I.314). The putative first Christian criminal trial in English legal history described in *MLT* is precisely a myth of origin for the courts of assizes, which emphasizes the king's role in those origins. In Chaucer's version, Alla the pagan king more or less accidentally invents the practice of swearing an oath on a Gospel book, which then in turn resolves the case before him with a literal miracle (II.662–6). A disembodied hand hits the knight on the neck and knocks his eyes from his head, and in case this symbolism was too subtle, a disembodied voice also explains that the knight is being punished for his slander (II.669–76). Such punitive miracles – which commonly involve the eyes – are widely attested in early English monastic historiography, likely reflecting the prevalence of mutilation in early English punishments.[61] One particularly noteworthy example here is Bede's description of the martyrdom of St. Alban in *Historia ecclesiastica* (I.7, 28–35), where the executioner's eyes fell out after beheading the saint. But where the villain of St. Alban's martyrdom is a representative of secular, imperial authority, the similar authority embodied by Alla serves here as the hero.

MLT differs from its analogues by detailing the extent of the king's investigations. The narrator strongly implies that Alla examines the crime scene himself (II.602–4), and his extended discussion of Custaunce's visible helplessness (II.631–43) is framed by the king's perception of it and his emotional response: both the internal pity he feels in his heart (II.614) and the external manifestation of that pity in the form of his tears (II.660–1).[62] His pronounced affect may be read in this sense as signs of his personal investment in the case, which has inspired his careful attention to the facts and so enabled him to notice the discrepancies between the knight's version of events and those offered by other witnesses (II.624–7). By implication, the miracle of blinding could not have happened without the king's diligence. The narrator's comparison of Custaunce to Susannah is telling: the equivalent to the prophetic Daniel who intervenes on Custaunce's behalf is Alla himself, who takes pity on his future wife and interrogates her accuser because he has paid close attention to the facts. Furthermore, the contrast between this trial and the Sultaness' assembly once again reflects the Man of Law's characterization in *GP*, as a royal authority working unilaterally to invent procedures out of thin air who is able to produce a better result than the community-oriented, tradition-bound *witan* of the Sultaness (and, crucially, of the Bedan conversion myth that *MLT* echoes and replaces).

Custaunce's trial is also a helpful point of contrast to the closing scene in the Monk's tragedy of Cenobia. Both scenes describe a woman who despite her nobility has been imprisoned and subjected to public view by a royal authority. Cenobia, the embodied law of monastic privilege, has been usurped and impoverished by Aurelius' worldly and imperial authority despite her moral excellence. Meanwhile Custaunce, the embodied law of mercantile customs, is falsely maligned by the earlier and more rigid laws of specific localities (the Muslim law of Syria, the gelds of early England), until the king applies his reason to elevate her, marry her, and demolish the old local laws in favour of a new imperial authority. Both of these narratives allegorize the ongoing processes of consolidation and centralization in English royal governance, which were facilitated in the asymmetrical recognition of monastic autonomy by the English crown that slowly but steadily erased monastic privilege and expropriated monastic wealth. At the same time, and not coincidentally, the symbolic vocabulary used to convey this allegory also figures the colonial modes of violence and subjugation that England would bring to the world in future centuries, and that continue to characterize the settler-colonial nations founded as English colonies to this day.

In the next and final chapter of this book I will bring this discussion to bear in a reading of the two actual prose *Canterbury Tales*: Chaucer's *Mel* and the concluding *ParsT*. In chapter 3 I discussed how the Friar and the Summoner allegorize in negative terms the heuristic of the text and gloss that Chaucer uses to frame his anxiety about literate institutions of education and government and their tendency to amplify violence and corruption. In the prose tales, we see Chaucer addressing

120   Chaucer's Problem of Prose

his own relation to those challenges head-on, and attempting to model a way forward despite them. In both cases, his method is a return to the point of origin. His Prudence is yet another woman-as-text, who in this instance embodies the corpus of proverbs and wisdom literature that articulate the principles that underwrite any attempt to formulate specific policies and laws. Though Prudence resembles the Friar and Man of Law in the way that she freely departs from the literal meaning of her texts, her gloss does not wander away from them either, as she consistently emphasizes a clear moral message about the importance of non-violence. The Parson, meanwhile, is a creature of the text like the Summoner and the Monk, but his treatise on confession avoids the punitive function of ecclesiastical law to advocate forgiveness, compassion, and community-mindedness.

Be that as it may, it would be a misreading of the prose tales if we were to reduce them to mere solutions to the problems that *The Canterbury Tales* introduces to its readers. On the contrary, their "resolutions" are primarily effective as provocations, which call readerly attention to the mediated effect of the written word and of poetic fictions in particular. The *Retraction* in particular functions not only as a warning about the moral hazards of Chaucer's writing but also as a sort of scribal colophon, which calls attention to the embodied material reality of the book in which one reads it and so the critical distance one ought to bring to it. In the next chapter I will conclude my survey of the "problem of prose" in *The Canterbury Tales* with an elaboration of these arguments.

Chapter Six

The Problem of Prose and the Prose
Canterbury Tales: *Melibee* and the Parson

In his study of the ordering of *The Canterbury Tales*, Larry Benson has observed that the cluster that runs from *Thopas* through the *Retraction* travels through the manuscript copies as a coherent unit.[1] This sequence is bookended by expressions of Chaucer's authorial anxiety about the quality of his poetry (in *Thopas* and the *Retraction*) and the two appearances of prose in the collection (*Mel* and *ParsT*). In both the beginning and the end of this sequence, we see Chaucer dramatizing his "failure" as a poet: first, in his poorly received poem that then leads him to tell a tale in prose; second, in the *Retraction* that withdraws the poems that "sownen into synne" (X.1086). In Chaucer's own tales, prose is the solution to a formal problem of Chaucer's "drasty" rhyming. In fragment X, prose creates a problem of content for the *Retraction* to resolve, through Chaucer's repentance of not only *The Canterbury Tales* but of his entire oeuvre, shifting his first-person voice from the text of his poetry to remediate it in the form of a (fictive) scribal colophon.[2] Both *Thopas* and the *Retraction* also echo the concerns about Chaucer's poetry raised in *MLI*, as in all three instances the lesson is that Chaucer should write less poetry and more prose. But as I will argue below, they also express the ethical vision that helps to explain why he wrote so much verse in *The Canterbury Tales* anyway. In this chapter I will turn finally to the prose tales that Chaucer did write to account for this strange theme and for its connection to the even stranger theme of Chaucer's implicit conversations with early English monastic historiography, unpacked in the preceding chapters.

As I have suggested, the balancing of *Mel* and *ParsT* is yet another figuration of the unproductive impasse between the more situational, circumstance-invested "gloss" of the Friar and Man of Law and the more legalistic, precedent-invested "text" of the Summoner and Monk – figures whose appearances are ordered in all three instances, we may

122   Chaucer's Problem of Prose

finally observe, so that the "gloss" speaks first. But where the Friar and the Summoner pose a formal problem that the Man of Law and the Monk reframe through English history, Chaucer and the Parson present prose as a formal solution. A potential Man of Law's tale, *Mel* expresses the loose relationship to textual authority embodied by the Friar,[3] as Prudence decontextualizes and reconfigures quotations and proverbs one after another in the course of her emphatic plea for peace. The text expresses not only an ethics of advice, as its readers have argued, but also an ethics of reading and applying authoritative texts to specific, embodied contexts – in other words, of glossing.[4] In contrast, *ParsT* is focused on the "text" of conventional penitential discourse, which covers the same sins policed by the Summoner but which is focused on contrition, redemption, and self-abnegation instead of obligation, punishment, and exploitation. Be that as it may, these best versions of text and gloss are nonetheless still troubled by the same destructive dynamic that we saw between the Friar and Summoner. We see this in *Thopas* and the *Retraction*, which are the self-aware counterparts to the Friar and Summoner's ironic self-negations in that they similarly point to a recursive relationship between the text/gloss polarities. *Thopas'* rigid poetic formalism and lack of content express the limitations of secular poetry as a medium of expression, while the *Retraction's* "gloss" on Chaucer's work calls attention to the limitations of para-textual authority. In this sense the balance between text and gloss presented by the two prose tales is ultimately no more satisfying than the symbolic marriages of the Wife of Bath and Jenkyn, and of the Loathly Lady and the Rapist Knight.

This chapter has three sections. The first section begins with my reading of Chaucer's tales. *Thopas* is a romance voided of history that parodies Chaucer's aspirations towards formal excellence: without context, the events of the story have no substance and cannot keep the pilgrims' attention. *Mel*, meanwhile, is a meditation on the historical forms of textual wisdom and their ideal application. The figure of Prudence is yet another woman personifying text-as-law with an allegorical name, here modelled as an ideal glossator on the traditional wisdom distilled in the ideal, originary form of the proverb. But unlike the more historically specific laws personified by "Cenobia," "Custaunce," and "Donegild," the law of "Prudence" is itself a law of interpretation and application, and so she provides a partial model for imagining what an ideal practice of glossing might look like.

The second section of this chapter will turn to *ParsT* and the *Retraction*. My reading of *ParsT* will focus in particular on the section on anger, which continues the themes of the tales studied in the previous

The Problem of Prose and the Prose *Canterbury Tales*   123

chapters to connect this sin to the problem of mediation. Anger and violence occasion the proliferation of written documents though they also frustrate communication, and so the solution to the problem of prose is to recognize one's anger, atone for it, and pursue "patience or suffraunce" (X.654) instead. But rather than resolve this frustration with communication, the *Retraction* ends the collection by forcing readers to confront and accept it. This reading follows Stephen Partridge's 2012 article "'The Makere of this Boke,'" which argues that Chaucer's *Retraction* is a simulated colophon that "works to emphasize the status of Chaucer's works, including the Tales, as books, in order to assert Chaucer's status as author."[5] This final abandonment of the collection's narrative conceit preforms precisely the authoritative abdication of authority described by Sharma. The colophonic form of the *Retraction* asserts authorial control over the compilation of the *Canterbury Tales* manuscript, precisely through the *Retraction*'s conventionally colophonic and penitential abdication of authority over future editorial decisions about the assembly of the tales into future manuscript collections and compilations.[6] Hence the second section of this chapter will argue on this basis that Chaucer's *Canterbury Tales* is not only a tale collection that imitates the form of the manuscript compilation, but also is an artwork expressing a profoundly materialist and situated disquiet about the political and economic conditions of textual production from which manuscript compilations emerge, which is to say the imperial institutions of church and crown that *The Canterbury Tales* satirizes so extensively.

The third and final section of this chapter will return to fragment II, and specifically *MLE*. Again, Helen Cooper has called this section "the greatest textual dilemma posed by the whole work."[7] The intimations of the Parson's "Lollardy" in this passage are telling in the way they help us to identify the tensions in the collection that this inhumanly perfect pastor helps to contain.[8] The project of monastic disendowment does not fit with the ethos of tolerance and community-mindedness that shapes *The Canterbury Tales*, which mandates generosity towards all fellow Christians. The ambitiously reformist agenda of Lollard preachers may advocate such generosity in the abstract, but the radical reforms they called for would necessarily break community ties and facilitate the commodification of land and workers – as, indeed, the Dissolution would accomplish in the sixteenth century, in its contribution to the processes that Marx would call the primitive accumulation of capital. *MLE*'s identification of the Parson as a Lollard instantiates the lingering ambivalence throughout the collection about its goals, which history would prove to be well founded.

124   Chaucer's Problem of Prose

Though *The Canterbury Tales* nominally resists the dehumanization and institutional violence that were accelerating in the fourteenth century, it ultimately recapitulates and contributes to them. Not only would the British Empire arising after Chaucer's death designate him the "father" of its own poetic forms, it would even bury its great poets beside him in a Westminster cathedral that had been vacated of monks but kept by the crown as a "royal peculiar" to serve as a site for future coronations.[9] Though this instrumentalization of Chaucer as a symbol of imperial greatness does not represent a particularly sensitive reading of *The Canterbury Tales*, it is not a particularly wrong reading either.

The Letter and the Spirit in Chaucer's Tales: *Thopas* and *Melibee*

By fragment VII of *The Canterbury Tales*, Chaucer has given his readers more than enough time to forget the conceit that he too is one of the pilgrims on the journey, who might also be called upon to tell a tale. Indeed, the Man of Law's meditations on "Chaucer" in the *MLI* imply that no one knew he was there: otherwise one would have expected the Man of Law to address Chaucer directly. Now, the Host addresses Chaucer the pilgrim with a metafictional joke about how quiet he is (VII.696–704), which leads immediately to the additional, more extended joke where the author tells a tale that all of his creations hate. When the Host interrupts him, Chaucer has no choice but to switch to prose, in what again is a radical abandonment of the organizing conceit of the poem's structural fiction – analogous, perhaps, to if a character in an opera stopped singing and started to speak. My reading of this tale will proceed from Chaucer's prefatory comment in lines VII.956–64 about his use of proverbs and the persistence of their meanings. But before I get to this passage and its implications, I must first describe *Thopas*, and explain the work it does as a preface to *Mel*'s protocols for glossing.

Many readers of *Thopas* have observed how the setting of mercantile Flanders (VII.721) is one of many indications that the tale is a parody of the romance genre, which is particularly concerned to expose how this genre serves to indulge bourgeois fantasies of sexual violence and wealth.[10] One example among many is the line where the narrator conveys the beauty of Thopas' robe through the flat assertion that it "cost many a jane" (VII.735). The tale is also, at the same time, one of the most subtle and complex metrical experiments in the entire Chaucerian corpus.[11] The close interconnection between the tale's descriptive flatness and its poetic intricacy is demonstrated for example at the moment of a

The Problem of Prose and the Prose *Canterbury Tales*   125

sudden change in the structure of his stanzas, beginning in the middle of Thopas' expository speech, as follows:

An elf-queene wol I love, ywis,
For in this world no womman is
Worthy to be my make
In towne;
Alle othere wommen I forsake,
And to an elf-queene I me take
By dale and eek by downe!   (VII.790–6)

This formal inventiveness appears, on the one hand, to signal an elevation in feeling attached to the introduction of the elf queen, in an effect equivalent to the key change in the third chorus of a popular song. On the other, the specific detail it introduces is a redundancy. Thopas has already said that there was no woman worthy of him in "this world," and so it is unnecessary for him to specify that there are no women worthy of him "in towne," when the town is presumably part of the world in question. The metrical innovation of *Thopas* is tightly linked here and throughout the poem to its consistently bourgeois failure of the imagination.

Scholars have identified many connections between *Thopas* and the commercially sold and traded romances of the late fourteenth century, which is suggested most strongly by the list of romance heroes in the text that overlaps with collections like the Auchinleck manuscript (VII.897–902).[12] Of these, perhaps the most suggestive is the allusion to Sir Percival in the final lines of the tale before the Host's interruption (VII.915–17). Though specific detail of drinking from a well appears to come from the romance *Sir Percevell of Galles*,[13] the character Percival himself originates in a far more famously unfinished quest romance, Chretien de Troyes' *Perceval*, whose episodic and endlessly deferrable quest narrative continues to inspire commercial fiction in all genres to this day.[14] These allusions mark the *Thopas* as a parody of not only a particular kind of bourgeois poem, but more largely of a particular kind of commercial media content intended for bourgeois consumption.

Unlike Chretien's unfinished romance, which breaks off with no explanation, Chaucer's own unfinished work here is cut off by the Host's irritable observation that "min eres aken of thy drasty speche" (VII.923). The Host's distaste is prefigured in the increasingly desperate beginnings of Chaucer's fits, culminating in the third: "Now holde youre mouth, par charitee, | Both knight and lady free, | and herkneth to my spelle" (VII.891–3).[15] These and other allusions to

126   Chaucer's Problem of Prose

speech and audience implies a critique of commercial romance that attends materially to the affordances and constraints of their written media format. Jessica Brantley has described how the manuscript layout of *Thopas* in Ellesmere is itself a part of the tale's formal joke.[16] Building on her work I would explain the joke as follows: however good the manuscripts of tail-rhyme romances may *look* as expensive books, they *sound* terrible when you read them aloud. The verse form's innovative flights of fancy help to reinforce this disconnect between form and content.

In context, then, *Thopas* serves as a metatextual comment on the gap between the embodied (secular, commercial) text of *The Canterbury Tales* and the narrative fiction that the text transcribes a spoken conversation between a group of pilgrims. If one analyzes the written text of *Thopas* closely for its form, one discovers a top-flight poet at the top of his game, working with and against the constraints of English verse as he received them.[17] In the fictional context of performance, meanwhile, the poem sounds like such a mess that it inspires the Host to say to Chaucer "thou doost noght elles but despendest tyme" (VII.931). The double valence of the word "time," which may mean specifically metrical rhythm, suggests both that the performed *Thopas* makes its audience impatient and that it wastes its metrical brilliance on a boring story. In this way, Thopas is a *reductio ad absurdum* for the notion that formal excellence in writing has anything to do with good poetry.

In all these formal features *Thopas* anticipates *MkT*, the interrupted tale with which it bookends *Mel*. *MkT* similarly deploys one of Chaucer's most innovative metrical forms, in the service of a story that similarly "anoyeth al this compaignye" (VII.2789). Certainly these two were connected by Edmund Spenser, who drew particularly from both in writing the *Faerie Queene*.[18] These interconnections between *Thopas* and *MkT* mark the pairing of *Thopas* and *Mel* as yet another instance of the text/gloss dilemma, with *Thopas* on the side of the overly formal and traditional text and *Mel* on the side of the overly informal and presentist gloss. By assigning both of these texts to himself, Chaucer suggests that he is both Friar and Summoner, Monk and Man of Law, slave to the strict formal rigidity of the text at the same time that he wanders far away from it. The implicit analogy between the formal conventions of commercial romance that are so rigidly applied in *Thopas* and the Boethian conventions of early English charters in *MkT* underscores how in both cases, the constraints in question paradoxically arise from market forces, though in both cases the Chaucerian audience rejects the very features of the texts that have made their forms so successful in the past.

The Problem of Prose and the Prose *Canterbury Tales* 127

After *Thopas* has been interrupted, Chaucer introduces *Mel* as follows:[19]

If that yow thynke I varie as in my speche,
As thus, though that I telle somwhat moore
Of proverbes than ye han herd bifoore
Comprehended in this litel tretys heere,
To enforce with th'effect of my mateere;
And though I nat the same words seye
As ye han herd, yet to yow alle I preye
Blameth me nat; for, as in my sentence,
Shul ye nowher fynden difference
Fro the sentence of this tretys lyte
After the which this murye tale I write.   (VII.954–64)

Chaucer tells his audience that even though he will include more proverbs than they have heard before, twice referring to a "little treatise" that may be either his source for *Mel* or the entirety of *The Canterbury Tales*.[20] Further, the metafictional contrast between speech and text in *Thopas* is replaced here with transparency, as Chaucer acknowledges that he writes *Mel* for not only auditors but also readers.[21] The strongest evidence for the latter reading is the use of the same phrase in the *Retraction* (X.1081), though here he may just be referring to *ParsT*.

Either way, Chaucer appears to anticipate that his readers will be surprised by not only the number of proverbs in *Mel* but also by the way he will phrase them. From the very outset, this framing of the tale applies the Pauline dictum quoted by Friar John, that the letter slays while the spirit gives life (III.1794). Though Chaucer will not follow the letter of his proverbs and quotations in the *Mel*, he will nonetheless honour their spirit of non-violence, and the resulting "glose" will be glorious.

Yet again, we see the text itself symbolized and personified in *Mel* in the form of a woman, in this case Dame Prudence. Chaucer's assignment of the name "Sophie" to her daughter by Melibee – unnamed in his sources – suggests that Prudence should be read as a personification of the virtue, and not just a woman who happens to have this relatively common given name.[22] Throughout Chaucer's work, "prudence" is consistently framed as a virtue connected to managing the future. In *Troilus and Criseyde*, Criseyde laments near the end that "Prudence, allas, oon of thyne eyen thre/Me lakked alwey, er that I come here!" (*TC* 5.744–5).[23] The three eyes of Prudence look towards the past, the present, and the future, in an image that likely derives from Dante

128   Chaucer's Problem of Prose

Purgatorio (29.130–2).[24] Hence in context, Criseyde is lamenting that she was always bad at anticipating the outcomes of her choices.

The word "prudence" also occurs several times in *The Canterbury Tales* outside of *Mel*, in contexts that draw attention to the situational contingency of this skill, and its ambivalent relationship to ethical virtue. In *The Shipman's Tale* (*ShT*), Daun John's "prudence" is the reason that his abbot gives him licence to leave the precincts of the abbey, and his exercise of this virtue in the tale that follows demonstrates how it may have more to do with achieving one's intentions than it has to do with Christian morality (VII.64). In *The Merchant's Tale* (*MerT*), Placebo flatters January with praise for his "heighe prudence" (IV.1482), in a use whose irony in this line is underscored by the common association of prudence with old age, for example in the Latin Vulgate translation of Job 12:12 – a passage quoted in *Mel* at VII.1164. In *The Canon's Yeoman's Prologue* (*CYP*), meanwhile, the Canon's Yeoman claims that his master could cover Canterbury entirely with silver and gold. The Host responds by asking: if he has such "heigh prudence" (VIII.630), then why does he look so poor? Finally, in *The Clerk's Tale* (*ClT*), Griselda is praised by Walter's subjects for her prudence when she cheerfully prepares his sham wedding to their daughter (IV.1022) – an occurrence of the term that fits with Griselda's representation, in that it is impossible to tell which of her actions seem prudent or why. But whether the term is used ironically or not in these appearances, it seems that "prudence" for Chaucer is a form of contingent, tactical awareness that verges on cunning, and that its absence is a sort of naivete.

A key passage for reading the character Prudence in *Mel* appears at the moment where she argues that Melibee should submit to the "maistrye" (VII.1081) of her women's advice, as follows: "if ye wole werken wikkednesse, and youre wif restreyneth thilke wikked purpos, and overcometh yow by reson and by good conseil, | certes youre wyf oghte rather to be preised than yblamed" (1091–2). Prudence then goes on to list a series of Biblical examples of wives from the Old Testament who have shown mastery over their husbands: Rebecca (from Genesis 27) the wife of Isaac, Judith (from Judith) the widow who saves Bethulia from the Assyrians, Abigail (from I Samuel 25) the prophetess and second wife of David, and Esther (from Esther) who saves the Jews of Persia from persecution by her husband's advisor Hamen (VII.1097–1100). These examples appear in the same order in *MerT* (at IV.1363–74), in the so-called marriage encomium that is a major interpretive crux in the latter tale's criticism of marriage.[25]

The obvious sarcasm of this passage in *MerT* draws attention to the implicit irony to these examples, that the wise actions of these women did

The Problem of Prose and the Prose *Canterbury Tales*   129

not particularly benefit their husbands. Isaac's wish to bless Esau is subverted, Judith's husband is dead before the action begins (and her likely sexual partner Holofernes is beheaded), Abigail's first husband is struck dead because of her actions, and Esther's husband loses both a major advisor and 75,000 soldiers. But while attention to the text in each of these instances may lead a listener away from Prudence's suggested course of action, the implication is that the literal meaning of her texts is incidental to her purpose, which is only to convince her husband that revenge is a bad idea. Hence in his response to this argument, Melibee stays true to his name when he tells Prudence he is convinced "by cause of thy sweete wordes" (VII.1113), and not by the logical integrity of her argument.

This message is the key difference between Prudence's "gloss" of scripture in the passage cited above and Friar John's glosses in *SumT*. In chapter 3, I followed Jill Mann to hold that the entire dialogue between the Friar and Summoner is an extended representation of anger and malice, which reaches it apotheosis in Friar John's deeply ironic sermon against anger. In contrast, the manifestation of Prudence's anger in *Mel* is brief, controlled, and explicitly intended to shock Melibee out of his own aggression and help him to calm down (VII.1684–1706).[26] As I will explain in the next section, anger in *ParsT* is similarly figured as a barrier to communication, and so a figure for the challenge posed to Chaucer's ambitions by the circumstances of embodied mediality that the formal problem of prose in *The Canterbury Tales* serves to represent.

Confession, Law, and *The Parson's Tale*

Like *MLI*, *ParsP* begins with a description of shadows and their proportions, which have changed considerably. The time is now 4:00 p.m., and as a result Chaucer's shadow is exactly eleven-sixths his height (X.6–9), a number that is almost exactly double the original height and one short of the numerologically and astrologically significant twelve of the apostles and the zodiac. Meanwhile Libra is in the moon's exaltation (X.11), and this sign of the scales foretells balance and proportionality, specifically of the approaching hour when the final tale will be finished and the shadows will again be exactly proportionate to the objects they shadow. Accordingly, the Host balances his earlier complaint about the fleeting past to discuss the fulfillment of his starting contract:

> Now lakketh us no tales mo than oon.
> Fulfilled is my sentence and my decree;
> I trowe that we han herd of ech degree;
> Almost fulfild is al myn ordinaunce.   (X.18–21)

130   Chaucer's Problem of Prose

In music, an octave may be concretized by the doubled length of the string that plays the note. The timing of *ParsP* suggests that by the time his tale is finished, the shadows of the pilgrims will have also doubled their length, and so the "song" of *The Canterbury Tales* will "resolve" where it began, now one octave lower.

Chaucer's representation of the Parson consistently emphasizes how deeply critical he is of mediating institutions, and how devoted he is in his professional practice to seeking out immediacy at every opportunity. In his Portrait, we learn that the Parson is constantly circulating in his parish and directly engaging with parishioners, and also that he does not take on additional work writing documents for cathedrals and guilds as a man of his profession could do to supplement his income (I.507–14). He chooses his simple life because he sees it as his responsibility to present the sheep in his flock with an unmediated example of Christ-like goodness for them to follow in their own lives. This same concern for direct, immediate communication informs his speech in the prologue to his tale.

In *MLI*, the Host's speech concludes with the Host turning to the Man of Law, using a series of legal terms that described their contract in precise terms to frame his request for a "tale." The Man of Law then agrees to the veracity of the contract and to the principle of upholding it, before he worms his way out of his obligation by citing the precedent of Chaucer. In precise contrast, the Parson denies the Host's request for a "fable" (X.29) on principle, thereby obviating any need to discuss the legal niceties of contractual obligations. Inattentive to such empty forms, the Parson will speak about "moralitee and vertuous mateere" (X.38) instead, repurposing the same image of the wheat and the chaff we saw in *MLT* (X.35–6). Again, this image distinguishes mediation from content, as the Parson promises to abandon the distortions of embodied media to offer pure immediacy instead.

Of course the Parson cannot finally deliver on this promised immediacy, and several ironies in this passage draw attention to his inability. His statement "I nam nat textueel" (X.57) is the most obvious, and it works in a manner that incidentally mirrors the dramatic irony of the Man of Law's evocation of Chaucer in *MLI* and so serves as another parallel between the sections. When the Man of Law claims that Chaucer has left him no tales to tell, he reminds readers that he is a character in a poem written by Chaucer. So also does the Parson's explicit denial that he is textual call attention to the truth that he is an authorial, textual creation.

The second irony appears when the Parson raises the possibility of using alliterative meter for his tale – like the Host suggests to Chaucer

The Problem of Prose and the Prose *Canterbury Tales*   131

in the *Thopas-Melibee Link* (VII.933) – but then rejects this form on the grounds of his regional identity as a "Southren man" (X.42). Given that the Parson's brother is a Plowman (I.529), this final statement about meter is one of many clues scattered throughout Chaucer's portrait of the Parson that *The Canterbury Tales* is in conversation with Langland's *Piers Plowman*. And as Kathryn Kerby-Fulton has recently argued, the Parson's characterization places him in the orbit of the so-called clerical proletariat who made up a large part of both the authors and audiences of that large corpus of Middle English poetry and prose satirizing, with great technical specificity, the many clerical abuses of institutional power, which readership appears to have been particularly enamoured of in *Piers Plowman* if the rates of manuscript survival are any indication.[27]

But instead of telling a tale that deploys Langland's apocalyptic, allegorical, and alliterative approach to discussing the structural problems of sin, repentance, and punishment in Christian law and theology, the Parson instead makes the final use of the word "prose" to appear in *The Canterbury Tales*:

> And therfore, if yow list – I wol nat glose –
> I wol yow telle a myrie tale in prose
> To knytte up al this feeste and make an ende.   (X.47–9)

The rhyming of "glose" and "prose" in these lines encapsulates in miniature the problem of prose that has structured the entire text.[28] On the level of content, the Parson asserts a contrast between "glose" and "prose" as modes of textual production, when he says that he will not do the former action but that he will use the latter form. Rhyme, in contrast, suggests a connection or even equivalence between the two, which fits into the pattern identified in the earlier chapters of this study. Thus the "glose"/"prose" rhyme makes two gestures: one of reconciliation between the poles of the Friar and Summoner, Man of Law and Monk, Chaucer and Parson, as fits the image of balanced Libra; and one of contrast, since the very balancing of these elements must accept the premise that they are opposites. In this alternative configuration, the tale does not "double" *Mel* in the sense of reflecting or balancing or otherwise "rhyming with" it, but in the sense of compounding the original problem of "lost time" introduced in *MLI* and reintroduced in the Host's criticism of *Thopas*.

The problem is compounded by two additional ironies in the passage. The first is the Parson's statement that he will not gloss his text is itself a gloss, citing scripture to explain why the text appears in prose and

132   Chaucer's Problem of Prose

not alliterative verse. The Parson's speech even cites the well-known trope of the pilgrimage to heavenly Jerusalem that so obviously informs the basic premise of *The Canterbury Tales* that critics have always recognized the passage as an important "gloss" on the entire collection (X.48–51). Second, the words "glose" and "prose" rhyme in the passage, which draws readerly attention yet again to the fact that the Parson is the fictional inhabitant of a poem where everybody speaks in heroic couplets, even when they are telling their audience that they don't want to speak in rhyme. Chaucer's Parson simply cannot disavow mediation for immediacy because the mediation of *The Canterbury Tales* creates the situation that makes the Parson's disavowal legible.

Again, it is helpful to return to the question of anger in *The Canterbury Tales*, which Jill Mann connects especially to "glosing" and flattery.[29] To Mann's analysis, I would add that the section *De Ira* in the *ParsT* (X.532–653) is a section that is particularly full of implicit references to *The Canterbury Tales* as a whole. Virtually this entire section on anger is concerned with the various kinds of false or inappropriate speech, which ends with three examples that pertain especially to Chaucer: first, "ydel words," which is to say "tho that been nedelees or withouten entente of natureel profit" (X.646) – a category of speech that clearly encompasses his *Thopas*, and the other "enditynges of worldly vanitees" (X.1085) cited in the *Retraction*. Second is "janglynge" (X.649), a term which connotes not only the gossip of the Wife and the Summoner but also the telling of amusing stories and the profession of the *jangleur*, closely cognate with that of the poet. Third and finally is "the synne of japeres, that been the develes apes, for they maken folk to laughe at hire japerie as folk doon the gawdes of an ape" (X.651). Japes are not only jokes but also illusions or fictions, and so the term in all of its senses applies to the many "fables" of *The Canterbury Tales*, which certainly appear to have been intended to make their audiences laugh.[30]

Also noteworthy are several more local parallels between *De Ira* and the particular tales discussed in the previous chapters of this book. In *MLT*, as I discussed in chapter 5, Custaunce (who, in my reading, may allegorize "customs") stands trial for homicide because one of the king's wicked knights has framed her. In *ParsT*, one crime associated with anger is homicide, and one example of homicide is "in yevynge of wikked conseil by fraude, as for to yeven conseil to areysen wrongful custumes and taillages" (X.567) – which reference to "customs" apparently alludes to the notorious Poll Tax that led to the Uprising of 1381, whose adoption was attributed in the complaint literature to Richard II's wicked knights.[31] Meanwhile in *FrT*, as I discussed in chapter 3, the demon explains his presence to the summoner he meets in the woods

The Problem of Prose and the Prose *Canterbury Tales*   133

through a brief speech about necromancy. Necromancy is also cited by the Parson as an example of angry "swearing" (X.603). Finally, the section offers advice about receiving advice that precisely echoes the message of *Mel*: "men shul understonde that man shal nat taken his conseil of fals folk, ne of angry folk, or grievous folk, ne of folk that loven specially to muchel hir owene profit, ne to muche worldly folk, namely in conseilynge of soules" (X.641). For the Parson "anger" is a sin linked especially to mediality and its abuses, and especially to the forms of mediality practiced in and by *The Canterbury Tales*.

Useful for understanding this representation of anger is Nicolette Zeeman's reading of the many angry passages in *Piers Plowman* – which, again, is an implicit intertext for *ParsT* and so a useful point of contrast. For Zeeman, anger in *Piers Plowman* often has an apophatic force, achieving a sort of mystical immediacy through negation.[32] In other words, for all that it may be occasioned by the frustration of communication, anger is also a pathway to possible solutions, as we see perhaps most dramatically represented in the scene from the B-version of the text where Piers rips Truth's pardon.[33] The Parson's description of anger makes no room for such productive gestures, in a manner that is consistent with his rejection of "fables" and allegory as a mode of representation. The affordances of allegorical representation discussed over the last chapters – that it can be useful for representing structures of harm as such – are precisely the affordances that the Parson's emphasis on immediacy forces him to reject, as his decision to avoid complicity in structures of harm amounts to an overall rejection of the idea that there is such a thing as a structural problem that cannot be reduced to the consequences of the individual sinful choices of individual sinful subjects. If the rest of the church all chose to do their work in the manner of the Parson, then there would be no ecclesiastical corruption anymore, and so perhaps the best path towards societal reform is to encourage the repentance of all the individual sinners who are members of the clergy.

This then leads us to the final, concluding, extratextual "gloss" on not only *ParsT* but the entire collection provided by the *Retraction*. When the implicit and explicit of the Ellesmere *Retraction* call Chaucer the "makere of this book" who "compiled" *The Canterbury Tales*, the word choice strongly indicates that Chaucer has "usurped the scribe's role throughout the work by taking responsibility for the arrangement and design" (134). More specifically, the *Retraction* and its framing both suggest to readers that Chaucer himself may have been the scribe of the very manuscript they hold in their hands. In this passage Chaucer, the authorial construct, claims not only the authority of the poet over the

134   Chaucer's Problem of Prose

contents of the text but also the authority of the scribe over the *ordinatio* of the book. This claim reframes the frame narrative's riff on the estates satire to reveal that it is only one aspect of the work's engagement with the structure of the mediating manuscript through which readers access that content. Accordingly, when the *Retraction* vaguely retracts only those tales "that sownen into synne" (X.1086), it authorizes readers not only to interpret the tales as they wish, but also to compile their own customized *Canterbury Tales* manuscripts in the future according to their visions of possible ethical benefits that such future collections might bring to its readers.

If we read the *Retraction* as a colophon, we may apply to it Scase's observation that colophons "draw attention to the text as a graphic product, as the output of scribal activity; if they are thresholds they give access not just to or primarily to a text, but to the copying of text."[34] Here, the *Retraction*'s colophon-like reframing of *ParsT* finally resolves the tension between the Parson's dislike for fables and other sinful speech and the conceit of *The Canterbury Tales* in which he appears. In fact, this work of poetry is *not* speech at all, but *writing*. The marks on the surface of the page may represent sounds, but ultimately this signification is just another fable; in fact the "wheat" is the mute book, the "chaff" the idea that it encodes any meaning beyond the material fact of its own existence. The Parson's attention to the text is therefore figured quite literally, as he leads not only his own author but the reader to contemplate the text of *The Canterbury Tales* in its material manifestation as text. In the same way that *Mel* solved the problem of the gloss by bringing attention to the ethical context of interpretation, so does *ParsT* solve the problem of the text by similarly situating it in the world as an object that one may use however one likes, whether that includes reading it or not.

In his survey of *ParsT* criticism at the cusp of the twenty-first century, Siegfried Wenzel identifies a tendency in critics to single out *ParsT* and see it as either a culmination or a final betrayal of Chaucer's vision, which either way must be considered separately from the collection as a whole.[35] In the next and final section, I will argue that this seeming separateness of *ParsT* stems from its inability to finally contain the profound disruption that the Man of Law/Monk dialogue introduces to the form of *The Canterbury Tales*. The earnest appeals for generosity, non-violence, and respect for neighbours that animates not only *Mel* and *ParsT* but the entirety of *The Canterbury Tales* are simply inconsistent with the Man of Law's violent reduction of England to "fee simple," especially as this reduction was predicated on the crown's imperial impulse to regularize its apparatus of power and spread it to

The Problem of Prose and the Prose *Canterbury Tales*   135

new territories. Though the identities of the Friar and the Summoner frame their argument as an anti-clerical satire of specifically ecclesiastical hypocrisy, in fact the structural problem they represent is endemic to institutional literacy itself. Hence as much as Chaucer may wish to authorize his project on the strength of his own poetic skill and secular authorship, his negative self-portraits in *MLI* and in *Thopas* tip past the edge of mere self-deprecation, to articulate quite compelling reasons to believe that the *Canterbury Tales'* project of envisioning an England that is more than the sum of its parts was doomed from the start.

The Parson in *The Man of Law's Epilogue*

In the spirit of the recursivity that the *ParsT*'s concluding gesture invites – bringing our attention back to the beginning of the collection to contemplate its structure and ordering, the texts that should be omitted and the texts that should be retained – I will now conclude this chapter with a reading of a passage buried far earlier in the text, the so-called *MLE* that might either colour or not colour our reading of the *ParsT*'s concluding gesture, depending on whether or not we think modern editors should have omitted or retained it. In the *GP*, the Parson's poverty and commitment to pastoral care place him in sharp contrast to all the other church officials on the pilgrimage, in a way that marks him as a relatively idealized and unrealistic figure. With his brother the Plowman, the Parson appears to model an aspirational moral excellence rather than an historical reality of medieval clericalism, and this self-evident fictionality sets him up as the only pilgrim who can speak with summary authority at the end of *The Canterbury Tales*.[36] As I will argue below, the Parson's apparent "Lollardy" in *MLE* brings him down to earth, as the evocation of Wycliffism transforms *ParsT* from a conclusion into another reiteration of its original animating problems of history, mediation, and prose.

Mishtooni Bose has made the point that Wycliffite and anti-Wycliffite rhetoric constituted "an uncomfortable confrontation between two branches growing from the same stem."[37] This "stem" is the reformism of fraternal mendicancy, which the fraternal orders claimed to maintain and their Lollard critics claimed to renew. The close, uncomfortable, often obscure distinction between these two reformist poles mark Wycliffism as part of a series of reformist divergences in English Christianity, which for example also included the Cistercian reforms of the eleventh century and the Benedictine Reform of the tenth. As Julia Barrow's study of the English Benedictine reform exemplifies, the problems that drove such reform movements were as likely to redress

136   Chaucer's Problem of Prose

administrative inefficiencies and unjust discrepancies in the adjudication of crimes as they were to renew theological rigour or Christian ethics.[38] For all that such reforms did to transform the lives of everyday Christians and the institutions they inhabited, their eternally recurrent reformism has always been itself a continuity in Christian practice that gives coherence to the religion, and traces back past Benedict's original drafting of his rule in the sixth century to Christ's own vexations at the prescriptivism of the scribes and Pharisees.

Against the backdrop of this long continuity in Christian writing, I will read the two prose tales as constituting two new reformist "branches" springing from a shared origin: the first is Chaucer's secular, literary, "proto-humanist" authorship, and the second is the Parson's simple, sincere, unmediated religious piety. Though this divergence is presented in *The Canterbury Tales* as a collaboration between the two figures rather than a confrontation, it nonetheless remains uncomfortable that the two authorities share their roots – as the humanists well knew and explicitly claimed – in the Roman forms of life that were preserved and renovated by the institutional Christian church, in a more or less explicit recapitulation of Rome's imperial aspirations towards global military and economic hegemony. It is commonly stated that at the time of the Reformation, one third of the arable land in England was owned by the church. How, then, could Wyclif and his followers have imagined a Dissolution of the monasteries to be anything but the profound disruption it would ultimately be when it was enacted in the sixteenth century? Given that (as Stephen Lahey has shown) Wyclif argued for the importance of "a strong, Grace-favored civil lord or king to reduce the office holders of the church to Christlike poverty," it makes sense that England's lawyers would be sympathetic to the Lollard cause; they stood to benefit directly and materially from their reforms.[39] But if the Parson's Lollardy meant that he too followed Wyclif to believe in the necessity of forcible disendowment carried out by secular authorities, how was he able to square this belief with its obvious ramifications for his own impoverished flock, who would find their lives radically disrupted by the ensuing chaos even if their lands already had secular owners? Either way, could a Lollard Parson play the role that Chaucer has set him up to play, of a fictional figure unshackled by the constraints of history who can imagine an alternative to the old status quo of text and gloss, interpretive literalism and interpretive freedom, Summoner and Friar, Monk and Man of Law, laws of Edward and Domesday Book, when Wyclif and his university-educated followers had only abandoned the old imperial politics of recognition to recommend far less subtle forms of dispossession that, when enacted, would mark in many

The Problem of Prose and the Prose *Canterbury Tales*   137

histories of England the end of the medieval period and the start of the British Empire?

To show how this problem is set up in the *MLE*, I will begin by briefly summarizing the relevant passage. It begins with the Host praising the "thrifty tale" (II.1165) of Custaunce that he just heard, using the precise phrase used by the Man of Law himself in the *MLI* to name the sort of tale he cannot tell (II.46). The Host then asks the Parson for a tale, swearing oaths twice – "for Goddes bones" (II.1166) and "by Goddes dignitee" (II.1169). The Parson responds with a rhetorical question: "what eyleth the man, so sinfully to swere?" (II.1171). This question leads the Host to twice identify the Parson as a "Lollere" (II.1173, 1177) who "wil prechen us somwhat" (II.1177). This then occasions the interruption by the other pilgrim (named differently in different manuscripts), who asserts that the Parson "schal no gospel glosen here ne teche" (1180) lest that teaching prove heretical (II.1182–3). The pilgrim then promises a tale that "schal nat ben of philosophie, | Ne phislyas, ne termes queinte of law" because "Ther nis but litel Latyn in my mawe!" (II.1188–90).

My reading of this passage focuses on the specific items that the interrupting pilgrim promises not to include. In Middle English, "philosophie" has a far more general meaning than it does in modern usage, and the word's particular association with natural science is reflected both by the fact that it occurs most frequently in *The Canon's Yeoman's Tale* (*CYT*) (VIII.505, 586, 820) and by its pairing with "phislyas," defined by the MED as a "mock-learned nonce word" meant to evoke the science of medicine.[40] In other words, the pilgrim's objection to the Parson's "Lollardy" appears to assume that if the Parson is a heretic, he has been made so by his overly strict and formal education in the philosophy, medicine, and law – which is to say the three major faculties of the medieval European university, which is indeed where the "Lollard" John Wyclif spent most of his professional life.

The third omission, "termes queinte of law," is particularly pointed context for reading the genre of *ParsT*. The Parson's original objection to the Host concerned his dislike for false oaths – a trait he shares with the summoner of *FrT*. As discussed in chapter 3, the Summoner's legalistic attention to the wording of oaths is not only a moral but also a juridical question about guilt before the ecclesiastical courts. Similarly, penitential handbooks like *ParsT* had been central to canon law back to the *Tractatus de penitentia* in Gratian's *Decretum*, as the pastoral techniques developed by confessors to assess and manage the guilt of sinners influenced and were influenced by the frameworks used to assess and manage guilt in ecclesiastical jurisprudence.[41]

138   Chaucer's Problem of Prose

In a recent study Arvind Thomas has argued compellingly that the representations of penance and penitential procedure in *Piers Plowman* demonstrate Langland's deep knowledge of canon law decretals, and so they participate in a "reinvention" of canon law discourse in this period.[42] And again, given especially the identity of the Parson's brother, *Piers Plowman* may be a useful model for imagining the kind of poem that the Parson might have told, had he not been a Southern man.[43] But instead of Langland's visionary, searching approach to the problems of sin, repentance, and punishment, *ParsT* gives us a competent summary of the text of penitential discourse with its emphasis on the personal responsibilities of individual sinners, while making no discernible attempt to name or address the structural problems that animate the versions of *Piers Plowman*.

One of the most puzzling aspects of the *ParsT* to critics is that it should be so conservative and conventional, though it is an original composition and not a translation.[44] As I've briefly stated above, I read this conservatism as an effort to present a law in familiar terms rather than the "queinte" ones anticipated by the other pilgrim in *MLE*. In place of the external, learned apparatus of institutional literacy and rarified procedure, the Parson uses the familiar, immediate, and deeply conservative prose of conventional penitential discourse to apply an immanent, affective law of personal responsibility and interpersonal relationships, modelled perhaps by his own high moral character but "written" by Chaucer's readers in their own hearts. The resulting emphasis on the personal responsibility of sinners to atone refuses to recognize the very existence of the structural problems that conventional medieval penitential discourse had helped to create – as if the corrupt bureaucracies of church and state were not themselves a cause of sin, and so their reform had no place in a consideration of sin's remedies. If the Parson is a Lollard who is committed in some way to the massive institutional reforms that Wyclif recommended, then *ParsT*'s framing of the problem of human sin is arguably misleading. Either institutions matter or they do not, and a basic premise of Wyclif's program is that they matter.

There is, then, an impasse in how we read the Parson that the ambiguous status of *MLE* as a work of Chaucer does not allow us to resolve. *ParsP* would frame the Parson's penitential prose as a summary of common-sense folk-law, which instrumentalizes conventional Christian morality to stabilize the social world that his frame narrative is designed to represent. *MLE*, meanwhile, frames it as a Lollard text, bound by the strictures of an intellectual movement and radical political agenda in a way that makes it partisan and so (in the opinion of at least one pilgrim)

The Problem of Prose and the Prose *Canterbury Tales*   139

predictable, boring, and overly specialized for a lay audience. Readers are stranded between these possible interpretations of the manuscripts, unable to decide on even the identity of the pilgrim who interrupts the Parson to make them both possible. In the meantime, the crux itself signifies how even though the Parson's portrait encourages us to read him as a fantasy of an ideal cleric, he ultimately remains just another clerk, who may make the ethical choice not to work at a cathedral or guild but who could get a job at one any time he wanted, so that he remains part of the system that remains the true source of the problem, whatever he personally chooses to believe.

As I have said, the colophonic Retraction both undercuts and fulfills the Parson's striving towards immediacy, by forcefully ejecting the reader from the organizing satirical fiction of *The Canterbury Tales* and asking them to contemplate instead the materiality of the fragmentary and incomplete manuscript compilation in which they have encountered this fiction. On the one hand, the Retraction finally allows the Parson to become the "not textual" man he claimed to be: the text that sustained him is over, and so he vanishes. On the other, we do not know the identity Chaucer intended for the pilgrim who critiques the Parson, nor even if the passage where the exchange occurs was intended to be included in the collection. The more we look for Chaucer's intention in the frame narrative of *The Canterbury Tales*, the more the manuscript compilation appears to be a mismatched assembly produced by a scribe after Chaucer's death. And yet the more we look for Chaucer's intention in the compilation's material organization (and especially the colophonic Retraction), the more it looks like the frame narrative is disordered because it was abandoned or even deliberately sabotaged by the author, in an expression of ambivalence about the text's imbrication in the clerical culture it satirizes. Both possibilities undermine the fantasy that began fragment X, that soon the shadows would double in size, the octave will be complete, and the pilgrimage would reach resolution. Then again, we have no evidence that Chaucer ever intended to return to the frame after the last tale, and so perhaps the discordance is intentional. Thus the ending of *The Canterbury Tales* reiterates one last time the larger collection's structural ambivalence about not only its author's authority as an English language poet, but about the ways that power worked through writing in late fourteenth-century England, whether in poetry, prose, text, gloss, or the back-and-forth between them.

Conclusion

One way of describing the sheer impressiveness of *The Canterbury Tales* is to observe that it is so densely self-referential, with so many echoes and connections across its great length, that a study of even the smallest portion of it leads naturally and without warning to a study of the entire Chaucerian corpus. I began writing the present study with the intention of discussing only three sections of the collection: fragment II, Chaucer's tales in fragment VII, and fragment X. To conclude it, I will briefly explain the process whereby *MkT* and fragment III came to be central to my argument, as a way of identifying some possible directions I see for any future studies that may wish to proceed on the basis of the work I've done here.

MLI in fragment II is a "second beginning" to *The Canterbury Tales* and also an apparent prologue to *Mel*. This introduction is echoed in many particulars by the *ParsP* in fragment X, down to the promise to tell a tale in prose. The *MLI* also sees the Man of Law subtly denigrate Chaucer's skills as a poet, in an expression of authorial self-doubt that anticipates both *Thopas* and the Retraction. My aim in reading across these selections has been to substantiate my claim that the Man of Law, Chaucer the pilgrim, and the Parson are not only structurally interconnected figures, but are also a tripod supporting the weight of the entire collection, whose analysis can empower readers to understand how the collection invites readers to examine and critique its vision of Christian English identity. The most obvious clue to this effect is the inclusion of prose tales, which do not so much abandon the structural fiction of the collection as they make that structural fiction the object of discussion. In *Mel*, we learn to cut through the noise of dialogue and confrontation to focus on a single moral message: vengeance is wrong, violence is self-defeating, and we should forgive the trespasses of others. In *ParsT*, we learn the same message from the

Conclusion   141

perspective of the offender, and we are urged to accept the forgiveness of others when we have trespassed, and to actively atone and cultivate community and fellowship. Of course the maddeningly neat, pat principles of virtuous living that are expressed in these two tales belie the complexity of the large collection, in a way that is well described indeed by the "authoritative abdication of authority" articulated by Manish Sharma.[1] When *ParsT* gives way to the retraction, it draws the reader's attention to the reality of what they are actually doing: reading a book, written by a stranger who was – even at the time of the text's original circulation – already dead. This reality means that readers can interpret what they read in any way they like and either apply the messages they've gleaned or not.

The critical question that remained for me, then, is where the current *MLT* fits in. What has Custaunce to do with prose? I thought the clue was in the early medieval setting of the tale. If *Mel* and *ParsT* contain within them a program for managing the future of English Christian identity, perhaps *MLT* commented on the origins of that identity in the age of Bede. My consideration of this question led me to the Monk for three reasons. First, *MkP* contains the only occurrence of the word "prose" in *The Canterbury Tales* outside of the texts listed above, and this is the only other occurrence that does not precede a prose tale. Second, the most authoritative primary sources for the time period depicted in *MLT* come from Bede, the major progenitor of English monastic historiography. Finally and most intriguingly, *MkP* followed directly on *Mel*, which might have been the Man of Law's original tale. Hence I found that my study of prose in *The Canterbury Tales* had wandered away from the prose tales to focus instead on the two pilgrims who talk about prose but never actually use it. I saw in these tales a movement towards diffusion and fragmentation that counteracted the movement towards unity and consolidation I saw in the two prose tales, to the degree that it seemed the prose tales were an attempted solution to an underlying problem.

As I have argued above, I believe that this problem is the uncomfortable mismatch between Chaucer's secular ambitions for English language poetry and the context of those ambitions, where English language writing had existed for centuries in monastic archives. On the one hand, Chaucer is a poet interested in "Englishness," as is clearly figured by the conceit of *The Canterbury Tales* that one person each for every kind of English job just so happened to travel together to the birthplace of English Christianity on the day Harry Bailey decided to sponsor a tale-telling contest. On the other, he is clearly concerned to generously represent the heterogeneity of the human experience, in the

142   Chaucer's Problem of Prose

course of attending to that famous contradiction he articulated between *auctoritee* and *experience*.

English monasteries, meanwhile, were closed, local institutions whose denizens were not normally allowed to travel, which existed despite a profound mismatch between their nominal adherence to the *auctoritee* of their monastic rules and the widely attested *experience* that many monks and especially many monastic officers did not follow their rules at all. Chaucer's project found its readership after his death because his work contributed to a modern imperial project that was openly hostile to the very idea of monastic asceticism, as was not unreasonable since Christian monastic asceticism began as a performance of rejecting Roman imperium. It is, then, an intriguing contradiction in Chaucer's reception that after his death, John Lydgate – a Benedictine monk who was Chaucer's most enthusiastic and prolific imitator – would translate the foundational charters of an English monastery into a passable pastiche of a verse form Chaucer popularized. What did Lydgate see in Chaucer's Monk that later readers missed? The additional alignment of the Man of Law with William the Conqueror (in *GP*) and of the Monk with Edward the Confessor (in *MkP*) strengthened my sense that the dialogue between the two figures was concerned in some way with the structural obstacle to the construction of "Englishness," that English was not only the spoken language of Chaucer's vibrant milieu but was also the institutional language of monastic property rights. Certainly this context seemed important for understanding how *MLT* related to its intertext *The Ecclesiastical History*, which is perhaps the most famous and influential text written by any English monk in history.

From here, I identified several possible ways of proceeding that have not made it into the study above. In the "literature group" of fragment VII,[2] *ShT* features a monk, and it likely followed *MLE* in an early draft of the collection; the Prioress is the only other Benedictine on the pilgrimage (exempting her entourage), and her tale directly precedes Chaucer's; and the Nun's Priest is plucked from anonymity to tell a tale that picks up on the Boethian themes of the *MkT* that proceeds it, which perhaps reflects his employment by a Benedictine institution. Indeed, monasticism and its discontents are a major recurrent theme of this longest continuous series of pilgrims after fragment I, and *The Nun's Priest's Tale* (*NPT*) that ends the sequence and deserves in particular to be read in relation to it.

Outside of fragment VII, the Knight interrupts *MkT* and tells his own Boethian tale; the Miller "quites" him and mentions the early English saint and abbess Frideswide (I.3459); the Manciple worked for men of law at a temple, and his juxtaposition with the Parson who follows

Conclusion 143

him is heightened by his claim that he is not "textueel" either (IX.316). Meanwhile the Pardoner interrupts the *WBP* before the Friar and Summoner do; he sings a love song with the latter of these two figures; he objects to swearing false oaths, as do the Summoner and the Parson; and he sells pardons and relics that are together perhaps the clearest symbols for the problem of mediality in the entire collection. Finally, the way my readings led me to consider connections between my chosen tales and *ClT*, *MerT*, and *CYT* suggested that they may provide other avenues for exploration.

Outside of *The Canterbury Tales* I have also identified possible resonances with the Boethian lyrics, *TC*, and of course the *Boece*, where Chaucer translates all of the "meters" into prose. So also is there more to say about the implicit conversation between Chaucer and Gower in *MLI*, and so by extension about the work of this important contemporary lawyer-poet. The same potential for future study applies to Lydgate – whose vast corpus of work is barely touched on in chapter 2 – and also to the royal official Thomas Hoccleve. As I have said, the present study is a continuation of the work in my previous book, which argued for a connection between Middle English alliterative poetry and Old English legal documents. Above I have highlighted a handful of connections to *Piers Plowman*: perhaps these might contribute to the ongoing efforts to read synthetically across these two major Middle English poetic works. Finally, my study bears expansion into a study of Edmund Spenser's reception of Chaucer, which may continue the many post-colonial readings of this early-modern poet.

In the first few years of working on this book, I considered writing chapters on these and other topics, and in many outlines I planned to address several. Ultimately the COVID-19 pandemic led me to abandon my every planned expansion except for my reading of fragment III. But before I reiterate my reasons for including this section, I will briefly describe one example of the new readings of other *Canterbury Tales* I believe my approach makes possible, through the example of the figure who comes most clearly into focus when he is read in relation to early English history: the Reeve.

The Old English word *gerefa* from which our word "reeve" derives appears to be related to the modern word "row," implying that the original function of a reeve was to line things up in rows and count them.[3] Because this activity covers a broad range of organizational activities, the term "reeve" remained fundamentally ambiguous throughout the medieval period, even as the proliferation of things that could be counted meant also a proliferation of reeve-like positions – often specified by compound words such as "land-reeve," "port-reeve," and most

144   Chaucer's Problem of Prose

famously, "shire-reeve" or "sheriff." As one would expect, there is a substantial discourse of complaint about every known kind of reeve in both Old and Middle English, reflecting the obvious possibilities for corruption and self-dealing that administrative positions of this kind have always had.[4]

One of the more striking patterns in the attested uses of Old English *gerefa* is in Old English Biblical and hagiographic literature, where the term was commonly used to translate the titles of wicked Roman officials and pagan villains. These include for example tax collectors, the "unjust steward" of the eponymous parable, and the various "judges" and "prefects" who ordered the executions of saints and prophets.[5] Pontius Pilate is called a reeve in Vercelli Homily I,[6] and the reeves of Ælfric's saints' lives include the wicked agents of pagan law in his legends of Sts. Peter and Paul, St. Lawrence, Sts. Cecilia and Valerian, St. Eugenia, St. Sebastian, St. Agnes, and the martyred bishop of Paris, St. Denis.[7]

Some context for this use of *gerefa* to refer to specifically pagan officials is provided by the preface to the *Codicellus possessionum* section of "Hemming's cartulary," briefly discussed in the introduction. Hemming explains that St. Wulfstan had ordered the cartulary to be created so that his successors to the see of Worcester could know about the lands that had been unjustly alienated, in the hopes that they might one day be able to get them back. Hemming lists four agents of this dispossession: Danes, unjust reeves, royal agents, and Normans (whose name, we should note, marked them as "North-men" and hence as relatives of the Danes).[8] Insofar as this sequence suggests an analogy between Danes and reeves, it therefore contextualizes the preference for the term "reeve" to refer to pagan villains. Danes were responsible for the martyrdom of important English saints like Edmund and Ælfheah of Canterbury, and their fondness for sacking monasteries is attested back to Lindisfarne in 793 CE. Given also the name of the "Danegeld" land tax described in chapter 5 – which, again, is not referred to by that name until after the Norman Conquest, and so may have been more pejorative than descriptive in origin – Hemming's list appears to attest a three-way connection between the Vikings, local administrators, and the crown, on the grounds that all three of them robbed monasteries of their possessions.

In a classic essay, J.R.R. Tolkien argued that *The Reeve's Tale* (*RvT*) contains one of the first recognizable instances of an English language author self-consciously imitating the dialect of another English-speaking region.[9] That region, Norfolk, is just above the border between Danish and Saxon territory established by the treaty of Alfred and Guthrum,

Conclusion   145

and so it is part of the Danelaw. Mann observes that the Reeve's portrait aligns with that "tradition of associating special characteristics with different counties" which "envisages Norfolk people as crafty and treacherous."[10] Perhaps this stereotype derives from the earlier English attitudes about the treacherous Danish ancestors of Norfolk's inhabitants, most famously attested by the Old English poem *The Battle of Maldon*.[11]

The Reeve's name, meanwhile, is the unusual "Osewold" (I.3860) – a pun perhaps on Latin *os*, and so a reference to his skeletal appearance. Two of the most famous Oswalds in medieval history are the seventh-century saint and king of Northumbria and the tenth-century saint and bishop of Worcester, St. Oswald. The first, King Oswald, is treated very differently by the contrasting histories of Bede and Geoffrey of Monmouth. Both chronicles describe the famous event where Oswald builds a cross at Heavenfield, prays to it before battle against King Cadwallon, and wins (*Historia ecclesiastica* book III ch. 2, *Historia regum Britanniae* ch. 199). In Bede's telling, Oswald is a blessed instrument of God who reigns for nine years after this victory (III.9). In Geoffrey's, the enraged Cadwallon seems to hunt down Oswald and kill him almost immediately – only one among many signs in *Historia regum Britanniae* of how its author's allegiances lay with the Britons (ch. 199).

The second, Bishop Oswald, is the figure from the Benedictine Reform discussed in the introduction. This second Oswald seems to be the more likely namesake of Chaucer's Reeve, for two reasons. First, Jill Mann has identified many indications that the Reeve is a sort of would-be member of the clergy.[12] Second, his Satanic associations connect him also to the Satans of *FrT* and *MkT*.[13] Taken together with his Norfolk qualities, these attributes suggest that he may be a satire of manorial exemption who flips Hemming's associations on their head. If Oswald, reeve of the Danelaw, is figured as a sort of marauder (or "reaver," perhaps), he is one who no longer robs independent manors on behalf of the crown, but rather one who robs the crown on behalf of himself.

This final point is suggested further by the key line from his description in the *GP*: "Ther was noon auditour koude on him wynne" (I.594).[14] Audits are typically commissioned on behalf of an external authority, who wishes to ensure that debts and taxes are being properly calculated and paid. An example of the principle appears in *RvT* itself, in which the two students from Soler ("King's") Hall perform an audit on the miller Symkyn to ensure that their wheat is being milled properly. Symkyn, meanwhile, is married to the daughter of the local priest, and according to the Reeve this makes her "noble kyn" (I.3942).[15] He steals

146   Chaucer's Problem of Prose

from King's Hall to save a dowry for his daughter, and as the Reeve comments:

hooly chirches good moot been despended
On hooly chirches blood, that is descended.
Therefore he wolde his hooly blood honoure,
Though that the hooly chirche sholde devoure.   (I.3983–6)

Symkyn is in this sense the sort of clergyman that the Host joked that the Monk might become: an agent of a thoroughly worldly institution that no longer has any connection to the spiritual church of Christ's body. Symkyn is also, for the same reason, not so different from the Reeve himself.[16] The Reeve has betrayed his tendency towards projection in *The Reeve's Prologue* (*RvP*) when he reverses the Biblical injunction to say of the Miller: "He kan wel in myn eye seen a stalke, | But in his owene he kan nat seen a balke" (I.3919–20). Just as the Friar and the Summoner would do in fragment III, so also does the Reeve's attempt to cast blame on the Miller only serve to betray his own foibles, the Reeve in effect auditing his own insecurities on behalf of his assembled audience.

In the *GP*, the Reeve is described as choleric (I.587), and this temperament marks him as a personification of that same anger whose tendency to frustrate communication I discussed in chapter 6. This inability to communicate is figured as a sort of impotence, both by his age and by his rusty sword (I.618).[17] These same images reveal an ambivalence in Chaucer's satire of the Reeve, related to the larger problem of prose in the entire collection. The Reeve here seems to be not only an impotent old man, but also an impotent old stock character, who no longer needs to be satirized because the social ills he represents are becoming increasingly irrelevant. Meanwhile new social ills are already on the horizon. Roughly thirty years after Chaucer's death, the Portuguese would arrive in Africa and begin the modern slave trade. Sixty years after that, Columbus would arrive in Hispaniola. In Chaucer's lifetime the international trade markets that would make these ventures so profitable were already falling into place. With such horrors on the horizon, how outraged can one be about an angry old manorial official who helps himself to more of his Lord's sheep, dairy, pigs, and poultry than he ought (I.597–8)? Similarly in *RvT*, Symkyn may be a crook, but what coherent values system would have us root against him for the clerks who raped his wife and daughter?[18] Though Patterson reads *RvT* as an attempt to contain the Miller's disruptive potential, I see him rather as the belated relic of a vanished age, who reminds the reader that in fact

Conclusion 147

the Miller's disruptions to the social order have already arrived and it is too late to contain them.

This unravelling of the satire in the Reeve's portrait, prologue, and tale leads me back to my reading of fragment III in chapter 3. Of all the possible departures from my four main tales that I had planned, this one seemed most crucial to the structure of the book, because it helped me to articulate the heuristic of text and gloss in *The Canterbury Tales* I had unpacked to frame the oppositions between *ParsT* and *Mel*, *MkT*, and *MLT* I found in my investigations. Institutional literacy in medieval England proceeded from the institutions of the church, which both the Friar and the Summoner served. The Friar worked for the fraternal orders, established almost 200 years before Chaucer's death as a reform movement that aimed to renovate the mission of Christ and the apostles recorded in the gospel. The Summoner, meanwhile, worked for the system that the Friar aimed to renovate, employed as he was by an archdeacon who oversaw an ecclesiastical court district on behalf of a bishop. The reformist intentions of the friars suggested that their purpose was to reconnect with the original spirit of Christian institutions that had moved away from their original purpose. The purpose of summoners, meanwhile, was to act as agents of those unreformed institutions, delivering summons and following procedures without question.

I have argued that the same basic opposition between the (dangerous) freedom of the gloss and the (dangerous) strictness of the text can be found in the dualisms of Chaucer and the Parson and of the Man of Law and the Monk. It seemed telling that in all three of these pairings, the reformist glossators (the Friar, Chaucer, and the Man of Law) all appeared earlier in the collection than the agents of the system they tried to reform (the Summoner, the Parson, and the Monk). Gestures towards the future are continually undercut in *The Canterbury Tales* by survivals from the past, and this reflects the fact that the possibilities for the future are always circumscribed by those perceptions of the past that demarcate the range of the possible. I believe Chaucer's authoritative abdication of authority attempts a rejection of this slavery to the past and a recognition that the future is circumscribed by neither the Man of Law's stars (II.194–6) nor the Monk's "ensamples trewe and olde" (VII.1998), but is re-opened at each moment to undetermined possibility. Hence, perhaps, the capacity of his work to continue to surprise its readers, myself included, and to invite them to perform their own self-audits for their own audiences when they attempt to describe what they have discovered.

Notes

Critical Introduction

1 The pilgrims speaking are Host (VII.934), Chaucer (VII.937), and the Parson (X.46). Here and throughout this study, claims about the appearances of a given word come from Henry Litwhiler's *Chaucer Concordance* (2017): http://www.columbia.edu/~hfl2110/cconcord.html.
2 For this case see Owen, "What the Manuscripts."
3 Colley, "Reclaiming Reason," p. iii. See also however Eleanor Johnson's study of the Middle English prosimetrum *Practicing Literary Theory*. On the particular utility of medieval prose for translation see, e.g., Chaytor, *From Script*, 89–114; Gordon, *The Movement*, 35–70.
4 Patterson, "What Man Artow?" On the importance of page formatting see Mak, *How the Page Matters*.
5 Sharma, *Logic of Love*, 3–8.
6 Sharma, *Logic of Love*, 8.
7 On the term "litel tretys" see Sharma, *Logic of Love*, 216–19 and 256–62.
8 On the application of media studies concepts and frameworks to medieval thought and writing see also Stock and Rasmussen, "Introduction"; Brylowe and Yeager, "Introduction." The term "media concept" comes from Guillory, "Genesis."
9 Nelson, "Ambient," 567. See also Nelson, "Premodern Media."
10 Nelson, "Ambient," 573.
11 Major touchstones remain Crane, "Writing Lesson"; Justice, *Writing and Rebellion*. On the larger context for the events of the summer of 1381 see for example Juliet Barker, *1381*; Prescott, "The Great and Horrible Rumour"; Bailey, "Injustice and Revolt"; Ormrod, "The Peasant's Revolt." As will be discussed below, the same connection persists in the settler-colonial nation of Canada, whose legal institutions are based in the same common law tradition whose early period is surveyed by the historians above. See, e.g., Maracle, *Memory Serves*; Coulthard, *Red Skins* and "From Wards."

150   Notes to pages 6–10

12 See the general discussion of these terms in chapter 3: 60–4. These terms may also be productively compared to the contrary control strategies of protocol and regulation, which I have written about elsewhere: Yeager, "Protocol and Regulation," and "Protocol, or 'The Chivalry.'" Chaucerian "glosing" corresponds to my notion of protocological control, and adherence to the text corresponds to my notion of regulatory control.

13 Here and throughout my abbreviated titles of Chaucer's works are taken from *Riverside*, 779.

14 Nakley, *Living in the Future*; Butterfield, *The Familiar Enemy*, 8–35, 273–6. On Englishness in Middle English poetry more generally see Turville-Petre, *England the Nation*.

15 Turner, *Chaucer*; Winthrop Weatherbee, "Chaucer and the European"; Butterfield, *The Familiar Enemy*; Gaston, *Reading Chaucer*.

16 Nakley, *Living in the Future*.

17 The phrase appears in Dryden's "Preface to Fables Ancient and Modern": Dryden, *Of Dramatic*, vol. 2, 280.

18 Scase, *Visible English*, 353; Kerby-Fulton, "Introduction."

19 *MED*, s.v. "Saxon," n., def. 2(b) and 4.

20 Referencing the title of Richard Firth Green's influential study, *Poets and Princepleasers*.

21 Spiegel, *Romancing*. Cited in Johnson, "English Law," 524 – a key touchstone for this study discussed in more detail in chapter 1: 39–41. On prose and its uses see also Chaytor, *From Script*, 89–114, and Gordon, *The Movement*.

22 Surveyed by Gillespie and Wakelin, eds., *Production of Books*.

23 Clegg and Reed, "Economic Decline." On medieval church estate management see Dobie, *Accounting*.

24 On Chaucer's biography see Turner, *Chaucer*; Strohm, *The Poet's Tale*; Crow and Olson, *Life-Records*.

25 Wool customs were not collected regularly in England until 1275: Lloyd, *English Wool Trade*, 60.

26 On the relationship between these achives and Middle English alliterative poetry see my previous monograph, *From Lawmen*.

27 The definitions and periodizations of "colonialism" are abundant and contradictory, within and outside of medieval studies. Here, I will use the word "settler-colonialism" to refer to modern nations like Canada, where external settlers have taken land and displaced Indigenous peoples, and the broader term "colonialism" to refer more generally to the exploitative global relations attending not only the first establishment of settler-colonial nations in the Western hemisphere following the fifteenth century but also the contemporary establishment of the trans-Atlantic slave trade. The earlier and related forms of subjugation, enslavement, and exploitation

practiced in medieval Europe and/or by medieval Europeans I will call "imperial" because they have been typically patterned on the practices and institutions of the Roman Empire, as indeed the Latin root of the word "colonial" itself attests.

28 Dor, "Chaucer's Viragos"; Hamaguchi, "Transgressing"; Schibanoff, "Worlds Apart"; Nakley, *Living in the Future*.

29 Patterson, *Chaucer and the Subject*, 26.

30 Patterson, *Chaucer and the Subject*, 32; Mann, *Chaucer and Medieval Estates Satire*; Leicester, *Disenchanted Self*.

31 Patterson, *Chaucer and the Subject*, 13. On the origins of liberalism in this period of English history see the work of James Simpson, most influentially *Reform and Cultural Revolution*.

32 Patterson, *Chaucer and the Subject*, 424.

33 On medieval prehistories of racial identity and their manifestations in Chaucer's poetry see for example Cord Whitaker, *Black Metaphors*, 68–88; Nakley, *Living in the Future*; Hsy, *Trading Tongues*, 27–57, 65–79; Akbari, *Idols*; Heffernan, *The Orient*; Heng, *Empires of Magic*, 181–238; Lampert-Weissig, *Medieval Literature*. On medieval race generally see Rambaran-Olm, Leake, and Goodrich, "Introduction"; Kim, "Introduction"; Heng, *Invention*; Hsy and Orlemanski, "Race and Medieval." On Indigenous studies approaches to medieval literature see Andrews, "Indigenous Futures."

34 Patterson, *Chaucer and the Subject*, 424–5.

35 Patterson, *Chaucer and the Subject*, 250–4; citing Aston and Philpin, *Brenner*. The original discussion in Marx appears in chapters 26–32 of *Capital* vol. 1.

36 See Holsinger and Knapp, "The Marxist Premodern," and the rest of this special issue, especially Rigby, "Historical Materialism."

37 Wynter, "Unsettling."

38 Wynter, "Unsettling," 259, in an epigraph quoting LeGoff, *Medieval Imagination*.

39 Wynter, "Unsettling," 262.

40 Lowe, *Intimacies*, 3. Major works by these thinkers include Hartman, *Wayward Lives*; Robinson, *Black Marxism*; James, *Black Jacobins*.

41 Lowe, *Intimacies*, 7.

42 Lowe, *Intimacies*, 4–5.

43 Lowe, *Intimacies*, 39.

44 Lowe, *Intimacies*, 74; quoting James, *Beyond*, 47.

45 Lowe, *Intimacies*, 81.

46 Gitelman, *Paper*, 1.

47 Gitelman, *Paper*, 5.

48 Gitelman, *Paper*, 9.

49 See also my discussion of this text in "Protocol and Regulation," 61–8.

152 Notes to pages 17–23

50 Davis, *Periodization*, 5.
51 Davis, *Periodization*, 23–50.
52 Davis, *Periodization*, 8.
53 Davis, *Periodization*, 59.
54 On the problems with this specific periodization of medieval history around the year 1066, see Treharne, *Living*. It is representative of the themes of this chapter that the most compelling defences of the Norman Conquest as a "revolutionary" dividing point now typically hinge on the Domesday book census, which indeed had important implications for the uses of the written word in England: Clanchy, *From Memory*.
55 Davis, *Periodization*, 52–3.
56 Davis, *Periodization*, 55.
57 Spelman, "Feuds," 5–6. For a recent consideration of a possible "feudal revolution" after William's reign, see Baxter, "Lordship and Labour."
58 Patterson, *Chaucer and the Subject*, 254.
59 On this massacre, troublingly downplayed by many scholarly accounts of 1381, see Spindler, "Flemings"; Prescott, "'Great and Horrible Rumour,'" 76–103. On Chaucer's representation of the Flemings see most recently Pattinson, "Ironic Imitations."
60 Reynolds, "Fiefs and Vassals after Twelve Years," 24; see also her *Kingdoms and Communities* and *Fiefs and Vassals*.
61 Coulthard, *Red Skins*, 17, 31–42, citing Fanon, *Black Skins*. On Fanon see also Gordon, "Through."
62 Coulthard, *Red Skins*, 15. See also his "From Wards." The phrase "politics of recognition" is typically attributed to Charles Taylor; see his *Multiculturalism*.
63 Marx, *Capital, Volume 1*, 873–6.
64 Coulthard, *Red Skins*, 13, citing Glassman, "Primitive Accumulation"; Federici, *Caliban and the Witch*; De Angelis, "Marx and Primitive." See also Gordon, "Canada."
65 Suggested for example by Rigby, "Historical Materialism." On monastic archives and the construction of the past see Geary, *Phantoms of Remembrance*; Remensyder, *Remembering Kings*; Ugé, *Creating*. On Indigenous and medieval studies see Andrews, "Indigenous Futures," and the remainder of this special issue.
66 Gransden, "Prologues," 66.
67 O'Brien, "Becket Conflict," 13–14. See also his *God's Peace*.
68 Coulthard, 58, citing Abel, *Drum Songs*, 250.
69 On the treaties see Fumoleau, *As Long*.
70 Coulthard, *Red Skins*, 59.
71 Coulthard, *Red Skins*, 75–6.
72 Coulthard, *Red Skins*, 78.

Notes to pages 23–30   153

73 Marsh and Baker, "Mackenzie."
74 Brooks and Cubitt, *St. Oswald*; Byrhtferth, *Lives of St. Oswald and St. Ecgwine.*
75 Tinti, *Sustaining Belief*, 60–1, citing Wormald, "Oswaldslow: An Immunity?" and "Lordship and Justice"; Baxter, "The Representation of Lordship" and "Lordship and Justice," 384–6.
76 Tinti, *Sustaining Belief*, 75. On the immediate causes for the drafting of this cartulary see Wareham, "The Redaction."
77 Tinti, *Sustaining Belief*, 61–2, citing Gransden, "Cultural Transition"; Mason, *St. Wulfstan*, 196–232; Tinti, "si litterali."
78 Crick, "Historical Literacy" and "St. Albans"; Clanchy, *From Memory*; Karn, "Information"; O'Brien, "Forgery." On the role of ecclesiastical institutions in early English charter production see also Smith, *Land and Book*, 22–8; Yeager, *From Lawmen*, 50–3; Thompson, *Royal Diplomas*, 5; Kelly, "Anglo-Saxon Lay Society."
79 Baxter, "Lordship and Labour," 108.
80 Yeager, *From Lawmen*, 102.
81 Wormald, *Making of English Law*, 159.
82 Thomas, *History*, 189–97 et passim.
83 Thomas, *History*, 203–19.
84 Boureau, "How Law."
85 Thomas, *History*, 431–65.
86 Mann, *Chaucer and Medieval Estates Satire*, 17–36.
87 Dinshaw, *Sexual Poetics*, 113–31.

1. The Problem of Prose in Fragments II and VII: An Overview

1 All quotations from *The Canterbury Tales* are from *Riverside.*
2 On the term and concept "purchasour" see Musson, "Sergeant of Law," 219; Green, "Chaucer's Man"; Lambkin, "Chaucer's Man of Law as Purchasour."
3 On this phrase see also Nolan, "Acquiteth," 147, citing Middleton, "Chaucer's New Men," n. 22.
4 Nolan, "Acquiteth," 137.
5 Hoyt, "Nature and Origins," 146–7; Clanchy, *From Memory*, 35–8.
6 Darby, *Domesday England*; Poole, *From Domesday Book*; Maitland, *Domesday Book and Beyond.*
7 Cameron et al. eds., *Dictionary of Old English*, s.v. "bocland." See further Abels, "Bookland and Fyrd"; Naismith, "Payments"; Smith, *Land and Book*, 8–11, 14; Baxter, *Earls of Mercia*, 145; Wood, *Proprietary Church*, 152–60; Reynolds, *Fiefs and Vassals*, 324–5, 331; Wormald, "Bede and the Conversion," 156; Kennedy, "Disputes about *Bocland.*"

154   Notes to pages 30–7

8 Cameron et al. eds., *Dictionary of Old English*, s.v. "folcland." In addition to the discussions of *bocland* above see Ryan, "Charters in Plenty"; Vinogradoff, "Folkland." A third form of title, *laenland*, is distinguished from *bocland* by being held by tenants for only three generations, though this distinction too was vexed and subject to revision.

9 Beginning with Havelock, *Preface to Plato*. A useful critique of this late twentieth-century "orality studies" remains Vail and White, *Power*, 1–39.

10 On these changes to court systems in particular see Beckerman, "Procedural Innovation."

11 For example, Patterson, *Chaucer and the Subject*, 281.

12 *Riverside*, 854.

13 Wallace, *Chaucerian Polity*, 200.

14 Dinshaw, *Sexual Poetics*, 65–87.

15 Nolan, "Acquiteth"; see also Musson, "Sergeant of Law," 212.

16 Wallace, *Chaucerian Polity*, 201–5.

17 As many readers have observed, this list is incorrect: see, e.g., Wallace, *Chaucerian Polity*, 204.

18 Hansen, *Chaucer and the Fictions*, 3.

19 Hansen, *Chaucer and the Fictions*, 9–10, citing Green, *Poets and Princepleasers*, 99–134.

20 Dinshaw, *Sexual Poetics*, 9.

21 Harris, *Obscene Pedagogies*, 30.

22 Nakley, *Living in the Future*, 184 n. 13, citing Davis, "Time Behind the Veil."

23 For the original documents see Crow and Olson, *Chaucer Life-Records*, 343–7. On the new documents see the special issue of *The Chaucer Review* 57.4 (2022), "The Case of Geoffrey Chaucer and Cecily Chaumpaigne: New Evidence," guest edited by Sebastian Sobecki and Euan Roger. Sobecki and Roger's conclusions have been criticized on the grounds that the word *raptus* had a very specific meaning of "rape," following Cannon, "Raptus." However legal historians of the period tend to disagree with literary scholars on this question, as, e.g., Shannon McSheffrey and Julia Pope write "[*raptus* and] ravishment could mean abduction or taking away with no sexual violence implied – children could be ravished by parents in custody disputes, for instance, and thieves could ravish goods" ("Ravishment," 818). See also Dunn, *Stolen Women*.

24 There have been many studies of sexual violence in Chaucer's poetry, life, and milieu. The approaches that most directly inform the arguments of the present book include Baechle, "Speaking Survival"; Harris, "On Servant Women" and *Obscene Pedagogies*; Katz Seal, "Whose Chaucer?"; Edwards, *Afterlife of Rape* and "The Rhetoric of Rape"; Bovaird-Abbo, "Is Geoffrey Chaucer's *Tale*"; Nakley, *Living in the Future*, 188–204; Kennedy, *Maintenance, Meed*, 31–60, esp. 54–7; Vines, "Invisible Woman";

Notes to pages 37–45   155

Goodspeed-Chadwick, "Sexual Politics"; Rose, "Reading Chaucer Reading Rape"; Weisl, "'Quiting' Eve"; Dinshaw, "Quarrels"; Saunders, "Woman Displaced"; Hansen, *Chaucer and the Fictions*.

25 Kisor, "Moments of Silence"; Goodall, "Unkynde"; Robertson, "Nonviolent Christianity," 337–8; Ashton, "Her Father's"; Dinshaw, *Sexual Poetics*, 95, 101–5; Scala, "Canacee"; Archibald, "The Flight."

26 *Riverside*, 862–3; Cooper, *Structure*.

27 On such problems see for example Blake, "On Editing."

28 See also Stevens, "Royal Stanza"; Kolve, *Chaucer and the Imagery*, 462–3; Edwards, "I speke."

29 Johnson, "English Law," 504.

30 Johnson, "English Law," 507.

31 Johnson, "English Law," 524. This concept of "prose" derives in part from her reading of Spiegel, *Romancing*.

32 See also Meyer-Lee, "Abandon the Fragments." The most influential arguments for and against the unity of the collection are Howard, *The Idea* and Leicester, *The Disenchanted Self* respectively.

33 Cooper, *Structure*, 123; Nolan, "Acquiteth," 139–44.

34 Caie, "Innocent III's *De Miseria*"; Lewis, "Chaucer's Artistic Use." See also *Riverside*, 856; Mann, 863.

35 David, "Man of Law Vs."

36 Turner, *Chaucer*, 454–7.

2. Saxon Script and Chaucerian Verse in London BL Add. MS 14848

1 Lowe, "Poetry of Privilege"; Webber, "*Judas*"; Hiatt, *Making*, 57–62. For an edition of the poems see Arnold, *Memorials*, vol. 3, 215–37. On Lydgate's links to the abbot Curteys who produced this register see Pearsall, *Lydgate*, 23–7.

2 Dean, "Gower," 251–2.

3 Stenton, *Latin Charters*, 19; cited by Crick, "Historical Literacy," 162.

4 The rubric in the Hyde Abbey cartulary says King Alfred's Old English will is written "in lingua Saxonica": London BL Add. MS 82931, f. 8v. Also, London Westminster W.A.M. 12752 glosses a charter of St. Edward an "item ex alia carta saxonica."

5 It should be noted that Crick is only one among many medievalists to argue against the attribution of an "historical sense" to early-modern literature and historiography which is distinct from medieval antecedents. Pertinent here also is Simpson's reading of early-modern Petrarchan poets like Wyatt: *Reform and Cultural Revolution*, 153–4.

6 Insley, "Where," 112. See also Stafford, "Political Ideas"; Reynolds, *Kingdoms and Communities*.

156   Notes to pages 45–7

7 The bibliography surveying these networks of influences is vast, but for Lydgate's place in particular see Mortimer, *Fall of Princes*; Nolan, *John Lydgate*; Pearsall, *Lydgate*, 49–82; Edwards, "The Influence."

8 All charters will be cited according to their "Sawyer numbers," as used on the Electronic Sawyer website: http://www.esawyer.org.uk. On S 980 see Lowe, "Bury St. Edmunds"; Keynes, *Facsimiles*, no. 33; Harmer, *Writs*, 433–4.

9 On S 995 see Ker, "Cnut's Earls," 60; Gransden, "Baldwin," 70–1; Harmer, *Writs*, 434–5. The third charter, S 1045, attributed to Edward the Confessor (ff. 251r.–255r.), also appears in an Old English version; on this document see Dumville, *English Caroline Script*, 36–7; Gransden, "Baldwin," 70–1; Harmer, *Writs*, 141 n. 2. Lydgate's translation of S 1045 continues with a translation of S 1068, and this is only some of the evidence that he was working from the Latin and not the Old English versions of the texts: Lowe, "Poetry of Privilege," 155–7. On Edward see chapter 4: 79–80.

10 Lydgate, *Lives of Ss Edmund & Fremund*. On this text's representation of kingship see Somerset, "Hard"; Ganim, "Lydgate, Location"; Gillespie, "The Later Lives"; Camp, *Saints' Lives*, 173–209. It is noteworthy in the current discussion that one of this text's manuscripts – Cambridge, University Library Ee.ii.15 – also witnesses Chaucer's *MLT*.

11 Kathryn Lowe has worked extensively on these documents: "Poetry of Privilege"; "Bury St. Edmunds"; "Post-Conquest"; "Linguistic Geography."

12 Ganim, "Lydgate, Location." Compare the concept of "tenurial discourse" in Smith, *Land & Book*.

13 See the introduction: 21–6.

14 As for example Julia Crick has argued about St. Albans: "Pristina libertas," "Liberty and Fraternity."

15 Witnessed for example on f. 244r.

16 The following overview of the history of European bookhands draws from Bischoff, *Latin Paleography*. See also Dumville, *English Caroline Script*.

17 Kelly, "Anglo-Saxon Lay Society," 46; Stenton, *Latin Charters*, 57. For single-sheet examples see Keynes, *Facsimiles*.

18 Gillespie, "Later Lives," 175–6; citing Scott, "*Caveat Lector*," 39–42; Reimer and Parvolden, "Of Arms"; Mooney, "Professional"; Doyle and Parkes, "The Production of Copies."

19 On the emergence of humanist scripts see Ullman, *Origin*; De La Mare, *Handwriting*; Derolez, *Paleography*, 176–82.

20 Wardrop, *Script*, 4.

21 I take the term "archaizing" from Parkes, "Archaizing Hands." See also Crick, "Historical Literacy"; Lucas, "Scribal Imitation"; Hector, *Paleography and Forgery*.

Notes to pages 48–51   157

22 Discussed in Lowe, "Bury St. Edmunds."
23 Lowe, "Bury St. Edmunds," 161.
24 It is a coincidence worth noting that this same Hyde Abbey also owned the Tabard Inn: Turner, *Chaucer*, 409.
25 Crick, "Historical Literacy," 163; Hiatt, *Making*, 52–7; Parkes, "Archaizing Hands," 103; Lucas, "Scribal Imitation"; Hector, *Paleography and Forgery*, 13–14; Hunter, "Facsimiles."
26 Crick, "Historical Literacy," 188–9.
27 Butler, "Recollecting." On the Tremulous Hand see also Franzen, *Tremulous Hand*.
28 Butler, "Recollecting," 148–9. See also Graham, "Beginnings"; Bjorklund, "Parker's Purpose"; de Hamel, "Archbishop."
29 Butler, "Recollecting," 151. On antiquarianism in fifteenth-century England see Gransden, "Antiquarian Studies."
30 Butler, "Recollecting," 151–2; Lucas, "Scribal Imitation."
31 Butler, "Recollecting," 152.
32 Butler, "Recollecting," 152, quoting Echard, *Printing*. See also Wendy Scase's discussion of facsimile-like "reprographics" in medieval manuscripts: *Visible English*, 283–349.
33 Treharne, *Living*.
34 Wiles, "Charters"; Crick, ""Historical Literacy," 161; Clanchy, *From Memory*, 148–9. Tollerton, *Wills*, 16, 38, citing *Chronicon Abbatiae Ramesiensis*, 1, 39; Tinti, *Sustaining Belief*, 136 n. 164.
35 On this manuscript see Conti, "Circulation" and "Individual Practice."
36 For examples of thirteenth-century charter-texts that imitate Old English letterforms see the Wilton cartulary London BL Harley 436 (dated c. 1250) and Keynes, *Facsimiles* nos. 41 (S 349) and 42 (S 1033).
37 Parkes, *English Cursive*, xiv–xvi, citing Neil Ker's original and more focused use of the term in *Medieval Manuscripts*, xi. On *anglicana* see also Derolez, *Palaeography*, 134–41.
38 For example, both letterforms may be found in the fourteenth-century single-sheet document Worcester, Cathedral Library, B 1599 (witnessing the charter S 1157): Harmer, *Writs*, 409, 528.
39 Either Lydgate himself or the scribe of his source text for the charters appears to make this error: Lowe, "Poetry of Privilege," 157.
40 On this archive see Thomson, *Archives*, and the forthcoming British Academy Anglo-Saxon Charters series volume *Charters of Bury St. Edmunds Abbey with St. Benet at Holme*, co-edited by Kathryn Lowe and Sarah Foot.
41 On Bury in this period see Gransden, *A History*; Jocelin of Brakelond, *Chronicle*.
42 Gransden, "Baldwin"; Lowe, "Bury St. Edmunds," 159–60.
43 Dunning, "John Lakenheath's Rearrangement"; Foot, "Internal and External."

158 Notes to pages 51–4

44 Thomson, *Archives*, 23; Dunning, "Death." On early charters and the Uprising see Justice, *Writing and Rebellion*, esp. chs. 1 and 5.

45 See for example Petrarch's comments on the script of one of his manuscripts in *Rerum Familiarum*, xxiii.19.8.

46 The touchstone for such arguments remains Eisenstein, *Printing Press*.

47 Dobbie, *Manuscripts*. See also more recently "Chapter 4: Manuscripts" in *Caedmon's Hymn: A Multimedia Edition:* https://caedmon.seenet.org/htm/introduction/ch4.html#CH4.

48 Dobbie, *Manuscripts*, 84–5.

49 On this manuscript see Robinson and Stanley, *Old English Verse Texts*, plate 2.11; *Bede's Ecclesiastical History*, lvi; Dobbie, *Manuscripts*, 38.

50 Dobbie, *Manuscripts*, 80.

51 On this manuscript see Cavill, "Manuscripts," 503–4; Robinson and Stanley, *Old English*, pl. 2.19; Dutschke, *Guide*, vol. 2, 705–7; *Bede's Ecclesiastical History*, lvii.

52 Trevisa, "Dialogue and Epistle," 133–4.

53 "Worschipful Bede in his first boke *De gestis Anglorum* [i.e., the *Historia ecclesiastica*] tellith that Seint Oswald, Kyng of Northehumberlond, axide of the Scottys a holi pischop, Aydan, to preche his puple, and the kynge of hymself interpreted it on Engliche to the puple." Wogan-Browne, Watson, Taylor, and Evan, *The Idea of the Vernacular*, 146–8, 147.

54 See for example Foot, "Reading"; Smith, *Land and Book*; Yeager, *From Lawmen*, 18–59.

55 Yeager, *From Lawmen*, 4–5.

56 I take the phrase "documentary poetics" from Steiner, *Documentary Culture*. For her reading of *The Charter of Christ* see 193–228. On *The Charter of the Abbey of the Holy Ghost* see Rice, "Spiritual Ambition"; Boffey, "The Charter"; Boening, "The Abbey."

57 Cervone, "John de Cobham."

58 This charter poem is S 451 and DIMEV 4183. Printed in Whitty, "Rhyming Charter"; see also Woodman, "The Forging." The medieval manuscripts of this text are London BL Cotton Charter IV 18 and Add MS 61901.

59 The Latin text translated by these lines reads: "Quoniam diuina scriptura multis in locis attestante liquet omnio cursum praesentis uitae in ualle lacrimarum constitutum fore, perspecta uolubili rota transeuntis mundi nulli cuiuslibet scientiae perspicati uigore pollenti hic inuestiganda est aut appetenda felicitas uer gaudii..."

60 Irvine and Godden, eds., *Old English Boethius*; Keynes and Lapidge, *Alfred*, 131–7.

61 On Chaucer and Boethius see Miller, *Philosophical Chaucer*.

62 Mann, 1016. Chaucer incorporates the same definition into *Boece*, book 2 prose 2 line 70: *Riverside*, 409–10.

63 *S&A*, II, 297–329.

Notes to pages 55–66   159

64 The word "transitory" also appears in *Boece*, 3.pr.8.37 (*Riverside*, 428).

65 On charter proems as literature see Smith, *Land and Book*, 36–50; Yeager, *From Lawmen*, 45–57.

66 Barrow, "The Chronology," 109; "William," 69.

67 *MED*, s.v. "Polyarke."

68 Hiatt, *The Making*, 60.

69 Lowe, "Bury St. Edmunds," 164. See also her fuller survey of the historical context in "Poetry of Privilege," 157–65.

70 Art. 10, "Contra privilegiorum abusiones": *Magnum oecumenicum Constantiense Concilium*, col. 1126–71.

3. The Text, the Gloss, and Fragment III

1 For the proverb in lines 835–6 see *Riverside*, 872; Mann, 898.

2 On tracing the bounds in Old English charters see Foot, "Reading," 50–1, and the discussion of the Old English poem *Christ and Satan* in chapter 4: 159, 162.

3 *MED*, s.v., "intromitten," def. 1.b.

4 Aston, "'Caim's Castles'"; Szittya, *Antifraternal Tradition*, 230.

5 Walling, "Friar Flatterer," citing Scattergood, *Politics*, 238–9; Clopper, *Songes*, 69–104; Mann, *Chaucer and Medieval Estates Satire*, 39. As Walling notes (58), "glossing" is such a persistent antifraternal motif in Wycliffite writing that Anne Hudson identifies it as a Wycliffite term: Hudson, "Lollard Sect Vocabulary," 170.

6 Mann, "Anger," 85–6. For a recent survey of medieval notions of anger see part 3 of Zeeman, *Arts of Disruption*.

7 In my reading of *ParsT*: 132–5, 137–8.

8 Guillory, "Genesis," 388.

9 Saltzman, "The Friar," 365.

10 Zeeman, *Arts of Disruption*.

11 Zeeman, *Arts of Disruption*, 136.

12 See also my earlier discussions in "Lollardy," 171–9, and *From Lawmen*, 190–2.

13 Patterson, *Chaucer and the Subject*, 289.

14 Dinshaw, *Sexual Poetics*, 113–31.

15 Patterson, *Chaucer and the Subject*, 283.

16 Kelly, *Charters of Bath*.

17 Walling, "Friar Flatterer," 62. See also Mann, "Anger," 81–2.

18 Saltzman, "The Friar," 368–70.

19 Robertson, *A Preface*, 331–2.

20 There is a long history of applying Augustinian reading practices to Chaucer, rooted primarily in the work of D.W. Robertson cited above. On Robertson and his influence see Justice, "Who Stole Robertson?"

160   Notes to pages 67–79

21 *Riverside*, 878; Mann, 916.
22 Mann, "Anger."
23 Leyerle, "Chaucer's Windy Eagle"; Mann, "Anger," 84. For a full discussion of media and the House of Fame see Nelson, "Ambient Media."
24 Hahn and Kaeuper, "Text and Context," 72–3.
25 Kline, "Myne by Right."
26 Weiskott, "Chaucer the Forester."
27 Mann, 907.
28 *Riverside*, 876; Mann, 906.
29 For a paraphrase of the debate and the key citations see Dubray, "Necromancy."
30 Mann, 918; *Riverside*, 879.
31 Somerset, "As Just," 207.
32 Finlayson, "Chaucer's Summoner's Tale"; Levitan, "Parody of the Pentecost."
33 Stafford, "The Laws," 179–80, 185–6; Jones, "The Significance."
34 For a depiction of St. Dunstan with his pincers see for example the marginal illustration in the early fifteenth-century *South English Legendaries* manuscript Oxford, Bodleian MS Tanner 17 f. 107v.
35 Dinshaw, *Sexual Poetics*, 113–31.
36 *AND*, s.v. "chose."
37 *MED*, s.v. "instrument."
38 A limitour is "[a] friar licensed to hear confession within a certain jurisdiction": Alford, *Piers Plowman*, 89. See also Williams, "Chaucer and the Friars."
39 Ingham, *Sovereign Fantasies*. See also Heng, *Empire of Magic*; Warren, *History on the Edge*.
40 Ullmann, "On the Influence."
41 Morris, "Edward I."
42 Some recent discussions (with helpful bibliographic summaries) of this redemption narrative include Turner, *Chaucer*, 422; Harris, "Rape Narratives," 263–4; Edwards, "Rhetoric of Rape"; Nakley, *Living in the Future*, 188–204; Vines, "Invisible Woman."
43 Nakley, *Living in the Future*, 199.
44 Mann, 900; *Riverside*, 873. On the incubus see Yamamoto, "Noon Oother." On fraternal promiscuity see also Mann, *Chaucer and Medieval Estates Satire*, 40–1.
45 Pugh, "'For to be Sworne.'" On the Wife and gossip see Lochrie, *Covert*, 56–92.
46 See introduction 13–14.
47 Lowe, *Intimacies*, 30.

4. Tragedy and the Law of Edward in *The Monk's Tale*

1 *Riverside*, 929; Mann, 1015–16.
2 Staley, *Languages*, 138.

Notes to pages 79–90   161

3 Camp, *Saints' Lives*, 133–72; Greenberg, "St. Edward's Ghost"; Legge, *Anglo-Norman Literature*, 60, 246–8.
4 In Anima's speech in B-version passus 15. See Steiner, *John Trevisa's Information Age*, 97–105.
5 O'Brien, *God's Peace*, 4–7, 105–30.
6 Dor, "Chaucer's Viragos," 172.
7 On Chaucer's time at Westminster see Turner, *Chaucer*, 486–505.
8 London, BL Add. 14848, ff. 251r.–255r.; Gransden, ed., *Chronicle*, xi–xiii; citing Cam, "The King's Government." See 44–51.
9 Cam, "The King's Government," 186, quoting her own translation from Cambridge, Cambridge University Library MS Ff.2.29, f. 65.
10 Dor, "Chaucer's Viragos"; see also Hamaguchi, "Transgressing"; Schibanoff, "Worlds Apart."
11 Nakley, *Living in the Future*, 214.
12 See 35–7 and 73–4.
13 Yeager, "Chaucer's Prudent Poetics." See also chapter 6: 126–9.
14 Zeeman, *Art of Disruption*. See 62–3.
15 Sharma, *Logic of Love*.
16 Discussed in chapter 2. Gransden, "Baldwin"; Lowe, "Bury St. Edmunds," 159–60.
17 *Riverside*, 930; Fradenburg, *Sacrifice Your Love*, 146–53; Wallace, *Chaucerian Polity*, 313.
18 Strohm, *Politique*, 88.
19 Patterson, *Chaucer and the Subject*, 242. See also Pauline Aiken's comparison of *MkT* to Vincent of Beauvais' *Speculum historiale*: "Vincent." On Chaucer and tragedy generally, key touchstones remain Herold, *Chaucer's Tragic*; Kelly, *Chaucerian Tragedy*; Boitani, *The Tragic and the Sublime*; Haas, "Chaucer's 'Monk's Tale'"; Robertson, "Chaucerian Tragedy."
20 Fradenburg, *Sacrifice Your Love*, 131.
21 Gerber, "'As olde bookes,'" 173.
22 Pope, "Critical Background," 35.
23 For my detailed reading of this passage see Yeager, "Chaucer's Prudent Poetics," 315–17.
24 Wallace, *Chaucerian Polity*, 308–10.
25 Mann, 805–6; *Riverside*, 806; Mann, *Chaucer and Medieval Estates Satire*, 34.
26 Berndt, "Monastic 'Acedia.'"
27 Fradenburg, *Sacrifice Your Love*, 151.
28 Falk, *Bright Ages*, 43.
29 *Riverside*, 929; Mann, 898, 1015.
30 Owst, *Preaching*, 270–9.
31 For an edition and commentary see Oliver, *Beginnings*.

162 Notes to pages 90–7

32 Maidstone, Kent Archives Office, DRb/Ar2 (14th c.); Rochester, Dioc. Reg., Episcopal Register 1 (14th c.): Keynes et al., *The Electronic Sawyer*.
33 Tyler, "The *Vita Ædwardi*"; Barlow, *The Life of King Edward*. On the historical circumstances of this text see Stafford, *Queen Emma*; Otter, "Closed Doors." On his canonization see Bozoky, "The Sanctity and Canonization."
34 Brooke and Kier, *London*, 293–8. See also Kyly Walker, "Westminster."
35 Bozoky, "The Sanctity and Canonization," 175–8.
36 Brooke and Kier, *London*, 295; Crick, "St. Albans."
37 Edward is also the apparent inventor of the Old English writ. On this format see Harmer, *Writs*.
38 Harmer, *Writs*, 307–8, 495; Brooke and Keir, *London*, 193, 369, 371; Gelling, *Early Charters*, no. 237.
39 Davis, *Medieval Cartularies*, 205.
40 O'Brien, *God's Peace*, 4.
41 On the Constitutions see O'Brien, *God's Peace*, 116–17; on Andrew Horn see 122.
42 On the law codes see O'Brien, *God's Peace*. Almost one in ten of the charters with Sawyer numbers (167 out of 1875) are attributed to Edward, and many of these are blatant forgeries: Keynes et al., *Electronic Sawyer*.
43 *S&A*, I, 414. The Monk's other sources include Petrarch (named at line VII.2325) and Dante (at line VII.2461): *Riverside*, 932–3; Mann, 1025, 1030–1.
44 See most recently Grimes, "Knowing Fortune."
45 Wenzel, "Why the Monk?" For compatible readings see also Claude Jones, "The Monk's Tale."
46 Grimes, "Knowing Fortune."
47 Described by Little, *Benedictine Maledictions*, 57. On the historical context of S 445 see Thacker, "Æthelwold," 45–6. For an exhaustive treatment of the subject of Satan in sanction clauses see Hoffmann, "Infernal Imagery."
48 Clayton, "Christ and Satan."
49 Harsh, "Christ and Satan"; Hill, "Measure."
50 Fitzgerald, "Rebel Angels," 244–55.
51 Harmer, *Select*, no. 14 (24–5, 56–7); Wormald, "Handlist," no. 21.
52 Miller, *Charters of the New Minster*, 105–11. Some of the differences between *Genesis A* and *B* and *Christ and Satan* are listed by Anzelark, "The Fall," 124–5.
53 On the Knight's interruption see Gaston, *Reading Chaucer*, 164–5; Terry Jones, "The Monk's Tale"; Knight, "Colloquium."
54 Lindeboom, "Chaucer's Monk Illuminated."
55 Nakley, *Living in the Future*, 225–8
56 Nakley, *Living in the Future*, 228.

Notes to pages 97–103   163

57 For a detailed discussion see McCluskey, "Black on the Outside." Heloise is directly referenced by Chaucer in *WBP*: III. 677–8.
58 Attested also for example in *Handlying Synne*, as is discussed by Whitaker, *Black Metaphors*, 101–2.
59 Dor, "Chaucer's Viragos," 169–72; Hamaguchi, "Transgressing," 189–90.
60 Baxter, "Edward the Confessor," 103–4.
61 Bozoky, "The Sanctity and Canonization," 175.
62 Hamaguchi, "Transgressing," 198; see also Dor, "Chaucer's Viragos," 169.
63 Hamaguchi, "Transgressing," 198.
64 Dor, "Chaucer's Viragos," 171.

5. Chronicles and Customary Law: Chaucer's Tale of Custaunce

1 Johnson, "English Law," 507. See above 38–40.
2 On the Man of Law's narration see Spearing, *Textual Subjectivity*, 101–23.
3 For a recent summary of this critical conversation see Stavsky, "Translating the Near East," 33–4. The post-colonial turn in the criticism of *MLT* is typically traced back to Schibanoff, "Worlds Apart."
4 Lavezzo, "Beyond Rome."
5 Nakley, "Anachronism," 371; see also *Living in the Future*, 151–79.
6 Nakley, "Anachronism," 396.
7 Wallace, *La Estoire*.
8 My account relies on the text and commentary in Swanton, *Lives*. On this text, its author, and the legend it records see also Martin, "The Lives"; Matthews, "Legends of Offa" and "Good King Offa," 9–12; Rickert, "Old English Offa"; Reader, "Matthew Paris," 184–272; Weiler, "Monastic Historical Culture"; Crick, "Offa."
9 Catto, "Andrew Horn."
10 Bahr, *Fragments*, 51.
11 Bahr, *Fragments*, 20.
12 Ker, "Liber Custumarum." These translations are called *Quadripartitus* and *Leges Henrici Primi* by modern editors.
13 Wormald, *Making of English Law*, 237–9. These include the so-called Laws of Edward the Confessor: O'Brien, *God's Peace*, 122.
14 Hanna, *London Literature*, 20.
15 Gransden, *Historical Writing*, 356–79, 508–17. Not to be confused with the *Flores historiarum* by the St. Albans historian Roger of Wendover, which was one of Matthew's sources. On manuscript production in late medieval St. Albans see Doyle, "Book Production," 3–4; Clark, *A Monastic Renaissance*.
16 Black, *Medieval Narratives*, 111.
17 *S&A* II, 280; Schlauch, *Chaucer's Constance*; Black, *Medieval Narratives*, 109–37.

164   Notes to pages 103–8

18 Krappe, "Offa-Constance." The parallel passages in *Beowulf, Widsith*, and elsewhere are presented as appendices of Swanton's edition, *The Lives*: 133–84.
19 Strohm, *Hochon's Arrow*, 4–5.
20 Lloyd, *English Wool Trade*, 1. On Chaucer's time as controller see Crow and Olson, *Life-Records*, 148–270.
21 Swanton, *Lives*, xxi–xxvi.
22 Fulk, Bjork, and Niles, *Klaeber's Beowulf*, 222–6.
23 The manuscripts of this poem are Edinburgh, National Library MS Advocates 19.2.1 (Auchinleck); Oxford Bodleian 3938 (Vernon), and London BL Additional 22283 (Simeon). On the connection to *King of Tars* see Lampert-Weissig, *Medieval*, 76–80; Calkin, *Saracens*, 97–132; Gilbert, "Unnatural Mothers"; Akbari, "Orientation," 118–21; Lynch, "Storytelling." On the problem with the uses of the term "Saracens" in this critical tradition see Rajabzadeh, "Depoliticized Saracen."
24 Quotations are from the Auchinleck text transcribed at the National Library of Scotland's Auchinleck website: http://auchinleck.nls.uk/mss /tars.html, accessed 2 April 2015.
25 Lamuto, "Mongol Princess," 187; see also Whitaker, *Black Metaphors*, 20–47.
26 *Dictionary of Medieval Latin from British Sources*, s.v. "Offa."
27 Rickert, "Offa Saga I," 75. For surveys of the scholarship on the "inglorious youth" of Beowulf see Fulk, Bjork, and Niles, *Klaeber's Beowulf*, 236.
28 Wermund's African origins are first recorded in a passage from Geoffrey of Monmouth's *Historia regum Britanniae* (Wright, ed., ch. 184, 133; Thorpe, trans., xi.8, 263), and his exploits are expanded upon by both Wace's *Roman de Brut* (ll.13385–420) and Laȝamon's *Brut* (ll.14414–62).
29 The latter of which is emphasized in Laȝamon's *Brut*, e.g., at line 14440: "Gurmunde, þan hæðene þrunge."
30 On Offa's Dyke see most recently Tyler, "Offa's Dyke."
31 Frankis, "King Ælle." On Chaucer's relation to Gower see also Nicholson, "The Man of Law's Tale." On Northumbria as a setting see Turner, *Chaucer*, 429–31.
32 Frankis, "King Ælle," 80–1. On Trevet's "De la noble femme Constance" as a conversion narrative see Spense, *Reimagining History*, 98–103; Wynn, "The Conversion."
33 Bately, *Anglo-Saxon Chronicle*.
34 Hsy, *Trading Tongues*, 68.
35 Wallace, *Chaucerian Polity*, 182–211, esp. 196–201; see also Kolve, *Chaucer and Imagery*, 297–358; Hsy, *Trading Tongues*, 65–79.
36 Stock, "Letter, Word." See also Brylowe and Yeager, "Introduction."
37 On these apostrophes in *MLT* see Astell, "Apostrophe"; Bloomfield, "The Man of Law's Tale."

Notes to pages 109–18   165

38 On this passage see Lim, "Counterfeit Correspondences."
39 All citations of Trevet's "De la noble femme Constance" and of Gower's *Confessio amantis* are taken from *S&A* II, 277–50.
40 For example, *Bede's Ecclesiastical History* I.23–4.
41 For an alternative reading of the Summoner's portrait see Phillips, "Language Lessons."
42 *DMF*, s.v. "Latin," adj. and n.
43 *OED*, s.v. "jargon," n.1. The word appears to be unattested in the Chaucerian corpus.
44 Mann, *Chaucer and Medieval Estates Satire*, 143.
45 Treharne, *Living*, 147–52, at 151. See also Thomas, *The English and the Normans*, 297–306; Machan, "Language and Society."
46 *Riverside*, 861, Mann, 872; Johnston, "The Exigencies"; Hamaguchi, "Cultural Otherness," 418–20; Hsy, *Trading Tongues*, 71–2.
47 Burrow, "A Manere Latyn."
48 On *lingua franca* see Rothwell, "Trilingual England," 54; Nakley, *Living in the Future*, 175–7; Rajendran, "Undoing," 8. On xenoglossia see Cooper, "But Algates."
49 Frankis, "King Ælle," 89.
50 *MED*, s.v. "corrupt," def. 4a: "To contaminate or corrupt (sb., the soul, etc.) morally or spiritually"; def. 6: "To pervert the meaning of (a text); corrupt (an expression)."
51 Stenton, *Latin Charters*, 53. On the so-called "hermeneutic" style of pre-Conquest Anglo-Latin see most recently Stephenson, *Politics of Language*.
52 For example, in the proem to the charter S 1166: Yeager, *From Lawmen*, 45–59.
53 See the discussion in chapter 1: 35–7.
54 Kolve, *Chaucer and the Imagery*, 300.
55 On Custaunce's ship as an archive see also Novacich, *Shaping the Archive*, 52–85.
56 The earliest mention of the Danegeld appears in Downer, *Leges Henrici Primi*, 15.1, 120–1. See also Green, "Last Century," 242; Lawson, "Collection of Danegeld."
57 *S&A*, II, 285.
58 It is noteworthy that in his *Mirror for Justices*, Andrew Horn refers to King Alfred's *witan* as a "parliament": Horn, *Mirror*, 8. On the early English *witan* see Roach, *Kingship and Consent*; Maddicott, *Origins*, 25–31.
59 On the significance of this oath to the Sultaness' characterization see Sottosanti, "We shul firste."
60 *Riverside*, 861; Mann, 872–3; Hamaguchi, "Cultural Otherness," 424–7; Nelson, "Premodern Media," 218–19; Lynch, "Diversiteee"; Dugas "Legitimization."

166   Notes to pages 118–25

61 Bartlett, *Why Can the Dead*, 401–9; Firth, "Broken Body," 72–4.
62 There is a large bibliography analyzing the many references to Custaunce's pale face; see for example Stavsky, "Translating," n. 63; Hamaguchi, "Cultural Otherness," 425; Erwin, "Why We Can't," 57–8; Robertson, "Nonviolent Christianity," 335; Dinshaw, "Pale Faces"; Kolve, *Chaucer and the Imagery*, 304.

6. The Problem of Prose and the Prose *Canterbury Tales*: *Melibee* and the Parson

1 Benson, "The Order," 94–5.
2 Partridge, "The Makere."
3 Wallace, *Chaucerian Polity*, 221–3.
4 Readings of *Mel* to this effect include Taylor, "Chaucer's *Tale of Melibee*"; Spencer, "Dialogue"; Staley, "Inverse Counsel"; Blamires, *Chaucer, Ethics*; Walling, "'In Her Tellynge Difference'"; Pakkala-Weckstrom, "Prudence"; Moore, "Apply Yourself"; Ferster, *Fictions*, 89–107; Collette, "Heeding"; Flynn, "Art of Telling"; Green, *Poets and Princepleasers*.
5 On the colophon genre see also Gameson, *The Scribe Speaks?* On the Retraction and Chaucer's authorship see also Minnis, *Medieval Theory*, 208–10; Cook, "Here Taketh."
6 Sharma, *Logic of Love*, 259–64.
7 Cooper, *Structure*, 123; Nolan, "Acquiteth," 139–44.
8 Though my discussion here will use "Lollard" as a synonym for Wycliffite, it does so on the basis of the Parson's expression of Wycliffite views, and not because I consider the terms to be interchangeable. See Cole, *Literature and Heresy*, 1–74; Somerset, "Wycliffite Spirituality"; Hudson, *Premature Reformation*.
9 On the history of Westminster see Carpenter, *House of Kings*.
10 On sexual violence in *Thopas* see Bovaird-Abbo, "Is Geoffrey Chaucer's *Tale*"; Weisl, "'Quiting' Eve," 123. On Mercantile fantasies of wealth see Scattergood, "Chaucer and the French War," 293; Burrow, "Chaucer's 'Sir Thopas.'" See also David Raybin's argument that the tale is children's literature: "*Sir Thopas*."
11 Stanley, "The Use of Bob-Lines."
12 Brantley, "Reading the Forms"; Cannon, "Chaucer and the Auchinleck."
13 *Riverside*, 923; Mann, 999.
14 Roach, *Le Roman de Perceval*; Cline, *Perceval*. One example of this story's continued influence as a formal model for commercial fiction is Michael Moorcock's famous advise to aspiring genre authors, that they should base their plot outlines on Dashiell Hammet's 1930 "grail" novel *The Maltese Falcon*: Moorcock and Greenland, *Death*, 3.

Notes to pages 125–41 167

15 Burrow, "*Sir Thopas.*"
16 Brantley, "Reading the Forms."
17 Jones, "'Lo, Lordes Myne.'"
18 Anderson, "'A Gentle Knight.'"
19 This reading of Mel proceeds from my article "Chaucer's Prudent Poetics."
20 Grace, "Chaucer's Little Treatises."
21 Foster, "Echoes."
22 *MED*, s.v. "Prudence," def. 4. On Prudence's gendered characterization see Jamie Taylor, "Chaucer's *Tale of Melibee*," 89–91; Crocker, *Chaucer's Visions*, 17–49; Blamires, *Chaucer, Ethics*, 66–7, 237; Walling, "'In Her Tellynge Difference'"; Collette, "Heeding"; Celia R. Daileader, "The Thopas-Melibee Sequence."
23 Burrow, "Third Eye."
24 *Riverside*, 1052.
25 *Riverside*, 885.
26 Yeager, "Chaucer's Prudent Poetics," 313.
27 Kerby-Fulton, "Introduction," 6–9. *Piers Plowman* survived in over 50 manuscripts.
28 On glosing and the Parson see Knapp, "The Words," 99–104.
29 Mann, "Anger," 95–101.
30 On the sexual violence of Chaucer's "japes" see Harris, *Obscene Pedagogies*, 31–55.
31 Ferster, "Chaucer's Parson," 137.
32 Zeeman, *Art of Disruption*, 187–242.
33 Zeeman, *Art of Disruption*, 188.
34 Scase, "Threshold Switching," 107.
35 Wenzel, "The Parson's Tale," 6–10.
36 Mann, *Chaucer and Medieval Estates Satire*, 55–67.
37 Bose, "Opponents." See also Clopper, "Franciscans, Lollards."
38 Barrow, "Ideology."
39 Lahey, *Philosophy and Politics*, 4; Jurkowski, "Lawyers and Lollardy."
40 *MED*, s.v. "phislias," n.
41 Larson, *Master of Penance*.
42 Thomas, *Piers Plowman and the Reinvention*.
43 Bowers, *Chaucer and Langland*.
44 *S&A* I, 531.

Conclusion

1 *The Logic of Love in The Canterbury Tales*. Thanks again to Manish for letting me read a pre-print version of this manuscript, whose influence on the present study bears repeating.

168   Notes to pages 142–6

2 Gaylord, "*Sentence* and *Solaas.*"

3 *OED*, s.v. "reeve," n.

4 On complaints about reeves see Bisson, *Crisis*, 177–8; O'Brien, *God's Peace, King's Peace*, 102; Mann, *Chaucer and Medieval Estates Satire*, 163–7.

5 Shields-Más, "The Reeve," 217–65.

6 Shields-Más, "The Reeve," 245, citing Scragg, *Vercelli Homilies*, 24.

7 Shields-Más, "The Reeve," 273–8.

8 Tinti, *Sustaining Belief*, 139.

9 Tolkien, "Chaucer the Philologist." On the Northern dialect of the Reeve's students, see also Horobin, "J.R.R. Tolkien"; Taylor, "Chaucer's Uncanny"; Epstein, "'Fer in the North.'"

10 Mann, *Chaucer and Medieval Estates Satire*, 166.

11 Pulsiano, "Danish Men's Words."

12 Mann, *Chaucer and Medieval Estates Satire*, 284 n. 70.

13 Ellis, "Chaucer's Devilish."

14 Blamires, "Chaucer the Reactionary," 532.

15 Plummer, "'Hooly Chirches Bloode.'"

16 Heffernan, "A Reconsideration," 41–2.

17 On his age see Smith, "Chaucer's Reeve"; Harley, "The Reeve's 'Foure Gleedes'"; Everest, "Sex and Old Age."

18 On rape in *RvT* see Harris, *Obscene Pedagogies*, 26–66.

Bibliography

Primary Texts

Arnold, Thomas, ed. *Memorials of St. Edmund's Abbey*. 3 vols. London: Rolls Series, 1890–6.

Barlow, Frank, ed. *The Life of King Edward Who Rests at Westminster*. Oxford: Clarendon Press, 1992.

Bede. *Bede's Ecclesiastical History of the English People*. Edited by Bertran Colgrave and R.A.B. Mynors. Oxford: Clarendon Press, 1969.

Byrhtferth of Ramsey. *The Lives of St. Oswald and St. Ecgwine*. Edited by Michael Lapidge. Clarendon Press: Oxford, 2009.

Caedmon. *Cædmon's Hymn: A Multimedia Study, Edition and Archive*. Edited by Daniel Paul O'Donnell. Cambridge: D.S. Brewer, 2005. Version 1.1 Internet Reprint, Vol. A.8. SEENET, 2018. http://caedmon.seenet.org/index.html.

Clayton, Mary, ed. and trans. "Christ and Satan." In *Old English Poems of Christ and His Saints*, 301–51. Cambridge, MA: Harvard University Press, 2013.

Cline, Ruth Harwood. *Perceval or The Story of the Grail*. Athens: University of Georgia Press, 1985.

Crow, Martin, and Clair Olson, eds. *Chaucer Life-Records*. Oxford: Clarendon Press, 1966.

Downer, L.J., ed. *Leges Henrici Primi*. Oxford: Oxford University Press, 1972.

Dryden, John. *Of Dramatic Poesy and Other Critical Essays in Two Volumes*. Edited by George Watson. London: J.M. Dent, 1962.

Fulk, R.D., Robert E. Bjork, and John D. Niles, eds. *Klaeber's Beowulf: Fourth Edition*. Toronto: University of Toronto Press, 2008.

Gelling, Margaret. *Early Charters of the Thames Valley*. London and New York: Leicester University Press, 1979.

Geoffrey of Monmouth. *The History of the Kings of Britain*. Translated by Lewis Thorpe. New York: Penguin Classics, 1966.

170   Bibliography

– *Historia Regum Britannie of Geoffrey of Monmouth: I. Bern, Burgerbibliothek, MS 568*. Edited by Neil Wright. Cambridge: D.S. Brewer, 1984.

Gransden, Antonia, ed. *Chronicle of Bury St. Edmunds, 1212–1301*. Walton-on-Thames: Thomas Nelson & Sons, 1964.

Harmer, Florence, ed. *Select English Historical Documents of the Ninth and Tenth Centuries*. Cambridge: Cambridge University Press, 1914.

– ed. *Anglo-Saxon Writs*. 2nd ed. Stamford: Watkins, 1989.

Horn, Andrew. *Mirror of Justices*. Edited by W.J. Whittaker. Selden Society 7 (1895).

Irvine, Susan, and Malcolm Godden, eds. and trans. *The Old English Boethius*. Cambridge, MA: Harvard University Press, 2012.

Jocelin of Brakelond. *The Chronicle of Jocelin of Brakelond*. Edited by H.E. Butler. London and Edinburgh: Nelson, 1949.

Kelly, Susan, ed. *Charters of Bath and Wells*. Oxford: Oxford University Press, 2008.

Keynes, Simon, ed. *Facsimiles of Anglo-Saxon Charters*. Oxford: Oxford University Press, 1991.

Keynes, Simon, and Michael Lapidge. *Alfred the Great: Asser's Life of Alfred and Other Contemporary Sources*. New York: Penguin, 1983.

Laȝamon. *Brut*. Edited by G.L. Brook and R.F. Leslie. 2 vols. EETS 277. London: Oxford University Press, 1978.

Lydgate, John. *John Lydgate's Lives of Ss Edmund & Fremund and the Extra Miracles of St Edmund*. Edited by Anthony Bale and A.S.G. Edwards. Heidelberg: Universitätsverlag Winter Heidelberg, 2009.

Macray, W.D., ed. *Chronicon Abbatiae Ramesiensis*. London: Rolls Series 83, 1886.

Miller, Sean. *Charters of the New Minster, Winchester*. Oxford: Oxford University Press, 2001.

Moorcock, Michael, and Colin Greenland. *Death Is No Obstacle*. Manchester, UK: Savoy, 1992.

Petrarch, Francesco. *Rerum Familiarum*. Edited by Ugo Dotti. Paris, Archivio Guido Izzi, 2002.

Roach, William, ed. *Le roman de Perceval ou le conte du Graal: Publié d'après le ms. fr. 12576 de la Bibliothèque Nationale*. Geneva: Librarie Droz, 1959.

Robinson, Fred C., and E.G. Stanley, eds. *Old English Verse Texts from Many Sources: A Comprehensive Collection*. Copenhagen: Rosenkilde and Bagger, 1991.

Scragg, Donald G., ed. *The Vercelli Homilies and Related Texts*. EETS, Original Series 300. Oxford: Oxford University Press, 1992.

Swanton, Michael, ed. and trans. *The Lives of Two Offas*. Devon: The Medieval Press, 2010.

Thomas of Marlborough. *History of the Abbey of Evesham*. Edited and translated by Jane Sayers and Leslie Watkiss. Oxford: Clarendon Press, 2003.

Trevisa, John. "Dialogue and Epistle." In *The Idea of the Vernacular: An Anthology of Middle English Literary Theory, 1280–1520*, edited by Jocelyn Wogan-Browne, Nicholas Watson, Andrew Taylor, and Ruth Evans, 130–8. Exeter: University of Exeter Press, 1999.

von der Hardt, Hermann, ed. *Magnum oecumenicum Constantiense Concilium de universali ecclesiae reformation unione et fide*. Volume 1. Frankfurt and Leipzig, 1696.

Wace. *Wace's Roman de Brut: A History of the British*. Edited by Judith Weiss. Exeter: University of Exeter Press, 1999.

Wallace, Kathryn Young, ed. *La Estoire de Seint Aedward le Rei Attributed to Matthew Paris*. London: Anglo-Norman Text Society, 1983.

Secondary Texts

Abel, Kerry Margaret. *Drum Songs: Glimpses of Dene History*. Montreal-Kingston: McGill-Queen's University Press, 2005.

Abels, Richard. "Bookland and Fyrd Service in Late Saxon England." In *Warfare in the Dark Ages*, edited by Kelly DeVries and John France, 347–71. New York: Routledge, 2008.

Aiken, Pauline. "Vincent of Beauvais and Chaucer's Monk's Tale." *Speculum* 17, no. 1 (1942): 56–68.

Akbari, Suzanne Conklin. "Orientation and Nation in Chaucer's Canterbury Tales." In *Chaucer's Cultural Geography*, edited by Kathryn L. Lynch, 102–34. New York: Routledge, 2002.

– *Idols in the East: European Representations of Islam and the Orient, 1100–1450*. Ithaca: Cornell University Press, 2009.

Alford, John. *Piers Plowman: A Glossary of Legal Diction*. Cambridge: D.S. Brewer, 1988.

Anderson, Judith H. "'A Gentle Knight Was Pricking on the Plaine:' The Chaucerian Connection." *English Literary Renaissance* 15, no. 2 (1985): 166–74.

Andrews, Tarren. "Indigenous Futures, Medieval Pasts." *English Language Notes* 58, no. 2 (2020): 1–20.

Anzelark, Daniel. "The Fall of the Angels in Solomon and Saturn II." In *Apocryphal Texts and Traditions in Anglo-Saxon England*, edited by Kathryn Powell and Donald Scragg, 121–33. Cambridge: Cambridge University Press, 2003.

Archibald, Elizabeth. "The Flight from Incest: Two Late Classical Precursors of the Constance Theme." *ChauR* 20 no.4 (1986): 259–72.

Ashton, Gail. "Her Father's Daughter: The Realignment of Father-Daughter Kinship in Three Romance Tales," *ChauR* 34.4 (2000): 416–27.

Askins, William. "*The Tale of Melibee* and the Crisis at Westminster, November, 1387." *SAC* 2 (1986): 103–12.

172   Bibliography

Astell, Anne W. "Apostrophe, Prayer, and the Structure of the *Man of Law's Tale.*" *SAC* 13 (1991): 81–97.

Aston, Margaret. "'Caim's Castles': Poverty, Politics, and Disendowment." In *Faith and Fire: Popular and Unpopular Religion, 1350–1600.* London: Humbledon, 1993.

Aston, T.H., and C.H.E. Philpin, eds. *The Brenner Debate.* Cambridge: Cambridge University Press, 1985.

Baechle, Sarah. "Speaking Survival: Chaucer Studies and the Discourses of Sexual Assault." *ChauR* 57, no. 4 (2022): 463–74.

Bahr, Arthur. *Fragments and Assemblages: Forming Compilations of Medieval London.* Chicago: University of Chicago Press, 2013.

Bailey, Mark. "Injustice and Revolt." In *After the Black Death: Economy, Society, and the Law in Fourteenth-Century England,* 186–233. Oxford: Oxford University Press, 2021.

Barker, Juliet. *1381: The Year of the Peasant's Revolt.* Harvard: Harvard University Press, 2014.

Barrow, Julia. "The Chronology of Forgery Production at Worcester from c. 1000 to the Early Twelfth Century." In *St. Wulfstan and His World,* edited by Julia Barrow and N.P. Brooks, 105–22. Aldershot: Ashgate, 2005.

– "William of Malmesbury's Use of Charters." In *Narrative and History in the Early Medieval West,* edited by Elizabeth M. Tyler and Ross Balzaretti, 67–89. Turnhout: Brepols, 2006.

– "The Ideology of the Tenth-Century English Benedictine 'Reform.'" In *Texts, Histories, Historiographies: The Medieval Worlds of Timothy Reuter,* edited by P. Skinner, 141–54. Turnhout: Brepols, 2010.

Bartlett, Robert. *Why Can the Dead Do Such Great Things? Saints and Worshippers from the Martyrs to the Reformation.* Princeton: Princeton University Press, 2013.

Bately, Janet. *The Anglo-Saxon Chronicle: Texts and Textual Relationships.* Reading: University of Reading, 1991.

Baxter, Stephen. "The Representation of Lordship and Land Tenure in Domesday Book." In *Domesday Book,* edited by Elizabeth Hallam and David Bates, 73–102. Gloucester: Tempus Publishing, 2001.

– *Earls of Mercia: Lordship and Power in Late Anglo-Saxon England.* Oxford: Oxford University Press, 2007.

– "Edward the Confessor and the Succession Question." In *Edward the Confessor: The Man and Legend,* edited by Richard Mortimer, 173–89. Woodbridge: Boydell Press, 2009.

– "Lordship and Justice in Late Anglo-Saxon England: The Judicial Function of Soke and Commendation Revisited." In *Early Medieval Studies in Memory of Patrick Wormald,* edited by Stephen Baxter, Catherine Karkov, Janet L. Nelson, and David Pelteret, 403–9. Farnham: Ashgate, 2009.

Bibliography   173

– "Lordship and Labour." In *A Social History of England 900–1200*, edited by Julia Crick and Elisabeth Van Houts, 98–114. Cambridge: Cambridge University Press, 2011.

Beckerman, John S. "Procedural Innovation and Institutional Change in Medieval English Manorial Courts." *Law and History Review* 10, no. 2 (1992): 197–252.

Benson, Larry D. "The Order of the Canterbury Tales." *Studies in the Age of Chaucer* 3 (1981): 77–120.

Berndt, David E. "Monastic 'Acedia' and Chaucer's Characterization of Daun Piers." *Studies in Philology* 68 (1971): 435–50.

Bischoff, Bernhard. *Latin Palaeography: Antiquity and the Middle Ages*, translated by Dáibhí Ó Cróinín and David Ganz. Cambridge: Cambridge University Press, 1990.

Bisson, Thomas N. *The Crisis of the Twelfth Century: Power, Lordship, and the Origins of European Government*. Princeton: Princeton University Press, 2009.

Bjorklund, Nancy Basler. "Parker's Purpose for His Manuscripts: Matthew Parker in the Context of His Early Career and Sixteenth-Century Church Reform." In *Old English Literature in Its Manuscript Context*, edited by Joyce Tally Lionarons, 217–41. Morgantown: West Virginia University Press, 2004.

Black, Nancy B. *Medieval Narratives of Accused Queens*. Gainesville: University Press of Florida, 2003.

Blake, Norman. "On Editing *The Canterbury Tales*." In *Medieval Studies for J.A.W. Bennett Aetatis Suae LXX*, edited by P.H. Heyworth, 101–19. Oxford: Oxford University Press, 1981.

Blamires, Alcuin. "Chaucer the Reactionary: Ideology and the *General Prologue* to the *Canterbury Tales*." *RES* 51.204 (2000): 523–39.

– *Chaucer, Ethics, and Gender*. Oxford: Oxford University Press, 2006.

Bloomfield, Morton W. "The Man of Law's Tale: A Tragedy of Victimization and a Christian Comedy." *PMLA* 87, no. 3 (1972): 384–90. https://doi.org/10.2307/460896.

Boenig, Robert E. "The Abbey of the Holy Ghost and the Charter of the Abbey of the Holy Ghost." *Studia Mystica* 1 (1995): 133–63.

Boffey, Julia. "The Charter of the Abbey of the Holy Ghost and Its Role in Manuscript Anthologies." *Yearbook of English Studies* 33 (2003): 120–30.

Boitani, Piero. *The Tragic and the Sublime in Medieval Literature*. Cambridge: Cambridge University Press, 1989.

Bose, Mishtooni. "The Opponents of John Wyclif." In *A Companion to John Wyclif*, edited by Ian Levy, 407–55. Leiden and Boston: Brill, 2006.

Boureau, Alain. "How Law Came to The Monks: The Use of Law in English Society at the Beginning of the Thirteenth Century." *Past and Present* 167 (2000): 29–74.

174 Bibliography

Bovaird-Abbo, Kristin. "Is Geoffrey Chaucer's *Tale of Sir Thopas* a Rape Narrative? Reading Thopas in Light of the 1382 Statutes of Rape." *Quidditas* 35 (2014): 7–28.

Bowers, John M. *Chaucer and Langland: The Antagonistic Tradition*. Notre Dame: Notre Dame University Press, 2007.

Bozoky, Edina. "The Sanctity and Canonization of Edward the Confessor." In *Edward the Confessor: The Man and Legend*, edited by Richard Mortimer, 173–89. Woodbridge: Boydell Press, 2009.

Brantley, Jessica. "Reading the Forms of *Sir Thopas*." *ChauR* 47, no. 4 (2013): 416–38.

Brooke, Christopher N., and Gillian Kier. *London 800–1216: The Shaping of a City*. London: Secker & Warburg, 1975.

Brooks, Nicholas, and Catherine Cubitt, eds. *St. Oswald of Worcester: Life and Influence*. Leicester: Leicester University Press, 1996.

Brylowe, Thora, and Stephen M. Yeager. "Introduction: The Medieval / Media Concept." In *Old Media and the Medieval Concept*, edited by Thora Brylowe and Stephen M. Yeager, 3–27. Montreal: Concordia University Press, 2021.

Burrow, John A. "A Maner Latyn Corrupt." *Medium Ævum* 30 (1961): 33–7.

– "*Sir Thopas*: An Agony in Three Fits." *RES* 22, no. 85 (1971): 54–8.

– "Chaucer's 'Sir Thopas' and 'La Prise de Neuvile.'" *Yearbook of English Studies* 14 (1984): 44–55.

– "The Third Eye of Prudence." In *Medieval Futures: Attitudes to the Future in the Middle Ages*, edited by J.A. Burrow and Ian P. Wei, 37–48. Woodbridge: Boydell Press, 2000.

Butler, Emily. "Recollecting Alfredian English in the Sixteenth Century." *Neophilologus* 98, no. 1 (2014): 145–59.

Butterfield, Ardis. *The Familiar Enemy: Chaucer, Language, and Nation in the Hundred Years War*. Oxford: Oxford University Press, 2009.

Caie, Graham. "Innocent III's *De Miseria* as a Gloss on the Man of Law's Prologue and Tale." *Neuphilologische Mitteilungen* 100 (1999): 175–85.

Calkin, Siobhain. *Saracens and the Making of English Identity: The Auchinleck Manuscript*. New York: Routledge, 2009.

Cam, Helen. "The King's Government as Administered by the Greater Abbots of East Anglia." In *Liberties and Communities in Medieval England: Collected Studies in Local Administration and Topography*, 183–205. Cambridge: Cambridge University Press, 1944.

Cameron, Angus, Ashley Crandell Amos, Antonette diPaolo Healey, Roy Liuzza, and Haruko Momma, eds. *Dictionary of Old English: A to I Online*. Toronto: Dictionary of Old English Project, 2018.

Camp, Cynthia Turner. *Anglo-Saxon Saints' Lives as History Writing in Late Medieval England*. Cambridge: Cambridge University Press, 2015.

Bibliography 175

Cannon, Christopher. "Raptus in the Chaumpaigne Release and a Newly Discovered Document Concerning the Life of Geoffrey Chaucer." *Speculum* 68 (1993): 74–94.

– *The Making of Chaucer's English: A Study of Words*. Cambridge: Cambridge University Press, 1998.

– "Chaucer and the Auchinleck Manuscript Revisited." *The ChauR* 46, no. 1 (2011): 131–46.

Carpenter, Edward. *House of Kings: The Official History of Westminster Abbey*. London: Westminster Abbey Bookshop, 1972.

Catto, Jeremy. "Andrew Horn: Law and History in Fourteenth-Century England." In *Writing History in the Middle Ages: Essays Presented to Richard William Southern*, edited by R.H.C. Davis and J.M. Wallace-Hadrill, 367–91. Oxford: Clarendon Press, 1981.

Cavill, Paul. "The Manuscripts of Cædmon's Hymn." *Anglia* 118 (2007): 499–530.

Cervone, C.M. "John de Cobham and Cooling Castle's Charter Poem." *Speculum* 83, no. 4 (2008): 884–916.

Chaytor, H.J. *From Script to Print: An Introduction to Medieval Literature*. Cambridge: Cambridge University Press, 1945.

Clanchy, Michael. *From Memory to Written Record*, 3rd ed. Oxford: Wiley Blackwell, 2012.

Clark, James G. *A Monastic Renaissance at St. Albans: Thomas Walsingham and His Circle, 1350–1440*. New York: Oxford University Press, 2004.

Clegg, Nancy W., and Reed Clyde. "The Economic Decline of the Church in Medieval England." *Explorations in Economic History* 31, no. 2 (1994): 261–80.

Clopper, Lawrence M. *Songes of Rechelesnesse: Langland and the Franciscans*. Ann Arbor MI: University of Michigan Press, 1997.

– "Franciscans, Lollards, and Reform." In *Lollards and Their Influence in Late Medieval England*, edited by Fiona Somerset, Jill Havens, and Derek Pitard, 177–96. Woodbridge: Boydell, 2003.

Cole, Andrew. *Literature and Heresy in the Age of Chaucer*. Cambridge: Cambridge University Press, 2008.

Collette, Carolyn P. "Heeding the Counsel of Prudence: A Context for the 'Melibee.'" *ChauR* 29 (1995): 416–33.

Colley, Dawn Fleurette. "Reclaiming Reason: Chaucer's Prose and the Path to Autonomy." PhD diss., University of Colorado at Boulder, 2012.

Conti, Aidan. "The Circulation of the Old English Homily in the Twelfth Century: New Evidence from Oxford, Bodleian Library, MS. Bodley 343." In *The Old English Homily: Precedent, Practice, and Appropriation*, edited by Aaron J. Kleist, 365–402. Turnhout: Brepols, 2007.

– "Individual Practice, Common Endeavour: Making Manuscript and Community in the Second Half of the Twelfth Century." *New Medieval Literature* 13 (2011): 253–72.

176 Bibliography

Cook, Megan L. "'Here Taketh the Makere of This Book His Leve': The 'Retraction' and Chaucer's Works in Tudor England." *Studies in Philology* 113, no. 1 (2016): 32–54.

Cooper, Christine F. "'But Algates Thereby Was She Understonde': Translating Constance in *The Man of Law's Tale*." *Yearbook of English Studies* 36 (2006): 27–38.

Cooper, Helen. *The Structure of the Canterbury Tales*. Athens: University of Georgia Press, 1983.

Coulthard, Glen S. "From Wards of the State to Subjects of Recognition? Marx, Indigenous Peoples, and the Politics of Dispossession in Denedeh." In *Theorizing Native Studies*, edited by A. Simpson and A. Smith, 56–98. Durham: Duke University Press, 2014.

– *Red Skins, White Masks: Rejecting the Colonial Politics of Recognition*. Minneapolis: University of Minnesota Press, 2014.

Crane, Susan. "The Writing Lesson of 1381." In *Chaucer's England*, edited by Barbara Hanawalt, 201–21. Minneapolis: University of Minnesota Press, 1992.

Crick, Julia. "Liberty and Fraternity: Creating and Defending the Liberty of St. Albans." In *Expectations of the Law in the Middle Ages*, edited by Anthony Musson, 91–103. Woodbridge: Boydell & Brewer, 2001.

– "Offa, Ilfric and the Refoundation of St. Albans." In *Alban and St. Albans: Roman and Medieval Architecture, Art, and Archaeology*, edited by Philip Lindley, 78–84. New York: Routledge, 2001.

– "St. Albans, Westminster and Some Twelfth-Century Views of the Anglo-Saxon Past." *Anglo-Norman Studies* 25 (2003 for 2002): 65–83.

– "*Pristina libertas*: Liberty and the Anglo-Saxons Revisited." *Transactions of the Royal Historical Society* 6, no. 14 (2004): 47–71.

– "Historical Literacy in the Archive: Post-Conquest Imitative Copies of Pre-Conquest Charters and Some French Comparanda." In *The Long Twelfth-Century View of the Anglo-Saxon Past*, edited by Martin Brett and David A. Woodman, 156–90. Burlington: Ashgate, 2015.

Crocker, Holly. *Chaucer's Visions of Manhood*. New York: Palgrave Macmillan, 2007.

Daileader, Celia. "The Thopas-Melibee Sequence and the Defeat of Antifeminism." *ChauR* 29 (1994): 26–39.

Darby, Henry Clifford. *Domesday England*. Cambridge: Cambridge University Press, 1986.

David, Alfred. "The Man of Law Vs. Chaucer: A Case in Poetics." *PMLA* 82, no. 2 (1967): 217–25.

Davis, G.R.C. *Medieval Cartularies of Great Britain and Ireland*. Revised by Claire Breay, Julian Harrison, and David M. Smith. London: The British Library, 2010.

Davis, Kathleen. "Time Behind the Veil: The Media, The Middle Ages, and Orientalism Now." In *Postcolonial Middle Ages*, edited by Jeffery Jerome Cohen, 105–22. New York: Palgrave, 2001.

– *Periodization and Sovereignty: How Ideas of Feudalism and Secularization Govern the Politics of Time*. Philadelphia: University of Pennsylvania Press, 2008.

Dean, James. "Gower, Chaucer, and Rhyme Royal." *Studies in Philology* 88, no. 3 (1991): 251–75.

De Angelis, Massimo. "Marx and Primitive Accumulation: The Continuous Character of Capital's 'Enclosures.'" *The Commoner* no. 2 (September 2001): 1–22.

de Hamel, Christopher. "Archbishop Matthew Parker and His Imaginary Library of Archbishop Theodore of Canterbury." *Lambeth Palace Library Annual Review* (2002): 52–68.

De La Mare, Albinia. *The Handwriting of Italian Humanists*. Oxford: University Press for the Association internationale de bibliophilie, 1973.

Derolez, Albert. *The Palaeography of Gothic Manuscript Books from the Twelfth to the Early Sixteenth Century*. Cambridge: Cambridge University Press, 2003.

Dharmaraj, Glory. "Multicultural Subjectivity in Reading Chaucer's 'Man of Law's Tale.'" *Medieval Feminist Newsletter* 16 (1993): 4–8.

The Dictionary of Medieval Latin from British Sources, edited by R.E. Latham, D.R. Howlett, and R.K. Ashdowne. London: British Academy, 1975–2013.

Dinshaw, Carolyn. *Chaucer's Sexual Poetics*. Madison: University of Wisconsin Press, 1989.

– "Quarrels, Rivals, and Rape: Gower and Chaucer." In *"A wyf ther was": Essays in honour of Paule Mertens-Fonck*, edited by Juliette Dor, 112–22. Liège: Université de Liège, 1992.

– "Pale Faces: Race, Religion, and Affect in Chaucer's Texts and Their Readers." SAC 23 (2001).

Dobbie, Elliott Van Kirk. *The Manuscripts of Caedmon's Hymn and Bede's Death Song, With a Critical Text of the Epistola Cuthberti de obitu Bedae*. New York: Columbia University Press, 1957.

Dobie, Alisdair. *Accounting at Durham Cathedral Priory: Management and Control of a Major Ecclesiastical Corporation 1083–1540*. New York: Palgrave Macmillan, 2015.

Dor, Juliette. "Chaucer's Viragos: A Postcolonial Engagement? A Case Study of the *Man of Law's Tale*, the *Monk's Tale*, and the *Knight's Tale*." In *Intersections of Gender, Religion and Ethnicity in the Middle Ages*, edited by Cordelia Beattie and Kirsten A. Fenton, 158–82. New York: Palgrave Macmillan, 2011.

Doyle, Antony I. "Book Production by the Monastic Orders in England (c. 1375–1530): Assessing the Evidence." In *Medieval Book Production: Assessing the Evidence – Proceedings of the Second Conference of the Seminar in the History*

178   Bibliography

of the Book to 1500, Oxford, July 1988, edited by Linda L. Brownrigg. Oxford: Anderson Lovelace, 1990.

Doyle, Anthony I., and Malcolm B. Parkes. "The Production of Copies of the *Canterbury Tales* and *The Confessio Amantis* in the Early Fifteenth Century." In *Medieval Scribes, Manuscripts and Libraries: Essays Presented to N.R. Ker,* edited by M.B. Parkes and A.G. Watson, 163–210. London: Scolar Press, 1978.

Dubray, Charles. "Necromancy." *The Catholic Encyclopedia.* Vol. 10. New York: Robert Appleton Company, 1911. http://www.newadvent.org /cathen/10735a.htm.

Dugas, Don-John. "The Legitimization of Royal Power in Chaucer's 'Man of Law's Tale.'" *Modern Philology* 95, no. 1 (1997): 27–43.

Dumville, David. *English Caroline Script and Monastic History: Studies in Benedictinism, A.D. 950–1030.* Woodbridge: Boydell & Brewer, 1993.

Dunn, Caroline. *Stolen Women in Medieval England: Rape, Abduction, and Adultery, 1100–1500.* Cambridge: Cambridge University Press, 2013.

Dunning, Andrew N.J. "Death to the Archivist: John Lakenheath's Register of Bury St. Edmunds." Humanities Commons, 2017. http://dx.doi.org /10.17613/M6SW6H.

– "John Lakenheath's Rearrangement of the Library of Bury St Edmunds Abbey, c. 1380." *The Library: The Transactions of the Bibliographic Society* 19, no. 1 (2018): 63–8.

Dutschke, C.W. *Guide to Medieval and Renaissance Manuscripts in the Huntington Library.* 2 vols. San Marino: Huntington Library Press, 1989.

Echard, Siân. *Printing the Middle Ages.* Philadelphia: University of Pennsylvania Press, 2008.

Edwards, A.S.G. "The Influence of Lydgate's *Fall of Princes.*" *Mediaeval Studies* 39 (1977): 424–39.

– "'I Speke in Prose': *Man of Law's Tale,* 96." *Neuphilologische Mitteilungen* 92 (1991): 469–70.

Edwards, Suzanne M. "The Rhetoric of Rape and the Politics of Gender in the Wife of Bath's Tale and the 1382 Statute of Rapes." *Exemplaria* 23, no. 1 (2011): 3–26.

– *The Afterlife of Rape in Medieval English Literature.* New York: Palgrave, 2016.

Eisenstein, Elizabeth. *The Printing Press as an Agent of Change: Communications and Cultural Transformations in Early-Modern Europe,* 2 vols. Cambridge: Cambridge University Press, 1979.

Elliott, Ralph W.V. *Chaucer's English.* London: Andre Deutsch, 1974.

Ellis, Deborah S. "Chaucer's Devilish Reeve." *ChauR* 27.2 (1992): 150–61.

Epstein, Robert. "'Fer in the North; I Kan Nat Telle Where': Dialect, Regionalism, and Philologism." *SAC* 30 (2008): 95–124.

Bibliography 179

Erwin, Bonnie J. "Why We Can't Stop Fighting about Chaucer's Man of Law." *Enarratio* 20 (2016): 41–66. https://doi.org/10.18061/1811/79857.

Everest, Carol A. "Sex and Old Age in Chaucer's *Reeve's Prologue*." *ChauR* 31.2 (1996): 99–114.

Falk, Seb. *The Bright Ages: The Surprising Story of Medieval Science*. New York: Norton, 2020.

Fanon, Frantz. *Black Skins, White Masks*. Translated by Charles Lam Markmann. New York: Grove Press, 1967, repr. 1991.

Federici, Silvia. *Caliban and the Witch: Women, the Body, and Primitive Accumulation*. New York: Autonomedia, 2004.

Ferster, Judith. *Fictions of Advice: The Literature and Politics of Counsel in Late Medieval England*. Philadelphia: University of Pennsylvania Press, 1996.

– "Chaucer's Parson and the 'Idiosyncracies of Fiction.'" In *Closure in The Canterbury Tales: The Role of the Parson's Tale*, edited by David Raybin and Linda Tarte Holley, 115–50. Kalamazoo MI: Medieval Institute Publications, 2000.

Finlayson, John. "Chaucer's *Summoner's Tale*: Flatulence, Blasphemy, and the Emperor's Clothes." *Studies in Philology* 101, no. 4 (2007): 455–70.

Firth, Matthew. "The Broken Body in Eleventh to Thirteenth-Century Anglo-Scandinavian Literature." *Comitatus* 50 (2019): 45–75.

Fitzgerald, Jill. "Rebel Angels: Political Theology and the Fall of the Angels Tradition in Old English Literature." PhD diss., University of Illinois at Urbana-Champaign, 2014.

Flynn, James. "The Art of Telling and the Prudence of Interpreting the *Tale of Melibee* in Its Context." *Medieval Perspectives* 7 (1992): 53–63.

Foot, Sarah. "Reading Anglo-Saxon Charters: Memory, Record, or Story?" In *Narrative and History in the Early Medieval West*, edited by Elizabeth M. Tyler and Ross Balzaretti, 39–65. Turnhout: Brepols 2006.

– "Internal and External Audiences: Reflections on the Anglo-Saxon Archive of Bury St. Edmunds Abbey in Suffolk." *Haskins Society Journal* 24 (2012): 163–94.

Foster, Michael. "Echoes of Communal Response in the *Tale of Melibee*." *ChauR* 42, no. 4 (2008): 409–30.

Fradenburg, L.O. Arranye. *Sacrifice Your Love*. Minneapolis: University of Minnesota Press, 2002.

Frankis, John. "King Ælle and the Conversion of the English." In *Literary Appropriations of the Anglo-Saxons from the Thirteenth to the Twentieth Century*, edited by Donald Scragg and Carole Weinberg, 74–92. Cambridge: Cambridge University Press, 2000.

Franzen, Christine. *The Tremulous Hand of Worcester: A Study of Old English in the Thirteenth Century*. Oxford: Oxford University Press, 1991.

180   Bibliography

Fumoleau, René. *As Long as This Land Shall Last: A History of Treaty 8 and Treaty 11, 1870–1939*. Vol. 6. Calgary: University of Calgary Press, 2004.

Gameson, Richard. *The Scribe Speaks? Colophons in Early English Manuscripts*. Cambridge: Department of Anglo-Saxon, Norse, and Celtic, 2002.

Ganim, John. "Lydgate, Location, and the Poetics of Exemption." In *Lydgate Matters*, edited by Lisa Cooper and Andrea Denny-Brown, 165–84. New York: Palgrave Macmillan. 2008.

Gaston, Kara. *Reading Chaucer in Time: Literary Formation in England and Italy*. Oxford: Oxford University Press, 2020.

Gaylord, Alan T. "*Sentence* and *Solaas* in Fragment VII of the *Canterbury Tales*: Harry Bailly as Horseback Editor," *PMLA* 82, no. 2 (1967): 226–35.

Geary, Patrick. *Phantoms of Remembrance: Memory and Oblivion at the End of the First Millennium*. Princeton: Princeton University Press, 1974.

Gerber, Amanda. "'As Olde Bookes Maken Us Memorie': Chaucer and the Clerical Commentary Tradition." *Florilegium* 29 (2012): 171–200.

Gilbert, Jane. "Unnatural Mothers and Monstrous Children in *The King of Tars* and *Sir Gowther*." In *Medieval Women – Texts and Contexts in Late Medieval Britain: Essays for Felicity Riddy*, edited by Jocelyn Wogan-Browne, Rosalynn Voaden, Arlyn Diamon, Ann Hutcison, Carol Meale, and Lesley Johnson, 329–44. Turnhout: Brepols, 2000. https://doi.org/10.1484/M.MWTC-EB.3.3650.

Gillespie, Alexandra. "The Later Lives of St. Edmund: John Lydgate to John Stow." In *St. Edmund, King and Martyr: Changing Images of a Medieval Saint*, edited by Anthony Bale, 163–86. Woodbridge: York Medieval Press, 2009.

Gillespie, Alexandra, and Daniel Wakelin, eds. *The Production of Books in England 1350–1500*. Cambridge: Cambridge University Press, 2011.

Gitelman, Lisa. *Paper Knowledge: Toward a Media History of Documents*. Raleigh: Duke University Press, 2014.

Glassman, Jim. "Primitive Accumulation, Accumulation by Dispossession, Accumulation by 'Extra-Economic' Means." *Progress in Human Geography* 30, no. 5 (2005): 608–25.

Goodall, Peter. "'Unkynde Abhomynaciouns' in Chaucer and Gower." *Parergon* 5 (1987): 94–102.

Goodspeed-Chadwick, Julie E. "Sexual Politics in 'The Wife of Bath's Prologue' and 'Tale': The Rhetorics of Domestic Violence and Rape." *Readerly/Writerly Texts* 11–12 (2004–5): 155–62.

Gordon, Ian A. *The Movement of English Prose*. Bloomington: Indiana University Press, 1966.

Gordon, Lewis R. "Through the Hellish Zone of Nonbeing: Thinking through Fanon, Disaster, and the Damned of the Earth," *Human Architecture: Journal of the Sociology of Self-Knowledge* 5, no. 3 (2007): Article 3.

Gordon, Todd. "Canada, Empire and Indigenous Peoples in the Americas." *Socialist Studies* 2, no. 1 (2006): 47–75.

Grace, Dominick M. "Chaucer's Little Treatises." *Florilegium* 14 (1995): 157–70. https://doi.org/10.3138/flor.14.010.

Graham, T. "The Beginnings of Old English Studies: Evidence from the Manuscripts of Matthew Parker." In *Back to the Manuscripts: Papers from the Symposium "The Integrated Approach to Manuscript Studies: A New Horizon" Held at the Eighth General Meeting of the Japan Society for Medieval English Studies, Tokyo, December 1992*, edited by S. Sato, 29–50. Tokyo, 1997.

Gransden, Antonia. *Historical Writing in England, c. 550–c. 1307*. London: Routledge & Kegan Paul, 1974.

– "Cultural Transition at Worcester in the Anglo-Norman Period." *British Archaeological Association Conference Transactions* 1 (1978): 1–14.

– "Antiquarian Studies in Fifteenth-Century England." *The Antiquaries Journal* 60, no. 1 (1980): 75–97. https://doi.org/10.1017/S0003581500035988.

– "Baldwin, Abbot of Bury St Edmunds, 1065–1097." *Anglo-Norman Studies* 4 (1982), 65–76 and 187–95.

– "Prologues in the Historiography of Twelfth-Century England." In *England in the Twelfth Century*, edited by D. Williams, 55–81. Woodbridge: Boydell & Brewer, 1990.

– *A History of the Abbey of Bury St. Edmunds 1182–1256*. Woodbridge: Boydell & Brewer, 2007.

Green, J.A. "The Last Century of Danegeld." *EHR* 96 (1981): 241–58.

Green, Richard Firth. *Poets and Princepleasers: Literature and the Court in the Late Middle Ages*. Toronto: University of Toronto Press, 1980.

– "Chaucer's Man of Law and Collusive Recovery." *Notes and Queries*, n.s., 40 (1993): 303–5.

Greenberg, Janelle. "St. Edward's Ghost': The Cult of St. Edward the Confessor and the *Leges Edwardi Confessoris* in English History." In *Felix Liebermann and Die Gesetze der Angelsachsen*, edited by Stefan Juranski, Lisi Oliver, and Andrew Rabin, 273–301. Leiden and Boston: Brill, 2010.

Grimes, Jodi. "Knowing Fortune: The Limits of Boethian Knowledge in 'The Monk's Tale.'" *Carmina Philosophiae* 19 (2010): 49–68.

Guillory, John. "Genesis of the Media Concept." *Critical Inquiry* 36 (2010): 321–62. https://doi.org/10.1086/648528.

Haas, Renate. "Chaucer's 'Monk's Tale': An Ingenious Criticism of Early Humanist Conceptions of Tragedy." *Humanistica Lovaniensia* 36 (1987): 44–70.

Hahn, Thomas, and Richard W. Kaeuper. "Text and Context: Chaucer's Friar's Tale." *SAC* 5 (1983): 67–101.

Hamaguchi, Keiko. "Transgressing the Borderline of Gender: Zenobia in the Monk's Tale." *ChauR* 40, no. 2 (2005): 183–205.

182 Bibliography

– "The Cultural Otherness of Custance as a Foreign Woman in the Man of Law's Tale." *ChauR* 54, no. 4 (2019): 411–40.

Hanna, Ralph. *London Literature 1300–1380*. Cambridge: Cambridge University Press, 2005.

Hansen, Elaine Tuttle. *Chaucer and the Fictions of Gender*. Berkeley: University of California Press, 1992.

Harley, Marta. "The Reeve's 'Foure Gleedes' and St. Fursey's Vision of the Four Fires of the Afterlife." *Medium Ævum* 56.1 (1987): 85–9.

Harris, Carissa. "Rape Narratives, Courtly Critique, and the Pedagogy of Sexual Negotiation in the Middle English Pastourelle." *Journal of Medieval and Early Modern Studies* 46, no. 2 (2016): 263–87. https://doi.org/10.1215/10829636-3491798.

– *Obscene Pedagogies: Transgressive Talk and Sexual Education in Late Medieval Britain*. Ithaca: Cornell University Press, 2018.

– "On Servant Women, Rape Culture, and Endurance." *ChauR* 57, no. 4 (2022): 475–83.

Harsh, Constance. "Christ and Satan: The Measured Power of Christ." *Neuphilologische Mitteilungen* 90, no. 3/4 (1989): 243–53.

Hartman, Saidiya. *Wayward Lives, Beautiful Experiments: Intimate Histories of Riotous Black Girls, Troublesome Women, and Queer Radicals*. New York: W.W. Norton & Company, 2019.

Havelock, Eric A. *Preface to Plato*. Cambridge, MA: Harvard University Press, 1963.

Hector, L.C. *Paleography and Forgery*. London and York: St. Anthony's Press, 1959.

Heffernan, Carol. "A Reconsideration of the Cask Figure in the *Reeve's Prologue*," *ChauR* 15.1 (1980): 37–43.

– *The Orient in Chaucer and Medieval Romance*. Woodbridge: Boydell and Brewer, 2003.

Heng, Geraldine. *Empires of Magic: Medieval Romances and the Politics of Cultural Fantasy*. New York, NY: Columbia University Press, 2003.

– *The Invention of Race in the Middle Ages*. Cambridge: Cambridge University Press, 2018.

Herold, Christine. *Chaucer's Tragic Muse: The Paganization of Christian Tragedy*. Lewiston NY: Edwin Mellen, 2003.

Hiatt, Alfred. *The Making of Medieval Forgeries: False Documents in Fifteenth-Century England*. Toronto: University of Toronto Press, 2004.

Hill, David, and Margaret Worthington, eds. *Æthelbald and Offa: Two Eighth-Century Kings of Mercia*. Manchester: Manchester University Press, 2005.

Hill, Thomas. "The Measure of Hell: Christ and Satan." *PQ* 60.3 (1981): 695–722.

Hoffmann, Petra. "Infernal Imagery in Anglo-Saxon Charters," PhD diss., University of St. Andrews, 2008.

Holsinger, Bruce W., and Ethan Knapp. "The Marxist Premodern." *Journal of Medieval and Early Modern Studies* 34, no. 3 (2004): 463–71.

Homar, Katie. "Chaucer's Novelized, Carnivalized Exemplum: A Bakhtinian Reading of the *Friar's Tale*." *ChauR* 45.1 (2010): 85–105.

Horobin, Simon. "J.R.R. Tolkien as a Philologist: A Reconsideration of the Northernisms in Chaucer's Reeve's Tale." *English Studies* 82 (2001): 97–105.

Howard, Donald. *The Idea of The Canterbury Tales*. Berkeley: University of California Press, 1976.

Hoyt, Robert S. "The Nature and Origins of the Ancient Demesne." *EHR* 65, no. 255 (1950): 145–74.

Hsy, Jonathan. *Trading Tongues: Merchants, Multilingualism, and Medieval Literature*. Columbus: Ohio State University Press, 2013.

Hsy, Jonathan, and Julie Orlemanski. "Race and Medieval Studies: A Partial Bibliography." *postmedieval* 8 (2017): 500–31.

Hudson, Anne. "A Lollard Sect Vocabulary?" In *Lollards and their Books*, 165–80. London: Hambledon Press, 1985.

– *The Premature Reformation: Wycliffite Texts and Lollard History*. Oxford: Clarendon Press, 1988.

Hunter, M. "The Facsimiles in Thomas Elmham's History of St. Augustine's Canterbury." *The Library* 5 ser. 28 (1973): 215–20.

Ingham, Patricia Clare. *Sovereign Fantasies: Arthurian Romance and the Making of Britain*. Philadelphia: University of Pennsylvania Press, 2001.

Insley, Charles. "Where Did All the Charters Go? Anglo-Saxon Charters and the New Politics of the Eleventh Century." *Anglo-Norman Studies* 24 (2002): 109–27.

James, C.L.R. *Beyond a Boundary*. New York: Pantheon, 1983.

– *Black Jacobins: Toussaint L'Overture and the San Domingo Revolution*. New York: Vintage, 1989.

Johnson, Eleanor. *Practicing Literary Theory in the Middle Ages: Ethics and the Mixed Form in Chaucer, Gower, Usk, and Hoccleve*. Chicago: University of Chicago Press, 2013.

– "English Law and the Man of Law's 'Prose' Tale." *JEGP* 114, no. 4 (2015): 504–25.

Johnston, Andrew James. "The Exigencies of 'Latyn Corrupt': Linguistic Change and Historical Consciousness in Chaucer's 'Man of Law's Tale.'" In *Communicative Spaces: Variation, Contact, and Change – Papers in Honour of Ursula Schaefer*, edited by Claudia Lange, Beatrix Weber, and Göran Wolf, 133–46. Frankfurt am Main: Peter Lang, 2012. https://doi.org/10.3726/978-3-653-02178-3.

Jones, Adrienne. "The Significance of the Regal Consecration of Edgar in 973." *The Journal of Ecclesiastical History* 33, no. 3 (1982): 375–90.

Jones, Claude. "The Monk's Tale: A Medieval Sermon." *Modern Language Notes* 52 (1937): 570–2.

Jones, E.A. "'Lo, Lordes Myne, Heere Is a Fit!': The Structure of Chaucer's *Sir Thopas*." *RES* 51, no. 202 (2000): 248–52.

184 Bibliography

Jones, Terry. "The Monk's Tale." *SAC* 22 (2000): 387–97.

Jurkowski, Maureen. "Lawyers and Lollardy in the Early Fifteenth Century." In *Lollardy and the Gentry in the Later Middle Ages*, edited by Margaret Aston and Colin Richmond, 155–82. New York: St. Martins, 1997.

Justice, Steven. *Writing and Rebellion: England in 1381*. Berkeley: University of California Press, 1996.

– "Who Stole Robertson?" *PMLA* 124, no. 2 (2009): 609–15.

Karn, Nicholas. "Information and Its Retrieval." In *A Social History of England 900–1200*, edited by Julia Crick and Elisabeth Van Houts, 373–80. Cambridge: Cambridge University Press, 2011.

Katz Seal, Samantha. "Whose Chaucer? On Cecily Chaumpaigne, Cancellation, and the English Literary Canon." *ChauR* 57, no. 4 (2022): 484–97.

Kelly, Henry Ansgar. *Chaucerian Tragedy*. Cambridge: D.S. Brewer, 2000.

Kelly, Susan. "Anglo-Saxon Lay Society and the Written Word." In *The Uses of Literacy in Medieval Europe*, edited by Rosamund McKitterick, 36–65. Cambridge: Cambridge University Press, 1990.

Kennedy, A.G. "Disputes about *Bocland*: The Forum for Their Adjudication." *ASE* 14 (1985): 175–95.

Kennedy, Kathleen E. *Maintenance, Meed, and Marriage in Medieval Literature*. New York: Palgrave, 2009.

Ker, Neil. "Liber Custumarum and Other Manuscripts Formerly at the Guildhall." *The Guildhall Miscellany* 1.3 (1954), 37–45.

– *Medieval Manuscripts in British Libraries, vol. 1: London*. Oxford: Clarendon Press, 1969.

– "Cnut's Earls." In *The Reign of Cnut, King of England, Denmark and Norway*, edited by A.R. Rumble, 43–88. London and New York: Leicester University Press, 1994.

Kerby-Fulton, Kathryn. "Introduction: The Clericus Class, Underemployment, and the Golden Age of Middle English Poetry." In *The Clerical Proletariat and the Resurgence of Medieval English Poetry*, edited by Kathryn Kerby-Fulton, 1–32. Philadelphia: University of Pennsylvania Press, 2021.

Keynes, Simon, et al., eds. *The Electronic Sawyer: Online Catalogue of Anglo-Saxon Charters*. https://esawyer.lib.cam.ac.uk/about/index.html.

Kim, Dorothy. "Introduction the Literature Compass Special Cluster: Critical Race and the Middle Ages," *Literature Compass* 16.9–10 (2019): e1249.

Kisor, Yvette. "Moments of Silence, Acts of Speech: Uncovering the Incest Motif in the Man of Law's Tale." *ChauR* 40, no. 2 (2005): 141–62.

Kline, Daniel T. "'Myne by Right': Oath-Making and Intent in The Friar's Tale." *Philological Quarterly* 77 (1998): 271–93.

Knapp, Peggy. "The Words of the Parson's 'Vertuous Sentence.'" In *Closure in The Canterbury Tales: The Role of the Parson's Tale*, edited by David Raybin and Linda Tarte Holley, 95–114. Kalamazoo MI: Medieval Institute Publications, 2000.

Bibliography 185

Knight, Stephen. "Colloquium on *The Monk's Tale*: 'My Lord, The Monk.'" *SAC* 22 (2000): 381–6.

Kolve, V.A. *Chaucer and the Imagery of Narrative: The First Five Canterbury Tales*. Stanford CA: Stanford University Press, 1984.

Krappe, A.H. "The Offa-Constance Legend." *Anglia* 61 (1937): 361–9.

Lahey, Stephen. *Philosophy and Politics in the Thought of John Wyclif*. Cambridge: Cambridge University Press, 2003.

Lambkin, Martha Dampf. "Chaucer's Man of Law as Purchasour." *Comitatus* 1, no. 1 (1970): 81–4.

Lampert-Weissig, Lisa. *Medieval Literature and Postcolonial Studies*. Edinburgh: Edinburgh University Press, 2010.

Lamuto, Sierra. "The Mongol Princess of Tars: Global Relations and Race Formation in *The King of Tars* (c. 1330)." *Exemplaria* 31, no. 3 (2019): 171–92.

Larson, Atria. *Master of Penance: Gratian and the Development of Penitential Thought and Law in the Twelfth Century*. Washington D.C.: Catholic University of America Press, 2014.

Lavezzo, Kathy. "Beyond Rome: Mapping Gender and Justice in *The Man of Law's Tale*." *SAC* 24 (2002): 149–80.

Lawson, M.K. "The Collection of Danegeld and Heregeld in the Reigns of Æthelred and Cnut." *EHR* 99 (1984): 721–38.

Legge, Dominica. *Anglo-Norman Literature and Its Background*. Oxford: Oxford University Press, 1963.

LeGoff, Jacques. *The Medieval Imagination*, translated by A. Goldhammer. Chicago: University of Chicago Press, 1985.

Leicester, H. Marshall. *The Disenchanted Self: Representing the Subject in The Canterbury Tales*. Berkeley: University of California Press, 1990.

Levitan, Alan. "The Parody of Pentecost in Chaucer's *Summoner's Tale*." *University of Toronto Quarterly* 40 (1971): 236–46.

Lewis, Robert E. "Chaucer's Artistic Use of Pope Innocent III's *De Miseria Humane Conditionis* in The Man of Law's Prologue and Tale. *PMLA* 81, no. 7 (1966): 485–92.

Leyerle, John. "Chaucer's Windy Eagle." *University of Toronto Quarterly* 40 (1971): 247–65.

Lim, Hyunyang K. "Counterfeit Correspondences: Documentary Manipulations and Textual Consciousness in Gloucester's Confession and *The Man of Law's Tale*." *Medieval and Early Modern Studies* 25 (2017): 67–97. https://doi.org/10.17054/MEMES.2017.25.1.67.

Lindeboom, B.W. "Chaucer's Monk Illuminated: Zenobia as Role Model." *Neophilologus* 92 (2008): 339–50.

Little, Lester. *Benedictine Maledictions*. Ithaca: Cornell University Press, 1993.

Lloyd, T.H. *The English Wool Trade in the Middle Ages*. Cambridge: Cambridge University Press, 1977.

186   Bibliography

Lochrie, Karma. *Covert Operations: The Medieval Uses of Secrecy*. Philadelphia: University of Pennsylvania Press, 1999.

Lowe, Kathryn A. "The Poetry of Privilege: Lydgate's *Cartae Versificatae*," *Nottingham Medieval Studies* 50 (2006): 151–65.

– "Post-Conquest Bilingual Memoranda from Bury St Edmunds," *RES* 59 (2008): 52–66.

– "Linguistic Geography, Demography, and Monastic Community: Scribal Language at Bury St Edmunds." In *Interfaces between Language and Culture in Medieval England: A Festschrift for Matti Kilpiö*, edited by Alaric Hall, Olga Timofeeva, Ágnes Kiricsi, and Bethany Fox, 147–78. Leiden: Brill, 2010.

– "Bury St. Edmunds and Its Liberty: A Charter-Text and Its Afterlife." In *English Manuscripts Before 1400*, edited by A.S.G. Edwards and Orietta Da Rold. *English Manuscript Studies 1100–1700* (17), 155–72. London: British Library, 2012.

Lowe, Lisa. *The Intimacies of Four Continents*. Raleigh: Duke University Press, 2015.

Lucas, Peter J. "Scribal Imitation of Earlier Handwriting: 'Bastard Saxon' and Its Impact." In *Le statut du scripteur au Moyen Age*, edited by Marie-Clotilde Hubert, Emmanuel Poulle, and Marc H. Smith, 151–6. Paris: École nationale des chartes, 2000.

Lynch, Kathryn. "Storytelling, Exchange, and Constancy: East and West in Chaucer's Man of Law's Tale." *The ChauR* 33 (1999): 409–22.

– "'Diverstieee bitwene Hir Bothe Lawes': Chaucer's Unlikely Alliance of a Lawyer and a Merchant." *The ChauR* 46 (2011): 74–92.

Machan, Tim. "Language and Society in Twelfth-Century England." In *Placing Middle English in Context: Selected Papers from the Second Middle English Conference*, edited by Irma Taavistainen, Terttu Nevalainen, Päivi Pahta, and Matti Rissanen, 43–66. Berlin: de Gruyter, 2000.

Maddicott, J.R. *Origins of English Parliament 924–1327*. Oxford: Oxford University Press, 2010.

Maitland, Frederic William. *Domesday Book and Beyond: Three Essays in the Early History of England*. Cambridge: Cambridge University Press, 1897.

Mak, Bonnie. *How the Page Matters*. Toronto: University of Toronto Press, 2011.

Mann, Jill. *Chaucer and Medieval Estates Satire*. Cambridge: Cambridge University Press, 1973.

– "Anger and 'Glosynge' in the Canterbury Tales." In *Life in Words: Essays on Chaucer, the Gawain-Poet, and Malory*, edited by Mark David Rasmussen, 80–101. Toronto: University of Toronto Press, 2014.

Maracle, Lee. *Memory Serves: Oratories*. Edmonton: NeWest Press, 2015.

Marsh, James H., and Nathan Baker. "Mackenzie Valley Pipeline Proposals." *The Canadian Encyclopedia*. Historica Canada. Article published 7 February 2006; last edited 21 March 2018.

Martin, Richard. "The Lives of the Offas: The Posthumous Reputation of Offa, King of the Mercians." In *Æthelbald and Offa: Two Eighth-Century Kings of Mercia*, edited by David Hill and Margaret Worthington, 49–54. Manchester: Manchester University Press, 2005.

Marx, Karl. *Capital, Volume 1*. Translated by Ben Fowkes. New York: Penguin Classics, 1976.

Mason, Emma. *St. Wulfstan of Worcester c. 1008–1095*. London: Blackwell, 1990.

Matthews, Stephen. "Good King Offa: Legends of a Pious King." *Transactions of the Lancashire and Cheshire Antiquarian Society* 98 (2002): 1–14.

– "Legends of Offa: The Journey to Rome." In *Æthelbald and Offa: Two Eighth-Century Kings of Mercia*, edited by David Hill and Margaret Worthington, 55–8. Manchester: Manchester University Press, 2005.

McCluskey, Colleen. "Black on the Outside, White on the Inside: Peter Abelard's Use of Race," *Critical Philosophy of Race* 6, no. 2 (2018): 135–63.

McSheffrey, Shannon, and Julia Pope. "Ravishment, Legal Narratives, and Chivalric Culture in Fifteenth-Century England." *Journal of British Studies* 48, no. 4 (2009): 818–36.

Meyer-Lee, Robert J. "Abandon the Fragments." *SAC* 35 (2013): 47–83.

Michelet, Fabienne. *Creation Migration and Conquest*. Oxford: Oxford University Press, 2006.

Middleton, Anne. "Chaucer's 'New Men' and the Good of Literature in the Canterbury Tales." In *Literature and Society, Selected Papers from the English Institute*, edited by Edward W. Said, 15–56. Baltimore: Johns Hopkins University Press, 1980.

Miller, Mark. *Philosophical Chaucer: Love, Sex, and Agency in the Canterbury Tales*. Cambridge: Cambridge University Press, 2005.

Minnis, Alistair. *Medieval Theory of Authorship: Scholastic Literary Attitudes in the Later Middle Ages*. 2nd ed. Philadelphia: University of Pennsylvania Press, 2012.

Mooney, Lynne. "Professional Scribes?: Identifying English Scribes Who Had a Hand in More Than One Manuscript." In *New Directions in Medieval Manuscript Studies: Essays from the 1998 Harvard Conference*, edited by Derek Pearsall, 131–41. Woodbridge: York Medieval Press, 2000.

Moore, Stephen. "Apply Yourself: Learning while Reading the 'Tale of Melibee.'" *ChauR* 38 (2003): 83–97.

Morris, Mark. "Edward I and the Knight of the Round Table." In *Foundations of Medieval Scholarship: Records Edited in Honour of David Crook*, edited by Sean Cunningham and Paul Brand, 57–76. York: Borthwick Publications, 2008.

Mortimer, Nigel. *John Lydgate's Fall of Princes: Narrative Tragedy in its Literary and Political Contexts*. Oxford: Oxford University Press, 2005.

Musson, Anthony. "The Sergeant of Law." In *Historians on Chaucer: The "General Prologue" to the Canterbury Tales*, edited by Stephen Rigby and

188 Bibliography

Alastair Minnis, 206–26. Oxford: Oxford University Press, 2014. https://doi.org/10.1093/acprof:oso/9780199689545.003.0012.

Naismith, Rory. "Payments for Land and Privilege in Anglo-Saxon England." *ASE* 41 (2012): 277–342.

Nakley, Susan. "Anachronism, Chaucer's Britain, and England's Future's Past." *ChauR* 44 (2010): 368–96.

– *Living in the Future: Sovereignty and Internationalism in The Canterbury Tales.* Ann Arbor: University of Michigan Press, 2017.

Nelson, Ingrid. "Premodern Media and Networks of Transmission in the *Man of Law's Tale*." *exemplaria* 25, no. 3 (2013): 211–30.

– "Ambient Media and Chaucer's House of Fame." *ELH* 88, no. 3 (2021): 551–78.

Nicholson, Peter. "The Man of Law's Tale: What Chaucer Really Owed to Gower." *ChauR* 26 (1991): 153–74.

Nolan, Maura. "'Acquiteth yow now': Textual Contradiction and Legal Discourse in The Man of Law's Introduction." In *The Letter of the Law*, edited by Emily Steiner and Candace Barrington, 136–53. Ithaca: Cornell University Press, 2002.

– *John Lydgate and the Making of Public Culture.* Cambridge: Cambridge University Press, 2005.

Novacich, Sarah Elliott. *Shaping the Archive in Late Medieval England: History, Poetry, and Performance.* Cambridge: Cambridge University Press, 2017.

O'Brien, Bruce. "Forgery and the Literacy of the Early Common Law." *Albion* 27 (1995): 1–18.

– "The Becket Conflict and the Invention of the Myth of Lex non scripta." In *Learning the Law: Teaching and the Transmission of Law in England, 1150–1900*, edited by Jonathan Bush and Alan Wijffels, 1–14. London: Hambledon Press, 1999.

– *God's Peace and King's Peace: The Laws of Edward the Confessor.* Philadelphia: University of Pennsylvania Press, 1999.

O'Connell, Brendan. "Chaucer's Counterfeit Exempla." In *Chaucer's Poetry: Words, Authority and Ethics*, edited by Clíodhna Carney and Frances McCormack, 134–45. Dublin: Four Courts, 2013.

Oliver, Lisi. *Beginnings of English Law.* Toronto: University of Toronto Press, 2002.

Olson, Paul A. "The *Reeve's Tale*: Chaucer's 'Measure for Measure." *Studies in Philology* 59.1 (1962): 1–17.

Ormrod, W.M. "The Peasants' Revolt and the Government of England." *Journal of British Studies* 29, no. 1 (1990): 1–30.

Otter, Monika. "Closed Doors: An Epithalamium for Queen Edith, Widow and Virgin." In *Constructions of Widowhood and Virginity in the Middle Ages*, edited by Angela J. Weisl and Cindy Carlson, 63–92. New York: St. Martin's Press, 1999.

Owen, Charles Jr. "What the Manuscripts Tell Us About the *Parson's Tale*." *Medium Aevum* 63, no. 2 (1994): 239–49.

Owst, Charles. *Preaching in Medieval England: An Introduction to Sermon Manuscripts of the Period c. 1350–1450*. Cambridge: Cambridge University Press, 1926; reprint, New York: Russell & Russell, 1965.

Pakkala-Weckstrom, Mari. "Prudence and the Power of Persuasion – Language and Maistrie in the *Tale of Melibee*." *ChauR* 35 (2001): 399–412.

Parkes, Malcolm. "Archaizing Hands in English Manuscripts." In *Books and Collectors 1200–1700: Essays Presented to Andrew Watson*, edited by James P. Carley and Colin G.C. Tite, 101–41. London: British Library, 1997.

– *English Cursive Book Hands 1250–1500*. Oxford: Oxford University Press, 1969, reprinted Farnham UK and Burlington VT: Ashgate, 2008.

Partridge, Stephen. "'The Makere of this Boke': Chaucer's Retraction and the Author as Scribe and Compiler." In *Author, Reader, Book: Medieval Authorship in Theory and Practice*, edited by Stephen Partridge and Erik Kwakkel, 106–53. Toronto: University of Toronto Press, 2018.

Patterson, Lee. "'What Man Artow?': Authorial Self-Definition in The Tale of Sir Thopas and The Tale of Melibee." *SAC* 11, no. 1 (1989): 117–75.

– *Chaucer and the Subject of History*. Madison: University of Wisconsin Press, 1991.

Pattison, Andrew John. "Ironic Imitations: Parody, Mockery, and the Barnyard Chase in the *Nun's Priest's Tale*." *ChauR* 54, no. 2 (2019): 141–61.

Pearsall, Derek. *John Lydgate*. Charlottesville: University Press of Virginia, 1970.

Phillips, S.E. "Chaucer's Language Lessons." *ChauR* 46, no. 1 (2011): 39–59.

Plummer, John F. "'Hooly Chirches Blood': Simony and Patrimony in Chaucer's *Reeve's Tale*," *ChauR* 18.1 (1983): 49–60.

Poole, Austin Lane. *From Domesday Book to Magna Carta, 1087–1216*. Oxford History of England vol. 3. Oxford: Oxford University Press, 1993.

Pope, Emma F. "The Critical Background of the Spenserian Stanza." *Modern Philology* 24, no. 1 (1926): 31–53.

Prescott, Andrew. "'The Great and Horrible Rumour': Shaping the English Revolt of 1381." In *The Routledge History Handbook of Medieval Revolt*, edited by Justine Firnhaber-Baker and Dirk Schoenaers, 90–117. London: Taylor & Francis Group, 2017.

Pugh, Tison. "'For to be Sworne Bretheren Til They Deye': Satirizing Queer Brotherhood in the Chaucerian Corpus." *ChauR* 43, no. 3 (2009): 282–310.

Pulsiano, Philip. "'Danish Men's Words Are Worse Than Murder': Viking Guile and 'The Battle of Maldon.'" *JEGP* 96.1 (1997): 13–25.

Rajabzadeh, Shokoofeh. "The Depoliticized Saracen and Muslim Erasure." *Literature Compass* 16, no. 9–10 (2019): e12548. https://doi.org/10.1111/lic3.12548.

Rajendran, Shyama. "Undoing 'the Vernacular': Dismantling Structures of Raciolinguistic Supremacy." *Literature Compass* 16, no. 9–10 (2019); 16:e12544. https://doi.org/10.1111/lic3.12544.

190   Bibliography

Rambaran-Olm, Mary, Breann Leake, and Micah Goodrich. "Medieval Studies: The Stakes of the Field." *postmedieval* 11 (2020): 356–70.

Raybin, David. "*Sir Thopas*: A Story for Young Children." *SAC* 39 (2017): 225–48.

Reader, Rebecca. "Matthew Paris and Anglo-Saxon England: A Thirteenth-Century Vision of the Distant Past." PhD diss., University of Durham, 1994.

Reimer, S.R., and P. Parvolden. "Of Arms and The Manuscript: The Date and Provenance of Harley 2255." *Journal of the Early Book Society* 8 (2005): 239–60.

Remensyder, Amy G. *Remembering Kings Past: Monastic Foundation Legends in Medieval Southern France*. Ithaca: Cornell University Press, 1995.

Reynolds, Susan. *Fiefs and Vassals: The Medieval Evidence Reinterpreted*. Oxford: Oxford University Press, 1994.

– *Kingdoms and Communities in Western Europe 900–1300*. Oxford: Oxford University Press, 1997.

– "Fiefs and Vassals after Twelve Years." In *Feudalism: New Landscapes of Debate*, edited by Sverre Bagge, Michael H. Gelting, and Thomas Lindkvist, 15–26. Turnhout: Brepols, 2011. https://doi.org/10.1484/M.TMC-EB.3.4972.

Rice, Nicole. "Spiritual Ambition and the Translation of the Cloister: The Abbey and the Charter of the Holy Ghost." *Viator* 33 (2002): 222–60.

Rickert, Edith. "The Old English Offa Saga I." *Modern Philology* 2, no. 1 (1904): 29–76. https://doi.org/10.1086/386628.

– "The Old English Offa Saga II." *Modern Philology* 2, no. 3 (1905): 321–76. https://doi.org/10.1086/386645.

Rigby, S.H. "Historical Materialism: Social Structure and Social Change in the Middle Ages." In "The Marxist Premodern," edited by Bruce Holsinger and Ethan Knapp. Special issue, *Journal of Medieval and Early Modern Studies* 34, no. 3 (2004): 473–522.

Roach, Levi. *Kingship and Consent in Anglo-Saxon England, 871–978*. Cambridge: Cambridge University Press, 2013.

Robertson, D.W. "Chaucerian Tragedy." *English Literary History* 19, no. 1 (1952): 1–37.

– *A Preface to Chaucer: Studies in Medieval Perspectives*. Princeton: Princeton University Press, 1962.

Robertson, Elizabeth. "Nonviolent Christianity and the Strangeness of Female Power in Geoffrey Chaucer's Man of Law's Tale." In *Gender and Difference in the Middle Ages*, edited by Sharon Farmer and Carol Braun Pasternack, 322–51. Minneapolis and London: University of Minnesota Press, 2003.

Robinson, Cedric. *Black Marxism: The Making of a Radical Black Tradition*. 2nd ed. Chapel Hill: University of North Carolina Press, 2000.

Rose, Christine M. "Reading Chaucer Reading Rape." In *Representing Rape in Medieval and Early Modern Literature*, edited by Elizabeth Robertson and Christine M. Rose, 21–60. New York: Palgrave Macmillan, 2001.

Bibliography   191

Rothwell, William. "The Trilingual England of Geoffrey Chaucer." *SAC* 14 (1994): 45–67.

Ryan, Martin J. "'Charters in Plenty, If Only They Were Good for Anything': The Problem of Bookland and Folkland in Pre-Viking England." In *Problems and Possibilities of Early Medieval Charters*, edited by Jonathan Jarrett and Allan Scott McKinley, 19–33. Turnhout: Brepols, 2013. https://doi.org/10.1484/M.IMR-EB.1.101675.

Saltzman, Benjamin A. "The Friar, The Summoner, and Their Techniques of Erasure." *ChauR* 52, no. 4 (2017): 363–95.

Saunders, Corinne. "Woman Displaced: Rape and Romance in Chaucer's Wife of Bath's Tale." *Arthurian Literature* 13 (1995): 115–31.

Scala, Elizabeth. "Canacee and the Chaucer Canon: Incest and Other Unnarratables." *ChauR* 30, no. 1 (1995): 15–39.

Scase, Wendy. "Threshold-Switching: Paratextual Functions of Scribal Colophons in Old and Middle English Manuscripts." In *The Dynamics of Text and Framing Phenomena: Historical Approaches to Paratext and Metadiscourse in English*, edited by Matti Peikola and Birte Bös, 91–113. Amsterdam: John Benjamins, 2020. https://doi.org/10.1075/pbns.317.04sca.

– *Visible English: Graphic Culture, Scribal Practice, and Identity, c. 700–c. 1550.* Turnhout: Brepols, 2022.

Scattergood, V.J. *Politics and Poetry in the Fifteenth Century, 1399–1485*. London: Blandford Press, 1971.

– "Chaucer and the French War: Sir Thopas and Melibee." In *Court and Poet: Selected Proceedings of the Third Congress of the International Courtly Literature Society*, edited by Glyn S. Burgess, 287–96. Liverpool: Francis Cairns, 1981.

Schibanoff, Susan. "Worlds Apart: Orientalism, Anti-Feminism and Heresy in Chaucer's Man of Law's Tale." *Exemplaria* 8 (1986): 59–96.

Schlauch, Margaret. *Chaucer's Constance and Accused Queens*. New York: Gordian Press, 1927.

Scott, Kathleen. "*Caveat Lector*: Ownership and Standardization in the illustration of Fifteenth-Century English Manuscripts." *English Manuscript Studies 1100–1700* 1 (1989): 19–63.

Sharma, Manish. *The Logic of Love in The Canterbury Tales*. Toronto: University of Toronto Press, 2022.

Shields-Más, Chelsea. "The Reeve in Late Anglo-Saxon England." PhD diss., The University of York, 2013.

Shippey, Thomas, and Andrew Haarder. *Beowulf: The Critical Heritage*. New York: Routledge, 1999.

Simpson, James. *Reform and Cultural Revolution, 1350–1547, Vol 2 of the Oxford English Literary History*. Oxford: Oxford University Press, 2002.

Smith, Charles R. "Chaucer's Reeve and St. Paul's Old Man." *ChauR* 30.1 (1995): 101–6.

192 Bibliography

Smith, Scott T. *Land & Book: Literature and Land Tenure in Anglo-Saxon England.* Toronto: Toronto University Press, 2012.

Somerset, Fiona. "'As Just as Is a Squyre': The Politics of 'Lewed Translacion' in Chaucer's Summoner's Tale." *SAC* 21 (1999): 187–207.

– "Wycliffite Spirituality." In *Texts and the Repression of Medieval Heresy*, edited by Caterina Bruschi and Peter Biller, 375–86. Woodbridge: York Medieval Press, 2002.

– "'Hard Is with Seyntis for to Make Affray': Lydgate the 'Poet-Propagandist' as Hagiographer." In *John Lydgate: Poetry, Culture, and Lancastrian England*, edited by Larry Scanlon and James Simpson, 258–78. Notre Dame: Notre Dame University Press, 2006.

Sottosanti, Danielle. "We shul first feyne us cristendom to take." *Studies in Philology* 117, no. 2 (2020): 240–60.

Spearing, A.C. *Textual Subjectivity*. Oxford: Oxford University Press. 2005.

Spelman, Henry. "Feuds and Tenure." In *Reliquiæ Spelmannianæ the Posthumous Works of Sir Henry Spelman, Kt., Relating to the Laws and Antiquities of England: Publish'd from the Original Manuscripts: With the Life of the Author.* Oxford, 1698.

Spencer, Alice. "Dialogue, Dialogics and Love: Problems of Chaucer's Poetics in the Melibee." In *The Canterbury Tales Revisited: 21st Century Interpretations*, edited by Kathleen Bishop, 228–55. Newcastle: Cambridge Scholars, 2008.

Spense, John. *Reimagining History in Anglo-Norman Prose Chronicles.* Woodbridge: York Medieval Press, 2013.

Spiegel, Gabrielle. *Romancing the Past: The Rise of Prose Historiography in Thirteenth-Century France.* Berkeley: University of California Press, 1993.

Spindler, Erik. "Flemings in the Peasants' Revolt, 1381." In *Contact and Exchange in Later Medieval Europe: Essays in Honour of Malcolm Vale*, edited by Hannah Skoda, Patrick Lantschner, and R.L.J. Shaw, 59–78. Woodbridge: Boydell, 2012

Stafford, Pauline. "The Laws of Cnut and the History of Anglo-Saxon Royal Promises." *ASE* 10 (1982): 173–90.

– "Political Ideas in Late Tenth-Century Charters as Evidence." In *Law, Laity and Solidarities: Essays in Honour of Susan Reynolds*. Ed. Pauline Stafford, Janet L. Nelson, and Jane Martindale, 68–82. Manchester: Manchester University Press, 2001.

– *Queen Emma and Queen Edith: Queenship and Women's Power in Eleventh-Century England.* Oxford: Wiley-Blackwell, 2001.

Staley, Lynn. "Inverse Counsel: Contexts for Melibee." *Studies in Philology* 86 (1990): 137–55.

– *Languages of Power in the Age of Richard II.* University Park, PA: Penn State University Press, 2005.

Stanley, E.G. "The Use of Bob-Lines in *Sir Thopas*." *Neuphilologische Mitteilungen* 73, no. 1/3 (1972), 417–26.

Stavsky, Jonathan. "Translating the Near East in *The Man of Law's Tale* and Its Analogues." *ChauR* 55, no. 1 (2020): 32–54.

Steiner, Emily. *Documentary Culture and the Making of Medieval English Literature*. Cambridge: Cambridge University Press, 2003.

– *John Trevisa's Information Age: Knowledge and the Pursuit of Literature c. 1400*. Oxford: Oxford University Press, 2021.

Stenton, Frank. *The Latin Charters of the Anglo-Saxon Period*. Oxford: Oxford University Press, 1955.

Stephenson, Rebecca. *The Politics of Language: Byrhtferth, Aelfric, and the Multilingual Identity in the Benedictine Reform*. Toronto: University of Toronto Press, 2015.

Stevens, Martin. "The Royal Stanza in Early English Literature." *PMLA* 94, no. 1 (1979): 62–76.

Stock, Markus. "Letter, Word, and Good Messengers: Towards an Archaeology of Remote Communication." *Interdisciplinary Science Reviews* 37, no. 4 (2012): 299–313.

Strohm, Paul. *Hochon's Arrow: The Social Imagination of Fourteenth-Century Texts*. Princeton: Princeton University Press, 1992.

– *Politique: Languages of Statescraft Between Chaucer and Shakespeare*. Notre Dame IN: University of Notre Dame Press, 2005.

– *The Poet's Tale: Chaucer and the Year That Made "The Canterbury Tales."* London: Profile Books, 2016.

Szittya, Paul. *The Antifraternal Tradition in Medieval Literature*. Princeton: Princeton University Press, 1986.

Taylor, Charles. *Multiculturalism: Examining the Politics of Recognition*. Princeton: Princeton University Press, 1994.

Taylor, Jamie. "Chaucer's *Tale of Melibee* and the Failure of Allegory." *Exemplaria* 21 (2009): 83–101.

Taylor, Joseph. "Chaucer's Uncanny Regionalism: Rereading the North in *The Reeve's Tale*." *JEGP* 109, no. 4 (2010): 468–89.

Thacker, A. "Æthelwold and Abingdon." In *Bishop Æthelwold: His Career and Influence*, edited by Barbara Yorke, 43–64. Woodbridge: Boydell & Brewer, 1988.

Thomas, Arvind. *Piers Plowman and the Reinvention of Church Law in the Late Middle Ages*. Toronto: University of Toronto Press, 2019.

Thomas, Hugh. *The English and the Normans: Ethnic Hostility, Assimilation, and Identity 1066–c. 1220*. Oxford: Oxford University Press, 2003.

Thompson, Susan D. *Anglo-Saxon Royal Diplomas: A Paleography*. Woodbridge: Boydell & Brewer, 2006.

Thomson, Rodney M. *The Archives of the Abbey of Bury St. Edmunds*. Woodbridge: Boydell & Brewer, 1980.

194   Bibliography

Tinti, Francesca. "*Si litterali memorię commendaretur*: Memory and Cartularies in Eleventh-Century Worcester." In *Early Medieval Studies in Memory of Patrick Wormald*, edited by Stephen Baxter, Catherine Karkov, Janet L. Nelson, and David Pelteret, 475–97. Farnham: Ashgate, 2009.

– *Sustaining Belief: The Church of Worcester from c. 870 to c. 1100*. Farnham, UK and Burlington, VT: Ashgate, 2010.

Tolkien, J.R.R. "Chaucer as a Philologist: *The Reeve's Tale*." *Transactions of the Philological Society* (1934), 1–70.

Tollerton, Linda. *Wills and Will-Making in Anglo-Saxon England*. Woodbridge: Boydell & Brewer, 2011.

Treharne, Elaine. *Living Through Conquest: The Politics of Early English 1020–1220*. Oxford: Oxford University Press, 2012.

Turner, Marion. *Chaucer: A European Life*. Princeton and Oxford: Princeton University Press, 2019.

Turville-Petre, Thorlac. *England the Nation: Language, Literature, and National Identity, 1290–1340*. Oxford: Clarendon Press, 1996.

Tyler, D.J. "Offa's Dyke: A Historiographical Appraisal." *Journal of Medieval History* 37 (2011): 145–61.

Tyler, Elizabeth. "The *Vita Ædwardi*: The Politics of Poetry at Wilton Abbey." *Anglo-Norman Studies* 31 (2009): 135–56.

Ugé, Karina. *Creating the Monastic Past in Medieval Flanders*. Woodbridge: York Medieval Press, 2005.

Ullman, Berthold L. *The Origin and Development of Humanistic Script*. Rome: Edizioni di Storia e Letteratura, 1960.

Ullmann, Walter. "On the Influence of Geoffrey of Monmouth in English History." In *Speculum Historiale*, edited by C. Bauer, L. Bohm, and M. Muller. Munich and Freiburg: K. Alber, 1965.

Vail, Leroy, and Landeg White. *Power and the Praise Poem: South African Voices in History*. Charlottesville: University Press of Virginia, 1991.

Vines, Amy N. "Invisible Woman: Rape as Chivalric Necessity in Medieval Romance." In *Sexual Culture in the Literature of Medieval Britain*, edited by Amanda Hopkins, Robert Allen Rouse, and Cory James Rushton, 164–7. Woodbridge: Boydell and Brewer, 2014.

Vinogradoff, Paul. "Folkland." *EHR* 8 (1893): 1–17.

Walker, Kyly. "Westminster Abbey, King Stephen and the Failure to Canonize King Edward in 1139." *Royal Studies Journal* 5, no. 2 (2018), 27–48.

Wallace, David. *Chaucerian Polity: Absolutist Lineages and Associational Forms in England and Italy*. Stanford, CA: Stanford University Press, 1997.

Walling, Amanda. "'In Her Tellynge Difference': Gender, Authority, and Interpretation," *ChauR* 40 (2005): 163–81.

– "Friar Flatterer: Glossing and the Hermeneutics of Flattery in Piers Plowman." *The Yearbook of Langland Studies* 21 (2007): 57–76.

Wardrop, James. *The Script of Humanism: Some Aspects of Humanist Script 1460–1560*. Oxford: Clarendon Press, 1963.

Wareham, Andrew. "The Redaction of Cartularies and Economic Upheaval in Western England c. 996–1096." *Anglo-Norman Studies* 36 (2013): 189–219.

Warren, Michelle R. *History on the Edge: Excalibur and the Borders of Britain, 1100–1300*. Minneapolis: University of Minnesota Press, 2000.

Weatherbee, Winthrop. "Chaucer and the European Tradition." *SAC* 27 (2005): 3–21.

Webber, Reginald. *"Judas Non Dormit:* John Lydgate and Late-Medieval Benedictine Episcopal Conflicts – Part II," *American Benedictine Review* 61, no. 1 (2010): 81–94.

Weiler, Bjorn. "Monastic Historical Culture and the Utility of a Remote Past: The Case of Matthew Paris." In *How the Past Was Used: Historical Cultures, c. 750–2000*, edited by Peter Lambert and Bjorn Weiler, 91–120. Oxford: British Academy, 2017.

Weiskott, Eric. "Chaucer the Forester: The Friar's Tale, Forest History, and Officialdom." *ChauR* 47, no. 3 (2013): 323–36.

– *English Alliterative Verse*. Cambridge University Press, 2016.

Weisl, Angela Jane. "'Quiting' Eve: Violence Against Women in the Canterbury Tales." In *Violence Against Women in Medieval Texts*, edited by Anna Roberts, 115–36. Gainsville: University of Florida Press, 1998.

Wenzel, Siegfried. "Why the Monk?" In *Words and Works*, edited by Peter Baker and Nicholas Howe, 261–9. Toronto: University of Toronto Press, 1998.

– "The Parson's Tale in Current Literary Studies." In *Closure in The Canterbury Tales: The Role of the Parson's Tale*, edited by David Raybin and Linda Tarte Holley, 1–10. Kalamazoo MI: Medieval Institute Publications, 2000.

Whitaker, Cord J. *Black Metaphors: How Modern Racism Emerged from Medieval Race-Thinking*. Philadelphia: University of Pennsylvania Press, 2019.

Whitty, J.R. "The Rhyming Charter of Beverley." *Transactions of the Yorkshire Dialect Society* 22 (1921): 36–44.

Wiles, Kate. "Charters and Cartularies, 1060–1220." In *The Production and Use of English Manuscripts*, edited by Orietta da Rold, Takako Kato, Mary Swan, and Elaine Treharne. First published 2010; updated 2013. https://www.le.ac.uk/english/em1060to1220/culturalcontexts/2_Charters.htm.

Williams, Arnold. "Chaucer and the Friars." *Studies in Philology* 57 (1960): 463–78.

Wogan-Browne, Jocelyn, Nicholas Watson, Andrew Taylor, and Ruth Evans, eds. *The Idea of the Vernacular: An Anthology of Middle English Literary Theory, 1280–1520*. Exeter: University of Exeter Press, 1999.

Wood, Susan. *The Proprietary Church in the Medieval West*. Oxford: Oxford University Press, 2006.

196   Bibliography

Woodman, D.A. "The Forging of the Anglo-Saxon Past in Fourteenth-Century Beverley." *English Manuscript Studies* 17 (2012): 26–42.

Wormald, Patrick. "Bede and the Conversion of England: The Charter Evidence." Jarrow Lecture, Parish of Jarrow and Simonside, England, 1984. Reprinted in *Times of Bede: Studies in Early English Christian Society and Its Historian*, edited by Stephen Baxter, 135–66. London: Wiley Blackwell, 2006.

– "A Handlist of Anglo-Saxon Lawsuits." *ASE* 17 (1988): 247–81.

– "Oswaldslow: An Immunity?" In *St. Oswald of Worcester*, edited by Nicholas Brooks and Catherine Cubitt, 117–28. London and New York: Leicester University Press, 1996.

– "Lordship and Justice in the Early English Kingdom: Oswaldslaw Revisited." In *Legal Culture in the Early Medieval West: Law as Text, Image and Experience*, 313–32. London: Hambledon, 1999.

– *The Making of English Law: King Alfred to the Twelfth Century*, vol. 1. Oxford: Wiley Blackwell, 2001.

Wynn, Phillip. "The Conversion Story in Nicholas Trevet's 'Tale of Constance.'" *Viator* 13 (1982): 259–74. https://doi.org/10.1484/J.VIATOR.2.301471.

Wynter, Sylvia. "Unsettling the Coloniality of Being/Power/Truth/Freedom: Towards the Human, After Man, Its Overrepresentation – An Argument." *CR: The New Centennial Review* 3, no. 3 (2003): 257–337.

Yamamoto, Dorothy. "Noon Oother Incubus but He: Lines 878–81 in the Wife of Bath's Tale." *ChauR* 28.3 (1994): 275–8.

Yeager, Stephen M. "Lollardy in *Mum and the Sothsegger*: A Reconsideration." *Yearbook of Langland Studies* 25 (2011): 161–90. https://doi.org/10.1484/J.YLS.1.102728.

– "Chaucer's Prudent Poetics: Allegory, the *Tale of Melibee*, and the Frame Narrative to the *Canterbury Tales*." *ChauR* 48, no. 3 (2014): 307–21. https://doi.org/10.5325/chaucerrev.48.3.0307.

– *From Lawmen to Plowmen: Anglo-Saxon Legal Tradition and the School of Langland*. Toronto: University of Toronto Press, 2014.

– "Protocol, or 'The Chivalry of the Object.'" *Critical Inquiry* 45, no. 2 (2019): 747–61. https://doi.org/10.1086/702615.

– "Protocol and Regulation: Controlling Media Histories." In *Old Media and the Medieval Concept: Media Ecologies Before Early Modernity*, edited by Thora Brylowe and Stephen M. Yeager, 54–78. Montreal QC: Concordia University Press, 2021.

Zeeman, Nicolette. *The Arts of Disruption: Allegory and Piers Plowman*. Oxford: Oxford University Press, 2020.

Index

Ælfgifu of Northampton, 57
Ælfheah, archbishop of Canterbury,
    144
Ælfric of Eynsham, 48, 49, 144;
    homilies 48, 49; saint's lives, 144
Æthelberht of Kent, 116
Æthelwold, Saint, 94, 162
Abelard and Heloise, 97
Aldhelm, of Malmesbury, Saint,
    113
Alfred, king of Wessex, 48, 52, 54, 57,
    106, 117, 144, 155, 165
alienation: and dispossession, 27;
    alienated estates, 20; land, 29–30,
    42, 144; territory, 94; of fallen
    angels in *Genesis A*, 94; of Adam,
    95; in *The Monk's Tale*, 96
allegorical names: Cenobia
    (Zenobia), 10, 28, 43, 80–2, 96–9,
    101, 113–15, 119, 122; Custaunce
    (Constance), 28, 39–41, 81, 99–102,
    104–8, 109, 112, 114–16, 118–19,
    132, 137, 141, 165–6; Donegild
    (Danegeld, Domild), 81, 101, 109,
    113, 115–16, 118, 122; Prudence,
    28, 42, 81, 85, 120, 122, 127–9, 167;
    Sophie, 81, 85, 127
alliterative meter and poetry, 130,
    131, 132, 143, 150

"Anglicana" script, 59
Anglo-Saxon charters: English
    translations, 50; literary quality of,
    53; proems, 56; scripts and letter
    forms, 48, 52; textuality 48
Anglo-Saxon Chronicle, 106
Anglo-Saxon Period, 111
anti-clericalism, in *The Canterbury
    Tales*, 5, 26, 59, 70, 73, 77, 135
anti-feminist tropes, 26
archive: of Bury St Edmunds,
    50–1, 157; of charters, 24; of the
    colonial and settler-colonial
    state, 13, 15, 17; contradictions
    in archival records, 82; of early
    English history, 30, 42, 46, 63, 82,
    111; of medieval England, 14, 16;
    of modern liberalism, 13, 16; of
    monasteries, 10, 49–50, 84, 104,
    113, 141, 152; of Old English laws
    and documents, 44, 103
Athelstan, king of England, 53
Augustine, Saint, archbishop of
    Canterbury, conversion mission,
    8, 106, 116
Augustine, Saint, of Hippo, 71; *de
    doctrina Christiana*, 66
Aurelius, Roman emperor, 96, 98–9,
    119

198   Index

Baldwin, Abbot of Bury St
   Edmunds, 50, 80
Barrow, Julia, 56, 135
Battle of Maldon, 145
Bede, 107, 113, 145; age of, 46, 73,
   111, 141; *Bede's Death Song*, 51–2;
   Caedmon's Hymn, 51; Chronicle, 18;
   on the conversion of King Edwin
   of Northumbria, 116; on the
   conversion of Northumbria, 106,
   117; Gospel of John, 52; *Historia
   ecclesiastica gentis Anglorum*, 52,
   102, 106, 116–18, 145, 158; on
   King Oswald, 145; in *Man of Law's
   Tale*, 116–18, 141; transcription of
   letters, 109
Benedictine black vestments, 97
Benedictine monastic libraries, 88
Benedictine Reform, 23, 47, 94, 135
Benedictine Rule, 25, 89, 98
Benson, Larry, 121
Beowulf, 103, 105, 164
Berger inquiry, 32, 34
Berndt, David, *Sacrifice Your Love*, 87
Bible: basic premise of, 63; translation
   of, 54; 2 Corinthians 3:6, 66; I Kings
   17, 67; I Samuel 25, 128; 1 Samuel
   28.7–20, 71; Genesis 27, 128
Boccaccio, Giovanni, 51, 57, 88
Boethius, *Consolation of Philosophy*,
   54, 92
Book of the Duchess (Chaucer), 35, 54
Bose, Mishtooni, 135
Boureau, Alain, 25
Bracciolini, Poggio, 47, 51
Brinton, Thomas, Bishop of
   Rochester, 90
bureaucracy: and documents, 15;
   ecclesiastical, 61, 65; imperial,
   77; literate, 7, 59; nascent of the
   English nation-state, 115
Butler, Emily, 48

Cadwallon, King, 145
Canada, 19, 20–2, 149–50; court
   of law, 19; settler-Canadian
   reconciliation politics, 19
Canterbury Tales (Chaucer):
– *Canon's Yeoman's Prologue* (CYP),
   128, 137
– *Clerk's Tale* (ClT), 128, 143
– Fragment II, 3, 26, 31, 39–40, 123,
   140
– Fragment III, 27, 58, 60, 62–4, 77,
   81, 140, 143, 146–7
– Fragment VII, 6, 83, 124, 140, 142
– Fragment X, 3, 139–40
– *Friar's Tale* (FrT), 63–4, 68–72, 74,
   76, 132, 137, 145
– *General Prologue* (GP), 5, 8, 11, 26,
   29, 34–6, 76, 86, 89, 97, 110, 119,
   135, 145–6
– *Knight's Tale* (KnT), 105–6
– *Man of Law's Introduction* (MLI),
   26, 30, 32, 34–5, 37–8, 41–2, 79, 83,
   88, 100–1, 114, 121, 124, 129–31,
   135, 137, 140, 143
– *Man of Law's Prologue* (MLP), 27,
   38–9, 41–2, 83, 85–6
– *Man of Law's Tale* (MLT), 3, 10, 27–8,
   34, 38, 41, 44, 80, 99–108, 110, 112–16,
   118–19, 122, 130, 132, 141–2, 147
– *Melibee* (Mel), 3–6, 27–8, 38–42,
   81–6, 119, 121–2, 124, 126–9, 131,
   133–4, 140–1, 147, 166–7
– *Merchant's Tale* (MerT), 128, 143
– *Monk's Prologue* (MKP), 3, 6, 27,
   38–9, 41–2, 54, 79–80, 84–6, 88–9,
   96, 110, 141–2
– *Monk's Tale* (MkT), 3, 10, 27, 38,
   79–80, 82–3, 87, 92–3, 95–6, 101,
   110, 126, 140, 142, 145, 147, 161
– *Nun's Priest's Tale* (NPT), 142
– *Parson's Prologue* (ParsP), 83,
   129–30, 138, 140

– *Parson's Tale (ParsT)*, 3–6, 28, 114, 119, 121–2, 127, 129, 132–5, 137–8, 140–1, 147; *De Ira*, 132
– *Reeve's Prologue (RvP)*, 146
– *Reeve's Tale (RvT)*, 144–6
– *Retraction*, 6, 28, 120–3, 127, 132–4, 139, 140–1
– *Shipman's Tale (ShT)*, 128, 142
– *Summoner's Tale (SumT)*, 63–8, 65, 70–2, 74, 76, 129
– *Tale of Sir Thopas (Thopas)*, 6, 28, 83, 121–2, 124, 126–7, 131–2, 135, 140
– *Wife of Bath's Prologue (WBP)*, 60, 64, 73–6, 117, 143
– *Wife of Bath's Tale (WBT)*, 64, 73–6
Caroline miniscule, 47
cartulary witnesses, 27
Ceys and Alcione, 35
Charlemagne, 104
charters (by Sawyer number):
    S 451 (Middle English Athelstan charter), 158; S 745 (Refoundation of New Minster), 94; S 980 (Cnut Charter of Bury), 46, 50, 56; S 995 (Harthacnut Charter of Bury), 50, 54–6; S 1045 (Edward Charter of Bury), 46, 50; S 1068, 156; S 1119 (Edward Writ of Westminster), 90–1; S 1166, 165; S 1157, 157; S 1441 (riding the bounds), 94
Charter of the Abbey of the Holy Ghost, 53, 158
Charter of Christ, 53, 158
Chaucer, Geoffrey: and the 1381 Uprising, 18; alleged feminism (representation of women), 35–8; and authority, 4–8, 16, 57, 82, 147; authorial anxiety, 121; anti-clerical critiques, 5, 14, 70, 73; as controller of wool customs, 9, 104; "father of English poetry," 7, 11, 14, 19, 124; modes of narration, 11; as

pilgrim (self-representation), 28, 32, 34–5, 124, 130–1, 136, 140, 147; "the Troilus-measure" or "Troilus-stanza," 44; use of allegory, 81–2
Chaumpaigne, Cecily, 154, 184
Chretien de Troyes, *Perceval*, 125
Christ, 5, 94, 130, 136, 146–7
Christ and Satan (OE poem), 94, 159, 162
Christianity, 8, 17, 56–7, 66, 77, 106–7, 116–17, 131, 135, 141; Christian ethics, 136; Christian identity, 140–1; Christian imperialism, 107; Christian monastic asceticism, 142; Christian morality, 128, 138
Chronicon ex chronicis, 24
Cistercian reform, 135
Codicellus possessionum, 144
Coleman, chaplain and chancellor to Wulfstan, 24
Colley, Dawn, 4
colonial politics of recognition, 21, 26, 77
Confessio amantis (Gower), 106, 165
conquests of England: Danish, 115, 145; Norman, 9, 24, 49, 106, 144, 152; Saxon, 9
Constitutions of Clarendon, 91
Cooper, Helen, 123
Corpus Christi College, 64
corruption, 22, 119, 144; clerical, 25, 62; of clerics in *The Canterbury Tales*, 26; institutional, 113; legal in *The Man of Law*, 39; and the politics of recognition, 22
Coulthard, Glen, 19–22, 24, 26, 30, 77, 117
Crick, Julia, 48, 155–6
Criseyde, 127–8

Danegeld, 115, 144, 165
David, Alfred, 41

200 Index

Davis, Kathleen, 16–17, 19, 36
Dene Nation (Denendeh), 19, 22–4
Dinshaw, Carolyn, 27, 36, 64, 73
dispossession, 20, 27, 87, 107, 136, 144; Chaucer's representation of, 20, 76; in English history, 20; settler-colonial processes of, 30
Domesday Book, 18, 23–4, 30, 32, 42, 92, 99, 116, 136, 152
Dor, Juliet, 79
Dunstan of Canterbury, Saint, 73, 94, 160

economy: of affirmation and forgetting, 13–14, 16; political, 14; symbolic, 79, 101
Edgar, King, 23, 73, 94
Edward I, King of England, 75
Edward II, King of England, 102, 106
Edward III, King of England, 90, 102
Edward the Confessor: Cenobia's embodiment of the laws and charters of, 82, 87–92, 96–9; charters, 46, 50, 82, 90–1, 156; in coronation oath, 21; endowing monasteries, 80, 87, 90; hunting, 97; Laws of Edward the Confessor, the (Leges Edwardi), 21, 79, 90–1, 136; Matthew Paris' verse life, 102; and Chaucer's Monk, 8, 18, 27, 73, 79–80, 90–2, 142; refusal/failure to procreate, 92, 98, 115; and Westminster, 9, 88, 90–1
Edwin, King of Northumbria, 116–18
Elmham, Thomas, Speculum Augustinianum, 48
English: Church, 9, 48, 73; Civil War, 18; reading and writing (literacy), 7–10, 14, 49
"Englishness," 7, 11, 77, 141–2, 150
Epistola Cuthberti de obitu Bedae, 52
export duties, 9
exploitation, 13, 20, 24, 36, 69, 122, 150

Fanon, Frantz, Black Skins White Masks, 19, 117
feudalism, 17–18
Fitzgerald, Jill, 94
formalism, 13; historical, 45, 51; of law and poetry, 58; literary and legal, 84; poetic, 122
formulae, legal: and dating documents, 84; "sake and soke," 8
Fradenburg, L.O. Aranye, 83, 87–8
frame narrative, 3, 11, 32, 134, 138–9
Frankis, John, 106, 112
Friar, the, 6, 27–8, 32, 58, 60–73, 76–7, 79, 81, 87, 96, 110, 119–22, 126, 129, 131, 135–6, 143, 146–7
Friar John, 61, 66–8, 70–2, 127, 129

Ganim, John, 46
gelds (taxes), 115, 119
Genesis A (OE poem), 94–5, 162
Geoffrey of Monmouth, 74–5, 145, 164
Gerber, Amanda, 83
Gilroy, Paul, 13
Gitelman, Lisa, 14–17
glossing, 28, 36, 122, 159; contextual, 6; creative, 16; "ideal practice of," 122; in Melibee, 124; in the Summoner's Tale, 64–5, 67, 70; text/gloss dualism, 6
Gospel of John, 52
Gower, John, 104, 106, 109, 112, 115, 143, 164
Gratian, Decretum, Tractatus de penitentia, 137
Green, Richard Firth, 35, 150
Gregorian reform, 12
Gregory the Great, 106, 109, 117
Grimes, Jodi, 93
Guillory, John, 61, 149

Hansen, Elaine Tuttle, 35
Harris, Carissa, 36
Hartman, Saidiya, 13, 151

"Hemming's cartulary," 144
Hercules, 92, 95–6
heterogeneity, 12, 141
hexameter, 3, 84, 90
Hiatt, Alfred, 57
historiography, 46, 88; critical, 10; early-modern, 17, 155; institutional, 104; Marxist, 12, 20; monastic, 25, 44, 104, 118, 121
History of the Abbey of Evesham, 25
Hoccleve, Thomas, 143
Horn, Andrew, 90, 102–3, 165
Host, the (Harry Bailey), 33–5, 37–9, 42, 79, 83, 85–92, 95–100, 124–6, 128–31, 137, 146, 149
House of Fame, The (Chaucer), 5–6, 68, 160
humanism, 136; (proto)-humanism, 12, 16, 136; scripts, 47, 156

iambic pentameter, 3
identity, Christian English, 140–1; civic, 103; community, 30; English national, 36, 74, 80; identity politics, 12; modern English forms of, 19; national collective forms of, 19, 26; political, 30; racial, 151; regional, 131; scribal, 7; as social function, 12
imperialism: proto-colonialism, 10–11, 107; Roman, 26
Indigenous studies, 10–11, 151
Industrial Revolution, 24
Ingham, Patricia, 74
Innocent III, 85; *De miseria*, 41
Insley, Charles, 45
institutions: Chaucer's critique of, 5, 130; ecclesiastical (religious), 9, 21, 24–5, 51, 53, 65, 72–5, 92, 105, 136, 147, 153; of government, 6, 8, 103; of manuscript production and archival authority, 16, 40, 61; of medieval media studies, 15; modern, 15; monastic, 23, 46,

82, 87, 90, 92, 110, 142; of power, 8–9, 111; political institutions of medieval Europe, 37, 123; royal, 10, 20, 91; secular, 9
insular miniscule script, 47, 49
Isidore of Seville, *Etymologiae*, 112
Islam, 107; Islamic state, 101

James, C.L.R., 13–14
Jenkyn, 27, 122
Jocelin of Brakelond, 50
John Lakenheath, Monk of Bury, 50–1, 80
John of Worcester, 24
Johnson, Eleanor, 38–40, 100, 149

Kerby-Fulton, Kathryn, 131
King of Tars, The, 105–6
Kline, Dan, 68
Knight, the, 18–19, 92, 95, 142

Lahey, Stephen, 136
Lamuto, Sierra, 105–6
Langland, William, *Piers Plowman*, 62–3, 67, 79, 81, 90, 131, 138
Latin: charters in, 44–6, 55–6, 64; "corrupt" in *Man of Law's Tale*, 112–13; "hermeneutic," 113; life of King Alfred, 48; reading and writing, 7, 47; and the Summoner, 102, 111–13; translations into / from, 24, 54, 103, 128
Lavezzo, Kathy, 101–2
law: "cenobial," 81–2; Canada, 19; canon, 66, 137–8; Christian, 131; civil, 25; early English (medieval), 9, 30–1; ecclesiastical, 68, 120; embodied as Custaunce and Cenobia, 107, 119, 122; English Common (*lex non scripta*), 16, 21, 26, 30, 44, 116, 149–50; feudal, 17–18; "Folklaw," 115, 138; imperial, 107; Lacanian, 87; models of recorded,

202 Index

101; Muslim, 119; Old English law codes, 8, 44, 103; pagan, 144; of personal responsibility, 138; pre-Conquest, 90, 102

Legend of Good Women (LGW), (Chaucer), 35, 38, 88

LeGoff, Jacques, 12, 151

Leicester, H. Marshall, 11

Liberalism, 11, 13, 151

life of St. Wulfstan (Coleman), 25

literacy, 7–8, 30, 45, 48–9, 51, 64, 135, 147

Lives of Ss. Edmund and Fremund, the (Lydgate), 46–7, 156

Loathly Lady, 27, 75–6, 122

Lollardy (Lollards), 52, 56, 123, 135–9, 166

London: city of, 91, 103; liberties, 102; port, 9

London Chronicles, 103

Lowe, Kathryn, 48, 58

Lowe, Lisa, 13–17, 77

Lydgate, John, 27, 44–7, 51, 53–7, 80, 110, 152–3, 155–7

Mackenzie Valley, 23

Magna Carta, 18, 75

Man of Law, the, 3, 6, 8–10, 17–18, 21, 26, 28–35, 37–44, 54, 58, 63–4, 73, 78–9, 82, 86, 100, 102, 106, 110, 113–15, 118–22, 124, 126, 130–1, 134, 136–7, 140–2, 147

Mann, Jill, 11, 61, 67, 111, 129, 132, 145

manuscript: culture, 16; production, 9, 16, 51; rates of survival, 131; storage, 16

manuscripts:

– Cambridge, Corpus Christi College 111, 64

– Cambridge, Trinity College MS R 5 22, 52

– Cambridge, Trinity Hall MS 1, 48

– Edinburgh, National Library of Scotland, Adv.ms.19.2.1 (Auchinleck manuscript), 125

– London British Library, Cotton Tiberius A.xiii.

– London, British Library, Additional 14848, 44–5, 47–50, 53, 56–8, 88, 171

– London, British Library, Additional 14850 (S 1219, f. 85r.), 48

– London, British Library, Additional 45951, 48

– London, British Library, Additional 82931, 48

– London, British Library, Cotton Augustus ii 8, 48

– London, British Library, Cotton Faustina A.III, 91

– London, British Library, Cotton Nero D I, 104

– London, British Library, Harley 743, 50

– London, Westminster Abbey, WA Muniment Book 11, 91

– Oxford, Bodleian Library, Bodley 343, 49

– Oxford, Bodleian MS Fairfax 6, 52

– San Marino, Huntingdon MS HM 35300 (Ellesmere manuscript), 52, 126, 133

Mauger, bishop of Worcester, 25

Mauritius, Roman emperor, 8, 106

Marx, 12, 14, 21, 123, 151; "Brenner Debate," 12, 151; Marxist historiography, 12, 20; "Primitive Accumulation," 12, 20–1

Mary of Woodstock, daughter of Edward I, benedictine nun, 116

media: documentary, 18; ecology, 16, 45; "media concept," 5, 61, 149; media studies, 10, 15, 17, 149; print, 15; women-as-media trope, 75

Melibee, 82, 127–9
Miller, the, 18–19, 142, 146–7
modernity, 12, 15–16, 48, 51
monasteries: Benedictine, 88; Bury
St Edmunds, 23, 27, 44, 46, 50,
52, 87–8, 103, 157; Dissolution of,
20–1, 87; Evesham, 25; St Albans,
23, 88, 103–6; Westminster, 9, 23,
79, 88, 90–1, 124
monastic chronicles, 109, 111, 123, 136
monastic exemption, 8, 10
Monk, the, 3, 6, 8–10, 17–18, 21, 27–8,
32, 38, 42–4, 54, 58, 63–4, 73, 78–98,
100, 110, 114–15, 119–20, 122,
141–2, 146–7
Morrow, Justice William G., 22

Nakley, Susan, 36, 75, 80–1, 97, 101–2
necromancy, 133
Nelson, Ingrid, 5
Niccoli, Niccolo, 47
Nolan, Maura, 30
Norreis, Roger, Abbot of Evesham, 25
Nun's Priest, the, 142

O'Brien, Bruce, 21
Offa I, founder of Anglian line, 104–6
Offa II of Mercia, 105–6
Old English: "bocland," 30–1, 153–4;
boundary clauses, 49; charters,
8, 27, 44, 47–8, 51–2, 57, 89;
chronicles, 8; documentary writing,
8; "folcland," 30–1, 154; insular
letterforms (scripts), 45, 47–9, 52,
56; language, 8, 48–50, 53, 90, 112,
143; law codes (legal documents),
8, 44, 50, 64, 90, 103, 143–4; "sake
and soke," 50; Satan in, 94–5;
translation of Bede's *Ecclesiastical
History*, 117; writs, 8, 52, 90
Olston, Paul, 79
orientalism, 10, 21

orientalist tropes, 80
Oswald, King, 145
Oswald, Saint, of Worcester, 23, 145
Oswaldslow, 23–4

Paris, Matthew, St. Albans historian,
102–4, 109; *Chronica maiora*, 103;
Flores historiarum, 103, 163; *Vitae
Offarum duorum*, 103
Parker, Matthew, archbishop of
Canterbury, 48, 52
Parson, the, 3, 28, 52, 114, 120–3,
130–40, 142–3, 147, 149, 166
patriarchy: patriarchal abuse, 37;
patriarchal society, 101
Partridge, Stephen, 123
patronage, 7, 91
Patterson, Lee, 10–14, 16–20, 64, 83,
146
Paulette, Francois, Fort Smith chief, 22
periodization, 27, 51, 150; Marxist,
20; of media history, 15–16, 27;
politics of, 19
*Petitiones quoad reformationis ecclesiae
militantis* (Ullerston), 58
Petrarch, 51, 57, 88, 158
Plato, 5, 31
poetics of exemption, 46
politics of recognition, 10, 19–21,
26–7, 44, 46, 77, 80, 82, 87, 92, 99,
116, 136, 152
Pontius Pilate, 144
post-colonialism and Chaucer, 11, 143
print: the Age of, 16; culture, 15, 47
proceduralism, 40, 69–70, 101
proto-colonial mercantilism, 107
Pseudo-Dionysius the Areopagite,
Ecclesiastical Hierarchy, 58

race, 151; critical race theory
(studies), 10–11, 14, 17;
representations of, 10

204   Index

Rapist Knight, the, 27, 75–6, 122
Reynolds, Susan, 18
Richard II, King, 79, 132
Robinson, Cedric, 23
Rochester, diocese, 88, 90
Roman de la Rose, 92

Saltzman, Benjamin, 62
Salutati, Coluccio, 47
Satan, 93–5, 117–18, 145
"Saxon," 7, 45, 50, 52–3, 56, 90
Scase, Wendy, 7, 134, 157
Selden, John, 17–18
self-determination, 22, 24, 101
self-governance, 82
self-representation, 5, 26, 32
Seneca, 33
Sharma, Manish, 5, 123, 141
Sir Percevell of Galles, 125
slavery, 13, 17–18, 118, 147
Somerset, Fiona, 72
Spelman, Henry, 17–18
Spenser, Edmund, 126, 143; *Faerie Queene*, 126
Spiegel, Gabrielle, 9
Stenton, Frank, 44
Stock, Markus, 107
Strohm, Paul, 83
Sultaness, the, 10, 101–2, 108, 113–19
Summoner, the, 6, 27, 32, 58, 60–73, 76–7, 79, 81, 87, 89, 110–11, 113, 119–22, 126, 129, 131–2, 135–7, 143, 146–7

testimony, 34
Textus Roffensis, 90
Thomas, Arvind, 138
Thomas of Marlborough, 25
Thopas, 124–5

Tolkien, J.R.R., 144
treaties 8, 11, 22
Treharne, Elaine, 111, 152
Tremulous Hand of Worcester, 48, 157
Trevet, Nicholas, Dominican friar, 54, 103, 106–7, 109, 112, 115, 164
Trevisa, John, 52
Troilus and Creseyde (TC), (Chaucer), 54–5, 57–8, 127, 143

Ullerston, Richard, 58
Ullmann, Walter, 84
uncial script, 47, 50

Venus, 95–6
Vercelli Homily I, 144
"virago," 28, 80, 115, 117

Wallace, David, 106
Walling, Amanda, 61, 65, 159
Walter, Hubert, 25
Wardrop, James, 47
Weiskott, Eric, 68
Wenzel, Siegfried, 93, 134
Wife of Bath, the, 27, 60, 64–5, 73–8, 82, 122, 132
William the Conqueror, 8, 18, 29, 99, 142
Wilton Diptych, 79
Worcester Cathedral (priory), 19, 23–5, 88, 144
Wormald, Patrick, 23, 25
Wulfstan, Saint, of Worcester, 24–5, 144
Wycliffism, 52, 135
Wynter, Sylvia, 12–13

Zeeman, Nicolette, 62, 133